MW01051278

Living Your Soul's Purpose™

Wellness and Passion with
Energy Psychology and Energy Medicine

Mary Hammond, MA, LPC

Diplomate Comprehensive Energy Psychology

Dynamic Energetic Healing® Developer

Become your own healer…or Enhance your practice

Rapid…Gentle…Drug-free

Let go of pain…depression…

stress…anxiety…chronic illness

Heal relationships and family patterns…

Live your dreams

Global Healing Press – Salem, Oregon

Global Healing Press
Global Healing Publications
PO Box 4215
Salem Oregon 97302

Changing the world with the energy of words...

Office:
835 Fran St. SE
Salem, Oregon 97306
Phone: 503-585-8992 or 866.628.1010
Fax: 503-304-0951

Mary Hammond, MA, LPC
mhnheart@comcast.net
onedynamicenergetichealing.org

ISBN: 978-1-4276-3148-0

Cover art by Willow Arlenea
willowarlenea .com

Photography by Eyes to the Soul
Elizabeth Sahdu Farwell

Graphic design by Carol Ann Munson
cagraphix@comcast.net

Kwan Yin designs by Rachel Kitterman
Rachelkitterman.com

To Mom
who always says,
"You can do it!"

Testimonials

Mary Hammond has written a magnificent contribution to the field of Energy Psychology. Living your Soul's Purpose™ not only walks you with ease through her innovative, creative and profound healing method DEH®. It is also a well-researched book on the breadth of the field. She is curious and dares to explore difficult arenas of thinking about the soul and the spirit, which will captivate the minds of the reader. Her honest and loving spirit portrays the vicissitudes of her own life as well of her clients to thoroughly describe the sequence of DEH®. She provides easy to follow step-by-step protocols of intervention for a wide variety of difficult to treat problems such as addictions, suicide, trauma etc. DEH® is an outstanding model of intervention accessible to anyone, producing profound and everlasting changes and transformation in people's lives.

Maria J. Becker, MD, FRCP(C) Psychiatry

Honest to the core, Hammond weaves together theory and compelling case histories to illuminate the intricacies of releasing the structures holding physical and emotional illness and in their place, creating the radiant joy of Living Your Soul's Purpose™!

Barbara Stone, PhD, LISW, DCEP, author of Invisible Roots: How Healing Past Life Trauma Can Liberate Your Present (Elite Books: Energy Psychology Press, 2008)

Mary Hammond's skill working within the DEH® model was instrumental in helping me to identify and heal long standing relationship patterns that had reached a crisis point in my life. The work was life changing and life affirming. The insights and healing I experienced provided the foundation for creating the life I lead now—one filled with joy and much love. The experience effected such a positive personal transformation that I trained with Mary and have incorporated DEH® into my own healing practice with clients. They too are experiencing the journey to wholeness.

Deborah Jones, MA, Professor of Dance, Healer and Intuitive

If you ever have an opportunity to have Mary work with you, you will be awed. Much of Energy Psychology is palliative, and the world desperately needs these quick fixes. But for in-depth clearing of huge long-term issues, we need more thorough and deeper protocols like DEH®. I cleared a lifelong issue in Mary's Living Your Soul's Purpose™ Training around my great great great great grandfather (among other issues) that I thought was WAY beyond the reach of Energy Psychology.

Dawson Church Ph.D., author of The Genie in Your Genes, soulmedicine.org

Of all the training I have done over 24 years as a clinician, nothing else has been so easy to use with clients and so effective. Mary's style and ability to teach such a comprehensive model in a short time, along with getting to experience the power of DEH can't be matched. I have taken many other seminars and trainings in which I came back to my practice and did not use, or integrate. I have been using this modality since I returned from the intensive, and feel very excited about it's potential to heal at so many levels. Thank you, Mary!

Constance S. Rodriguez Ph.D., www.soulmatters.com
Gifts of the Soul: Experiencing the Mystical in Everyday Life (Llewellyn, 2008)

Mary Hammond's "Living Your Soul's Purpose™" is a welcome, user-friendly contribution to the burgeoning field of Energy Psychology. I particularly appreciated the chapter on "The Energetic Blocks" where the author streamlined the material on the complex concepts of energetic reversal and disorganization in ways that benefit the beginning as well as the advanced EP practitioner. This same balance was evident in other chapters including "Energetic Boundaries," where the author was able to include basic information as well as advanced applications. Throughout the book, Hammond includes helpful features such as sections on resonance for the practitioner and "points of interest for discussion" at the end of each chapter. I recommend this book as a useful addition to any energy practitioner's bookshelf.

Maggie Phillips, author of Reversing Chronic Pain and Finding the Energy to Heal

Dynamic Energetic Healing is an impressively thorough approach to resolving depression, anxiety, and stress, as well as healing relationships and much more. *Living Your Soul's Purpose*™ offers a clear framework for moving through each of the steps involved in this transformation. This book is a gift to everyone who is interested in deep healing—therapists and laypeople alike.

Debby Vajda, LCSW, Energy Psychotherapist, www.DebbyVajda.com

After the five day intensive training, I had a plan to introduce DEH to two of my clients —and I brought it to just about all of them. Because it's needed, called for, appropriate, provides a more solid container than I have had. It energizes and focuses me, my clients, the work. Ok, I think it is becoming (has become) my work.

Paula McGuire, LMFT

I am a psychotherapist of 31 years and an experienced energy therapist. DEH® is the most comprehensive healing approach to emotional and physical healing that I have experienced. Results are profound and the Spiritual aspect clarifies the true nature of the cause and effect of illness, resulting in immediate healing and recovery. I have personally benefited from this work and truly love it's stellar approach. This clears the emotional burdens & conflicts, replacing such with peace & health; producing a harmonious consciousness.

Roberta Roth, LCSW, International Teacher and Healing Guide

I am grateful for the sacred space…the demonstrations are such a great way to learn. I liked how the protocol was delivered from least complicated to the more complex. Enjoyed group opportunities for personal release of trauma…I got it all on a sub-conscious level and in time will get it all on a conscious level! Mary lives her soul's purpose. You are a wonderful, warm, open, loving, caring, and nurturing being. It has been transforming to be in her presence.

Sharon Viehdorfor, Reiki Master, Unity Children's Director and Author

Dynamic Energetic Healing has totally changed my life. It has allowed me to discover who I am and accept myself completely. I have found joy, peace, happiness and acceptance of who I am.

K. Olson, Homemaker, Computer Programmer, Webmaster for Lavender Women, www.lavenderwomyn.com—See her story in the book, Living Your Soul's Purpose™

Finding Dynamic Energetic Healing was probably one of the best things that has happened to me. I was in a place of desperation and isolation, and this therapy provided me with tools to help myself climb up and out of my place. It just makes sense, and is such a relief! I absolutely recommend it to someone who is motivated to change their life for the better, but may not know how.

Brionna, Salem, OR
See her case at soulmedicine.org/cliniciandatabase

The DEH® Intensive Training is awesome! Mary provided intention, information and experiences to learn the framework for DEH®. All learning styles were provided for, and feedback was available throughout. It was fun as well as professional. Mary is a dynamic healer and teacher whose energy and expertise is evident. She is passionate about sharing this work with others. The protocol is profound in its results as it is used with clearly held intention and spiritual foundation. Both needs for professional and personal are addressed and energetic boundaries are sustained. Profound respect for each person was modeled creating a genuine, safe place to grow and learn.

Diane Wade, LCSW, dwade22@msn.com

Mary Hammond has changed my life dramatically. She is a warm, compassionate and nurturing person, whose life models what she teaches. On a personal level, she taught me to use Dynamic Energetic Healing to cope with deep grief and health issues. It was so effective that I was moved to share this treasure with others. With her encouragement, I am learning to use DEH® in my professional life. Words just aren't adequate to express my gratitude!

Marlene Boltman, Reading Specialist

Mary's healing techniques and skills are absolutely astonishing. She is a true healing master and DEH® training will greatly enhance my healing skills.

Glenn Ackerman, Los Angeles, glack43@yahoo.com

The effect of learning DEH® is difficult to put into words. It has changed my life in a most profound way. In a very short time I have done some deep healing work and I am so grateful. I truly believe this is the healing method of the future and I am looking forward to becoming proficient at it and offering it as a gift of love.

Rev. Mary Tiwari, New Thought Minister, revmary@centerforinnerawareness.org

Wow! I had a sense that all of my training and all of the books I have read on Energy Psychology over the past year that I had been preparing for Mary's DEH® training. I was right! Everything has come together in this comprehensive, dynamic energy healing process.

Jaynie Clark, Vancouver BC, Canada

Excellent presentation! Great material! Dynamic Energetic Healing is the wave of the future...I am impressed by your clarity, compassion, and skill...you obviously "walk the talk." ...Quick, direct results.

Jim McMillan, Business Owner

DEH® has been nothing short of miraculous for me! Not only has working with Mary helped release many emotional blocks but it also relieved me from my lifelong stomach problems. I love having these simple but profound tools at my disposal whenever I need them. Mary is an incredible shining soul whose joy in her work always shines through in everything she does.

Rachel Kitterman, Artist

Table of Contents

In Gratitude

As always with such a project there are so many to thank; Mother and Nana for their lifetime of love and encouragement, and my father for his love and challenges which strengthened me. My familial sisters, Nancy Jessup, Barbara Wagner, and Sioux Plummer (our sister-cousin); we offer mutual support through life's triumphs and tragedies. Thanks to my brother Bill for his quiet support.

Love to my two generations of children, Lynnann Salisbury and Matt Chesnut who have taught me so much about love and life, and I am also blessed to be the mother of Amber and Jewel Newman who help me with my computer and find their own projects while I write, and their father Ben Newman who supports me by caring for them.

My thank you to my teachers from the past, Antonia Bercovici, Ph.D.; Betty Jones, Ed.D.; and Molly Worthington, MA, who nurtured the developmentalist within me, and to my teachers in the energy world—Tapas Fleming, Lac.; Helen Tuggy, Ph.D.; Judith Swack, Ph.D.; Ragani Michaels, MS; Fred Gallo, Ph.D.; Gary Craig; Donna Eden, LMT; and David Feinstein, Ph.D. All have forged the way for Energy Psychology and Energy Medicine to birth the models that inspired me.

My deep gratitude to Howard Brockman, LCSW, and Nancy Gordon, LCSW, who for three years met weekly with me as we healed ourselves and discovered the path that became the roots of Dynamic Energetic Healing®.

For seven years plus I have met with Nancy Gordon, LCSW; Kim Holman, LMT; and Sharon Rommel, LMT, to commune with the healing guides in the Medical Assistance Program developed by Machaelle Small Wright, peralandragardens.com and I am so grateful for the support for my health from both sides.

In the Mid-Willamette Valley in Oregon I am blessed with a community of healers who are either Energy Psychology-Medicine/DEH practitioners or EP-EM/DEH enthusiasts, and my friends. We meet in circles and pairs for healing, share tea, and celebrations, and discover and are given new material for this work. Berta Aronson, LCSW, Integrative mental health leader; Marybeth Carden, Shaman; Julia Doermann, Shaman, Teacher; Deborah Farrell, Healer; Deborah Jones, MFA, EHP, Shaman; Rachel Kitterman, Healer; Photograper of the photos in this book, Elizabeth Sadhu-Farwell; Healer Wendy Jensen, LCSW, D.CEP; Scott Johnson, Shaman; Garuka Khalsa, DC; Jennifer Krumm, LPC, EHP; Nancy Link, LPC; Linda Morley, PMHNP; Vicki McLean, LMT; Kathy Outland, LCSW; Eileen Foster-Sakai, LMT; Carolynne Sybelle, LMFT (now in Santa Rosa); Daryl Thomas, MA, LMT; Diane Wade, LCSW; Holly Williams, LPC, D.CEP.

Long time beloved healer friends, Roxanne Whitelight, D.D., MSW, and her partner Ruth Laangstraat, MD, sustain me and goddess-parent Amber and Jewel.

More gratitude and joy to the Association for Comprehensive Energy Psychology Board who have challenged me intellectually, emotionally, and spiritually not only to serve, but to be a better person and to laugh more often: Maria Becker, MD; Mary Jo Bolbrock, Ph.D.; Dawson Church, Ph.D.; John Freedom; Michael Galvin, Ph.D.; Jim Klopman; Greg Nicosia, Ph.D.; Mary Sise, MSW; Robert Schwartz, Ph.D.; and to my energetic brother, 2006-07 President Larry Stoler, Ph.D. In addition, thanks to the other members of my national support team, David Gruder, Ph.D.; Dorothea Hover-Kramer, Ed.D.; Pat Koestner, PsyD., RN; Barbara Stone, Ph.D.; Sharon Toole, MS; and Debby Vajda, LCSW.

And, of course I give my love and thanks to my conspirators to change the world with words, Ruth Crowley, Ph.D., who smoothed the rough edges of my writing line by line and paragraph by paragraph adding concise language, clearer meaning, and a consistent voice. Further gratitude to Megan Trow-Garcia who did the final editing, perfecting, and correcting the details, and reminded me that commas are not to be intuitively placed, and for cheerleading me to the finish with her enthusiasm and loving spirit. Deep thanks to Linda Morley, PMHNP and Barabara Stone who infused their gifts of writing and editing after we thought all was done!

Finally, thank you from my heart to my clients who engaged in this simple process of healing while sharing with me their pain, their secrets, their emerging gifts of their spirits, and pieces of this work. I extend a special thanks to all of you who agreed to bless our lives with your stories throughout this book.

Introduction

"... The other fork of the road—the one "less traveled by"—offers our last, our only chance to reach a destination that assures the preservation of the earth."

Rachel Carson

When my granddaughters' grandchild is a grandmother she will gently hold her granddaughters' forehead and say, "Of course this feels good dear one, and I am happy to share the divine within me, through my hands with you. But please remember that all you have to do is simply ask your energy system to activate and it will. Brush your field right after you brush your teeth, and then you won't forget." I imagine that when my granddaughter is a grandmother she will be telling her grandchildren about how we used to manipulate our energy field with tapping, holding and body postures.

She will still hold her grandchild's forehead as grandmothers have done through the ages, and she will say, "Your energy system is part of your body like your blood and your bones. It is part of your relationship with spirit and your family and friends. I know you will care for it."

My work puts together that which is natural—living our purpose and caring for our energy field.

To naturally care for yourself, do some form of prayer or spiritual practice every morning. I will show you my path and you will eventually find your own way with your path. This will lead to further clarity about your purpose here.

To build this awareness into the future generations, we now tap and hold to adjust the energy field, and this book is one of several written in the last decade to instruct you in this process that was second nature a few centuries ago and will become second nature for my granddaughter's grandchildren.

Until then…we must address our current healthcare crisis by teaching as many people as possible about their internal healing system and that it can be activated simply and easily. There is no question to most people that we are in the midst of a healthcare crisis. Everyday I talk to people who need something from western medicine that they cannot get because they are uninsured, or because healthcare has compartmentalized people into symptoms and systems—organic and structural. They want someone to listen. They so appreciate it when they are helped to understand that there are emotions and thought patterns that connect the pain in their heart and the pain in their lower back and that these two areas of pain are related.

Energy medicine and energy psychology are emerging as the new healthcare. It is not the whole answer or the end all by any means, but it offers simple, drug-free, powerful methods that replace and enhance current medicine and psychology. Try these methods for a year or two, and have your annual traditional check-up, and see if energy medicine and energy psychology can make a difference with your health. If it does not, the old ways will be around for a long time. In a year or two if you experience what many are experiencing, you won't be sorry for the hours you spend learning to care for your energy field. Join me in the journey.

This work is meant to be a comprehensive approach to energy psychology and energy medicine and healing. Currently, many energy models claim instant healing. I do not, although any energy model is usually more rapid than most traditional methods.

What I do experience with the people I work with is deep and thorough healing of complex illnesses and issues.

I am also told by some colleagues to keep it simple for "clients." My experience is that if most of my clients have the same training—which takes about 40 hours or more—that I do for practitioners, clients can heal themselves of many illnesses, and emotional discomfort and prevent future illness. If they cannot we have a growing list of gifted practitioners that can assist them.

Also the energy professions in general have been criticized for a lack of research. That is changing, and these pages reveal much of the exciting research on energy for healing. There is still some of this work that is intuitively guided and these pages further reveal when and how this occurs. Whether researched or intuitively guided many more people are finding their purpose in life and experiencing wellness in my office, more frequently than ever before.

Become your own healing practitioner or enhance your professional healing practice. This book provides the information and is a good precursor to taking some of my classes.

If you are moved by this book, with about 40 hours of training you can learn to become your own healer or enhance your healthcare practice beyond what you ever imagined.

You will be guided from illness or discomfort to wellness and comfort, and then to the passion of your purpose.

Why I am Here

My eyes opened from a deep sleep recovering from the surgery that had taken my womb. Right away I replaced it with the womb of the Light the Divine Mother had generously offered, and I heard the familiar whisper say, "If you are to live, complete the healing with your kids (my grown up kids had suffered the consequences of the addictions of their young mother), give up anger, finish your books, live in passion, love fully."

I had been teaching the soul's purpose work for a decade now, and I knew the divine had just prescribed the next steps in my soul's purpose. We have to live in alignment to stay well. Over the years, I realized that when healing deep pain in my life, a period of transformation and ecstacy followed. The depth of my pain was an indication of the leap my soul would take in the next adventure of my life. I am here writing to you because a major part of my soul's purpose is to teach about soul's purpose.

I was five when my loving, playful Daddy had his on-set of bi-polar disease, although it was not named until much later in our lives. It seemed in an instant to change our family dynamics and the course of my life. My soul's purpose had begun—to help families survive the devastation of unnamed, denied adult disorders. My father was my greatest challenge and my greatest teacher. Since his death he has, to my surprise, become one of my brightest guides in living a passionate life!

There would be other lessons on my way to the higher education of soul's purpose.

I was 23 when cancer first visited to attack my thyroid, parathyroid and lymph glands and my soul was stirred to greater urgency and passion. My first daughter was two and neither my first young husband nor I or our families were equipped to face the prospect of young death. So, as the person next to me died in ICU and the nurse silently pulled the curtain so I would not know, I decided to live. Choosing life in these circumstances sparked a depth of acceptance of my immortality that aged me spiritually several decades beyond young adulthood.

Passion and purpose found its home in my soul through my studies and work in early childhood education. Near young death created a fervor in me from then on to pack much into my life because I just never knew when the curtain might be pulled.

The dark side of passion, addiction, crept in also. My first marriage did not survive this.

I found myself directing child development programs for 500 children by day, and by night drinking would take over and my own children would have to fend for themselves. Again, I awakened one day with the choice once more to live or to die. Again I chose life with all of its challenges. That was over two decades ago, and my passion for helping people heal grew quickly out of these early life experiences; I found myself in the chemical dependency and mental health fields forging innovative treatments. Heroin addicts participating in art therapy on the floor and children of alcoholics displaying their dreams with toys in the sand tray began to teach me about the shifts of energy within and in the room as healing occurs. I could feel it, but I could not name it. Clearly Spirit had intervened.

Restless in life and in work I continued to long for that which was deeper and deeper. My desire to fully merge psychology and spirit led me to energy psychology. My colleagues and I studied energy and studied the spiritual realm, and in the process experienced the interplay of energy and spirit and this book resulted.

This coincided with deepening my soul's purpose with family—healing with my now grown daughter and son, cherishing my grandchildren, and adopting two young children from China.

Healers must heal in order to achieve an energetic vibrational level to be optimally effective. After several years of happily practicing energy psychology, cancer entered my womb silently like a dark conception, and grew fetus-like for a couple of years feigning other illness and injury. According to the western oncologist, even after surgery, I still carried an imminent, untreatable, incurable death sentence. Five years ago again I said no to death and yes to life, and through the energy psychology, energy medicine tools presented in this book, which we call Dynamic Energetic Healing®, I expect to live a long life.

The callings then became crystal clear—merge with Divine Mother; carry her message sometimes gently, sometimes strongly. Serve others more broadly, especially through energy psychology. Do soul work with people. Love your children deeply. Develop passionate relationships that support your higher callings.

This is my soul's purpose, and I will guide you while you strive to find yours.

Why Are You Here?

This book is for all of you who have something to heal and a desire to know and live your soul's purpose—why you are on this planet now and how to achieve your dreams. Live your soul's purpose with these simple but powerful tools that create clarity for your unfolding, evolving path.

We take for granted for most of our lives that we are born into a family, go to school, have another family, go to work, and then die. In the midst we have challenges and successes. Somewhere in our spiritual development we may begin to realize that the process of our birth, the families we were born into, the work that we do, the families we marry into and even how we will die can be a conscious process.

We could, of course, move through life based solely on the rules of culture and learned values, or we might choose to deepen our experience by becoming consciously aware of our soul's purpose and align our life decisions accordingly.

This book will provide you with the design to consciously engage in the journey of wellness and your soul's purpose with the best of energy psychology and energy medicine.

What is Dynamic Energetic Healing® (DEH)

DEH is a model in the larger field of energy psychology and energy medicine. DEH guides people through a process for healing, change or increased performance.

We prepare the room as sacred and our energy fields as sacred to begin. We use manual muscle (energy) testing from kinesiology for assessment and guidance. We establish that the body's energy flow is directionally correct and strong. We energetically determine if the left and right brain are communicating for optimal wellness, and if the energy is crossing over the midline. We develop energetic intentions for healing where the words of the intention are treated as energy for change. The intentions involve healing mental, emotional, and physical illness, as well as relationship issues and blocks to soul's purpose.

We begin the healing for change by energetically working with conscious, and unconscious, resistance, denial, and objections to the desired change. Next, we access the energy for change through your current life events, and sub-consciously through your birth and pre-birth material, your ancestry, and your karmic history.

We establish a strong personal energy field to hold the changes. We use energy meridians and energy centers in the body called chakras as interventions for healing individual, family and collective trauma and loss. We clear blocks to healing—death energy, resentment patterns, energetic soul loss, shattered energy fields, and dark energy, dissociated and disconnected parts, limiting thoughts, beliefs, and contracts. We travel through stories and tunnels of light to access the information.

You will tap or hold the meridians and the chakras to release unhealthy patterns. You may use sacred sound, light or visual imagery and aspects of your spiritual tradition for healing. You will have energetic access to gifts of the past. As you work, insight and intuition increase, and emotional and physical healing beyond your imagination will occur.

When Nancy Gordon, Howard Brockman and I developed and then trademarked and registered this model, it did not have all of these pieces. In working with clients and students more has been added or shifted. Further, DEH was not intended to be applied only with shamanism as Howard Brockman writes about it in his book. We developed it before he became a shaman, and he then later decided to couple DEH exclusively with shamanism in his work.

Nancy and I have taken the work in different directions.

I hope her book will be completed soon. This book is my perspective.

This simple but thorough protocol can be coupled with many spiritual resources or it can stand alone. Either way, you will find healing, changes for the better, and connection with your soul's purpose.

The DEH protocol belongs to all and there are practitioners trained in many paths—Christianity in all persuasions, Judaism, Buddhism, Sikhs, nature lovers, participants in the sacred feminine traditions, as well as those who embrace indigenous, shamanic practices.

This book is written for practitioners and lay people alike. If you are a practitioner, incorporating energy psychology and energy medicine into your practice is essential in this era, and if you are a lay person, taking as much responsibility as possible for your well-being is essential. Living your purpose is essential. For this reason all are invited to read this book and to attend my classes.

Many of the energy points we work with are natural. We grab our chest in anguish, rub our temples when we are stressed, we rest our hand on our under nose or chin point. We hold our head for relief.

In the end what DEH ultimately does is clear and strengthen the individual energy field so that you become a healer for yourself and for others if you wish.

How to Use This Book

This book is created in a feminine style like a piecework quilt. The quilt patterns piece together my story with concepts and information and my clients stories with the model presented.

Use this book wisely. Read the whole thing before you begin work on

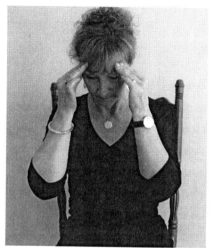
Fingers to temples, "worry" or headache.

Finger on lip pondering, "secret."

Hand to chin, "hmmm."

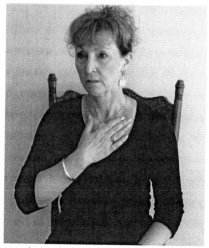
Hand over heart center, "sadness."

Sit hug, "despair." *Body hug, "joy."*

yourself. Create sacred space for yourself as you read or work. Work with positive intention. Do reversal correction, and practice meridian tapping, heart center tapping, and Tapas Acupressure Technique, for quite awhile. When you feel comfortable with those, then begin practicing the DEH protocol. When you get stuck or need more support go to onedynamicenergetichealing.org and call one of our practitioners for an appointment (they also work by phone), and to become proficient, sign up for classes listed on my training page at onedynamicenergetichealing.org.

Energy work is moving into the mainstream at four levels much like natural supplements have. You can hear about a supplement from a friend and go to the nearest nutrition center or health food store and try it for yourself. You might be shown tapping or Tapas Acupressure Technique by a friend and try it for yourself. With supplements you might see a TV program or read a book and put yourself on a supplement regimen. And so with energy work, this book and others and a DVD or two may introduce you to this work and you begin to try it for yourself. You may go to a nutritionist or a naturopath or chiropractor, or acupuncturist as a client and be prescribed nutritional supplements or herbs in the course of your treatment. Again with energy work you may learn it while you are healing a chronic condition with a professional. And of course as a professional you may choose to become a supplement prescriber or you may decide to become fully trained in energy psychology or energy medicine.

DEH® Disclaimer

Nothing in the following disclaimer is intended to absolve DEH® or The Heart Center Inc. (DBA Dynamic Energetic Healing Institute and Global Healing Press, Global Healing Publications) Mary Hammond from the requirements of local, national or state law.

Be aware that when using DEH®, emotional, physical sensations or unresolved memories may surface. Previously vivid or traumatic memories may fade, which could adversely impact the ability to provide detailed legal testimony regarding a traumatic incident.

Emotional material may continue to surface after a session, indicating other issues that may need to be addressed.

Before following or implementing any protocol or opinion expressed in this book, first discuss the protocol or opinion with an appropriate physician, therapist or other licensed medical professional and follow all their directions precisely and heed all warnings and cautionary Information. DEH® is not a substitute for medical treatment.

By continuing to read this document and utilizing these techniques, you agree to all of the above. If any court of law rules that any parts of this disclaimer are invalid in law, the disclaimer stands as if those parts were struck out.

Please explore our website, onedynamicenergetichealing.org, where you'll find a calendar of upcoming training events, a listing of Certified Professionals, and books and other products to purchase—all great ways to deepen your understanding of DEH® and connect with our community.

Use DEH® with love.

Section One

The Many Facets of Energy

Chapter One
The Energy of Soul

The soul is its own source of unfolding.

Greek Sage, Heraclitus

The Energetics of Soul's Purpose

To my surprise and delight I discovered in my work with energy psychology in Dynamic Energetic Healing® that the most direct route to your healing and your soul's purpose is energetic.

The principle is simply this, that everything is energy, and if everything is energy, then thoughts, feelings, illnesses, and even your soul's purpose is energetic. Energy is easily transmuted. If all is energy, then all can be changed, enhanced, and finally transformed by working with your personal energy system and your connection to the collective energy systems.

I also discovered that there is an energetic overlap to healing illness and other major issues and aligning with your soul's purpose. The illness or issues often hold the blocks to your soul's purpose and when your illness or major issues are healed, you can align more easily with your purpose.

In the stillness and quiet of my office Marlene's tears spilled down her cheeks as she spoke about Karen's passing and the presence she had seen leave her body. She was sure she had seen soul. Karen, 52, had courageously lived for several years and then succumbed to a ravaging cancer. She had done it with grace and tears, laughter and friendship. Marlene, her teaching colleague and soul sister, had lived the courageous vigil sharing last field trips, what teachers call

ıal life, chairside chemo support, and bedside companionship. She held
, hand as her soul left.

Marlene was thrilled a year later when I asked if her experience as healer
with her dying friend could be part of this book. She said it would honor Karen's
life. "As well as your life, as her friend," I said.

And of course, all the story tellers in this book have granted permission for
their inspiring stories to be shared with you.

When you have had an experience like Marlene's—knowing soul so
personally, it is easier to grasp the notion of soul. Otherwise it is a challenge to
find the words to describe soul. It is not important for your own soul alignment
that you have a definite definition of soul. It is much more important to form
the questions, to ponder what the great ones have said, and to have a sensory
awareness of your personal soul shifts

This chapter poses perspectives and questions and may stimulate an inner
conversation for you about the nature of soul.

We use and confuse the term "soul" in our culture.

We go to churches that proclaim that our souls need saving. The
presumption is that soul is not okay as it is or not on course, or not developing
as it should. My experience with life, the divine and energy work is that soul is
in fact an aspect of God and that when we work with intention toward healing
and soul's purpose, we are partnered with the divine for our soul's growth.

We hope that our growth will be enhanced by a soul mate. When I ask
people what they mean by soul mate, they tell me it is the partner to whom they
do not have to explain themselves, and who understands what they want and
need without having to ask, and who loves them unconditionally. Ah, a mythic
partner who is clairvoyant and magic! She or he does not exist, of course, and
some go from disappointment to disappointment trying to create this myth as
truth. Our karmic work described later in this book would indicate that soul mates
actually are those souls with which we have uncompleted business. Yes, there can
be deep love, but there are also challenges that the unfinished business demands.

Soul is about development. Soul comes to the earth plane for the Graduate
School of Soul Development. It lives in this body for awhile to heal from past
soul damage—karmic and ancestral, and to develop gifts with the single,
focused purpose of expanding the ability to love.

4

The sacred energy of healing blesses my life daily, and the individuals that do their healing work with me have allowed me to expand my abilities to feel, and see and shift energy and to expand the energy of love.

Let's explore what soul is and what others say about soul.

I set out to do research on what soul is, and to my surprise I found many references to soul but few definitions. It seemed that the great books, the soul scholars, all but a few, were hesitant to define "soul."

Psychology

For decades soul has been sorely neglected in the field of psychology as psychology strived to be scientific. We looked at the observable behaviors and expressed thoughts and feelings to make neat packages for the scientific world. In mainstream psychology only Jung's work remained as soul work until Transpersonal Psychology emerged later.

Carl Jung, MD (1981), prolific author and thinker of the last century, has shaped how we think about dreams, symbols and their relationship to us. He fostered notions of a collective unconscious that energy psychology translates to collective energy. He defines soul as the psyche, and psyche as soul. No matter what model of psychology we use, the goal is always a more functional life and the outcome in addition can be a more authentic life and a strengthened spiritual connection.

Could it be that in working with thought, emotions and energy we actually strengthen the soul and become more present to it?

The roots of the word "psychology" can be translated to "soul knowledge." (Zukav, 2000) Energy psychology honors that meaning by recognizing that thoughts, cognition, and feelings, long the foundational roots for change in psychological theory, have energy fields. We use the ancient tools of indigenous medicines, energy strategies, to shift and create positive change to the thoughts, feelings and cognition. We experience change in our actions as well as emotionally and spiritually, at the soul level.

James Hillman, Ph.D., (1996) began working with the psyche more directly and writes about those psychological experiences that move us beyond the personal. There had long been unrecognized psychologies that allowed people to explore their birth, the impact of their families, their dream life and past lives. Hillman gave this a conceptual structure in Transpersonal Psychology. Thus, it became more accepted to use the images of the mind from dreams and altered states for healing.

ın Theology

ımanism

Indigenous religion knew the connection with soul and healing. All have a form of soul journeying and repairing soul loss, and soul damage.

Shaman Sondra Ingerman, in her book, *Soul Retrieval*, calls the soul "vital essence" (p. 11). In her work she teaches the medicine of the ancients where shamans gain access to the

Sage

spirit world and assistance with lost souls and soul parts. The body loses some of this vital essence resulting in ill health and when the lost soul parts are reclaimed, health returns. This concept is reflected in our energetic soul work in DEH.

Recent Religions

As modern religion became more dogma than inspiration, soul became more elusive, mysterious and less tangible.

Christianity

I interviewed my dear friend Linda Morley, PMHNP, who has a strong presence in our Christian energy psychology community in Oregon. She reflected on the teachings of Wayne Jackson, DD (greatfaith.org), a more conservative theologian than I am usually drawn to, but who does support gays in the Christian church, and who was one of the few sources I found on Christianity and the soul.

Cross

The Soul

"The Hebrew term for "soul" is nephesh, found more than 780 times in the Old Testament. Because of the variety of contextual meanings, it is not always rendered by the English word "soul." The King James Version uses 28 different words by which to translate the original term. Nephesh, therefore, signifies different things, depending upon the passage in which it occurs.

Similarly, in the Greek New Testament, the original word for "soul" is psyche, found 103 times. Our modern word "psychology" derives from this Greek term.

Here are some uses of "soul" in the Scriptures.

A Person

"Soul" may signify merely an individual person.. Peter writes, 'eight souls' were saved by water in the days of Noah (1 Pet. 3:20).

The Mind

"Soul" can have to do with that aspect of man that is characterized by the intellectual and emotional (Gen. 27:25; Job 30:16). It is the eternal component of man that is fashioned in the very image of God (Gen. 1:26), and that can exist apart from the physical body (Mt. 10:28; Rev. 6:9).

The Spirit

In the Old Testament, "spirit" is ruach, found some 378 times in the Hebrew Old Testament, and literally meaning "breath," "wind," etc. The corresponding Greek term is pneuma, occurring 379 times in the New Testament (the original form being found in our English word, pneumonia). Again, though, as with "soul," the word "spirit" may take on different senses, depending upon its contextual setting.

The Air We Breathe

Ruach can literally denote a person's "breath." The queen of Sheba was "breathless" when she viewed the splendor of Solomon's kingdom (see 1 Kgs. 10:4-5). The word can also signify the "wind." For instance, some people, pursuing empty goals, are but striving after the "wind" (Eccl. 1:14,17, etc.).

A Non-physical Being

The term "spirit" can be employed, however, in a higher sense. It also is used to depict the nature of a non-material being, e.g. God. God (the Father), as to his essence, is spirit (Jn. 4:24), i.e., he is not a physical or material being (Lk. 24:39; Mt. 16:17; cf. also the expression, "Holy Spirit"). Similarly, angels are "spirit" in nature—though they are not deity in kind (Heb. 1:14).

A Person

"Spirit" can be used, by way of the figure of speech known as the synecdoche (part for the whole, or vice versa) for a person himself. John wrote: "Beloved, believe not every spirit, but prove the spirits, whether they are of God; because many false prophets are gone out into the world" (1 Jn. 4:1). Note that the term "spirits" is the equivalent of "false prophets" in this text.

The Soul

"Spirit" may refer to the "inward man" (2 Cor. 4:16) that is fashioned in God's image (Gen. 1:26-27), and thus be a synonym of "soul." A sacred writer noted that the "spirit of man is the lamp of Jehovah" (Prov. 20:27); this is an allusion to that element of man that distinguishes him from the beasts of the earth.

Mary's Thought

Genesis 2:7 in the Bible says, ..."God breathed on man's face the breath of life, so that man became a living soul."

I wonder then, If God's breath created the individual soul, then the Bible is saying we are all a part of God because breath is life-giving, sustaining and universal.

Judaism

In the Lunaric version of the Jewish Kabbalah, the concept of soul is that the universal soul sends a spark of itself to the individual soul. Strictly speaking the soul remains above connecting with the spark. So then the spark, our individual energy field, is a part of soul. And, of course the citings from the Old Testament above embrace Judaism also.

The Sacred Feminine

Working with energy has always been our natural way. Before the split in the fifth century delegating medicine to male physicians, and religion to male priests, women were healers and led ceremony in circles and temples. Working with the energy of ritual and the human energy system was everyday living.

Divine Mother

My personal theology is based on a balance of the divine masculine and divine feminine. Christ consciousness, and the presence of Divine Mother are my daily guides. Divine Mother gives me messages when I ask, so I asked about soul and energy.

Message from Divine Mother

Soul is the energy of union, the individuality and the oneness, the collective and the parts, the human and divine. Soul holds the information about all that has been, all that is and all that will be. Energy is the fabric of soul, and soul is the form of the fabric.

It is my sense that when I am working with energy that I am working with soul, and that the changes in thoughts, emotions and the body manifest through the soul. At the same time I sense the changes in the soul also.

The Collective Soul

Throughout our work with assisting people with wellness and purpose, we became more attuned to the collective effect of working with energy, with soul.

Norm Shealy, MD, and Dawson Church, Ph.D., in their book *Soul Medicine* state that,

Buddah

"The soul may be thought of as a personalized expression of the universal field, as the divine aspect of a human being, of God expressed at the level of a single being, or as personhood made manifest through pure consciousness, as opposed to physical or mental form."

Jungian theory, Shamanism and soul medicine all support the notion of oneness and a collective field. While I worked over time with various individuals, they would report changes in friends, co-workers and family members that had not done energy work and who might not embrace energy work if they were introduced to it. Energy testing the body's wisdom confirmed that when we shift the energy-soul, we also shift collectives—relationships, families, communities and nations.

The more we work at the collective level, the more hopeful we are that we can shift pollution of waters, and the toxins of hate and violence.

So, if soul is psyche and psyche is the seat of thoughts and feelings, and thoughts and feelings have energy fields and energy is soul then we are with energy work rearranging parts of our soul, and strengthening the soul for greater health. When we do soul's purpose work, we are simply returning the soul to natural alignment with Creator, much as a chiropractor aligns our spine with our body.

Energy is soul. Soul is energy. Everything is energy, and everything is soul. Soul is our vital essence, our connection with the holy spirit and the divine collective soul. When we are aligned and merged with soul, there is a feeling of flow in our endeavors and our relationships; challenges are energizing instead of draining, and joyous pursuits bring ecstasy.

Points of interest for discussion from this chapter:

- Energy is easily transmitted. Your personal energy system, along with collective energy systems, can be changed, enhanced and transformed.
- We are in partnership with the Divine when we work with INTENTION toward healing and soul's purpose.
- Soul's earth plane purpose is to develop gifts with the single focused purpose of expanding the ability to love.
- Practitioners of energy psychology and energy medicine use ancient tools of medicine to shift thoughts and feelings
- Soul is the energy of union, oneness

Chapter Two
Working in the Great Mystery

Energy is the currency of all interactions in Nature. To leave energetic considerations out of the equations of life and medicine is to ignore 99 percent of what is happening...

James Oschman, Ph.D.

Science, Spirit and Energy

Psychology, science, the ancient and modern energy traditions, and spirituality create the streams that flow together to create DEH as a model in energy psychology. From the psychological viewpoint, energy is thought form, the individual and collective unconscious, the force in the developmental process. From the quantum scientific point of view, energy is an electromagnetic field and the foundational form for air/gas, liquid and matter which holds the material of creation at a biochemical level. From the ancient Chinese medicine point of view, energy is chi, the Chinese term synonymous with energy flow or life force. From the spiritual point of view, energy is Spirit, prana, and light, the Holy Spirit. The work in Dynamic Energetic Healing® draws from all of these streams to transform thought form for deep healing.

What is Energy?

The Scientist's Answer

The most obvious evidence of energy is heat. We identify the elements that we use for heat—gas, steam and electricity—energy. When we do energy work in the psychological, spiritual or physical realm with therapeutic touch, or acupressure, the body heats up as healing occurs and feels warmer.

Let's experiment for a moment. Pause for a moment from reading this and hold your hands together about a 1/4 or 1/2 inch apart. Notice that you begin to feel a build up of warmth between them, and an invisible pressure pushing them apart. This is energy and evidence of your energy field. When energy is shifted through body work such as massage, acupressure, acupuncture, or through trance states such as past life therapy, people report a feeling of warmth throughout their bodies. Thirst for water often accompanies the dehydration produced by the release of body heat that occurs with energy work.

The energy or auric field, within and around the individual is approximately eight to twenty feet in diameter. The assumption is that our energy field's purpose is to support our optimum health. Most people report to me that they feel energy as tingling or warmth surrounding the body. Some people feel or sense energy. When one feels that sense that someone is crowding their space, their energy field has been entered. Some people "see" energy as colors or light.

The energy field is electromagnetic. When operating smoothly, it is like the ripple of minute particles attracting a magnetic flow. When it is not operating optimally, it behaves like magnets pushing apart. Westerners have harnessed the ability to measure energy with tools such as the Galvanic Skin Response used in polygraphs, which tests the strength of the electrical field of the skin. In the 1970s Jeffrey Mishlove, Ph.D., (1975) studied energy's qualities with black light and found that it was readily observable.

Those who read auras see the energy field as colors shifting with various moods and states. (Eden, 1999)

When the energy field positively shifts using the energy strategies outlined in this book, and the electromagnetic field is balanced, the body feels warm. The potential for greater spiritual, physical, emotional, or mental health occurs. While participating in energy work to the point of healing, people describe images, or colors of light. They also report elevated body warmth accompanied by increased mental and emotional awareness.

12

This scientist's question is further answered in the quantum sciences in the last decade, popularized in the 2004 film, *What the Bleep Do We Know*. The film states that the quantum world represents "the science of possibilities." The film goes on to talk about the power of thought as being the specialized energy of human beings. Quantum science and energy psychology come together in the precept that we as humans are our thoughts, and that thoughts are energy. And if they are energy they are easily changed.

Quantum Botanist Rupert Sheldrake, Ph.D., recorded his theories in *New Science of Life* and *Presence of the Past,* describing an energy field that holds memory which he calls the morphic field and morphic resonance. These theories support the notion that any given energy field reverberates with information from the past. He realized that plants' abilities to regenerate are a factor of memory or information held in the morphic field of the lost part. It is the simple explanation to the now well-researched fact that when something occurs several times, others begin to "pick it up." The morphic field is the archetypal structure that holds the memory of the lost part. The field of the lost part, he proposes, holds the resonance from the past. Thought forms, we were to learn through a decade of work with clients, also hold memory, resonance of the past (Sheldrake, 1994, 2007). DEH relies on this theory as clients access the resonance of their ancestry for healing.

In 2007 several of us got to spend time with Dr. Sheldrake at the Association for Comprehensive Energy Psychology where he shared his wisdom again about morphic fields, but also about taking the maverick stance in the new sciences and the new medicine. Even though he is a Cambridge professor and scholar he receives much criticism of his unusual work. He has met this challenge by starting a website to investigate journalists who criticize him! I had the privilege of joining small groups after hours for provocative conversations with him.

Sheldrake's work compliments Fritjof Capra's now classic *Tao of Physics*. Capra discusses the influence of Eastern religion on modern science, and the necessity for heart as well as intellect in scientific pursuit. He suggests merging mysticism with the science of studying the prana energy, the Hindu term for auric and meridian energy. He, too, supports the idea that this field, which he describes as energy waves and particles, is the carrier of information from the past to the present. (Capra, 1975)

Thus the energy field remembers and is directly affected when it is hurt, injured, lost, stuck, or traumatized. It remembers consciously forgotten stories, and family denial patterns. It remembers the victim stances, poverty, racism, and the power of our grandmothers. It remembers forgotten loves and forgotten losses. It remembers its emotional and intellectual past, its ancestry and karmic history. The field also remembers creativity, successes, abundance, healing, wellness and gifts, and just under the soul's disturbance lies our soul's purpose.

In Dynamic Energetic Healing we access the memory of the loss, grief or trauma, and negative thoughts and strengthen the field to the point that the negativity dissipates, and then we return to the times when the field holds memories of health and well-being.

The New Biology

Revolutionary cellular biologist and author of *The Biology of Belief* Bruce Lipton, Ph.D., discovered through his focus on cell biology that the cell has a "magic membrane" that is the interface between thought and biology. Lipton calls himself a spiritual scientist and emphasizes the cell's preference for carrying positive thought.

Energy psychology provides, he says, "a profound new understanding of psychology: The environment along with the perceptions of the mind controls behavior and the genetics of biology. Rather than being programmed by our genes our lives are controlled by our perceptions of life experiences…Energy psychology focuses on the programmed consciousness rather than the physiochemical hardware that mechanistically expresses behavior." (Lipton, 2005)

Daily as energy clearings are accomplished by tapping on the meridians, clearing the chakras, and the aura or biofield, negative thoughts are released and the positives almost always automatically remain. If not, then we find the words in the subconscious that are the opposite positive and ask the person to merge with them and use an energy intervention to complete this merge. I like to imagine the humming of the happy cells during this shift.

Eileen, a gifted massage therapist and healer found that a shadow of uncleared negative thoughts was creating anger at her family members. We found the core of this anger at family in a past life betrayal, and with this awareness she tapped the meridians regarding the anger and she has had little problem with inappropriate anger since. What remained at the end of that session was the energy of LOVE that she could carry to her family in place of the anger.

This work corroborates Lipton's work where he observed in his laboratory that human cells gravitate toward that which is nurturing and life sustaining and actually retreat from destructive toxins. The body wants to hold love rather than fear or anger.

Dawson Church, Ph.D., in *The Genie in your Genes* traces the research that describes how consciousness changes DNA, supporting what the ancestors tell us in our EP/DEH work that as we move through healing family energy that DNA/genetics are shifted.

The ancient traditions and the new sciences teach us that the anatomy of energy is easily changeable. DEH® and other EP provides a process that changes these structures for permanent health. As the energy field clears of trauma and strengthens, our perceptions are mirrored by the universal energy reflecting new ideas about ourselves, further altering perceptions for deeper healing and awareness, and clearing the way to realize our soul's purpose.

While Lipton worked on the biology of belief and thought, Candace Pert, Ph.D., was working on the biology of emotion. I was thrilled and touched when Pert published *Molecules of Emotion: Why We Feel the Way We Feel* (1994). Through years of study and research she discovered that emotion did not just reside in the brain but in the cells carried throughout the body by neuropeptides. Therapists had long known that the body carried memories. Often feelings come to the body as pain or tension before the mind captures them. I had worked with many clients who remembered previous abuse and trauma in their bodies, but this was the session that describes this vividly; that our emotions and memories are in the cells.

In the mid 1980's I was working with a 36 year old woman who had a history of severe abuse and had recurrent nightmares of being choked. We did guided imagery to work on bringing in other positive images to heal the experience, and to dissipate the nightmares. She sat quietly in a chair across the room, her eyes were closed and her hands relaxed in her lap.

In those days I found that repeating the words of the experience in a trance state created release and relief.

On this particular day as we were working on healing the choking experience, finger prints appeared on her neck. We went to a mirror so I could be sure I was not hallucinating, and then we got her calmed down. This was a decade before I was introduced to energy psychology, and without the DEH tools the finger prints remained on her neck for several hours. She visited a friend after our session who took one look at her and said, "Where have you been, what happened to you?!" When she told me about this exchange with her friend, she leaned forward toward me and laughed and said, "Oh, I told her I was with my counselor, Mary!"

Her nightmares did get less frequent, and we both eventually recovered from that session.

> **With the tools of energy psychology any physical disturbance**
> **that comes up in the session can, most of the time,**
> **be immediately relieved.**

The scientist's discoveries of the interplay of form and thought teach us the essence of change; that consciousness is the mirror of the physical and the physical is the mirror of consciousness. What reflects in our body/energy, reflects in our consciousness and what reflects in our consciousness, reflects in our body/energy.

Energy and Spirit

To create the ambience for change in consciousness, DEH® calls the sacred into the room and through the practitioner. We use light in many colors and forms throughout the sessions. As trauma clears, all participants find a greater sense of peace, and inspiration and many clients find a deepened connection with the divine. All religious and spiritual traditions speak of some mystical energy that holds power.

Working with the human energy field traces back to ancient times in theology. The phenomenon that we experience as energy is acknowledged and described in many spiritual traditions although the labels and explanations vary. Celtic women laid their hands on their children and family members asking for Creator's energy to come through them for healing. Ancient Asians knew spirit in the herbal plants. Shamans invoke, then and now, the energy of spirit through the elements.

In Eastern traditions this energy is called prana or the breath of life by the Hindus, and chi by the Chinese Buddhists. It was accepted as substantive, but mysterious, defying explanation. Touch, prayer and chants invoked this energy for spontaneous healing, as we do in DEH.

The Hindu tradition also identified energy centers called "chakras" from the top of the head, down the spine to the tailbone that are used extensively throughout DEH. Balancing the chakras creates at the very least a feeling of peace and harmony and emotional balance, and at the very most physical healing and intuitive insight and enlightenment. It seems these energy centers may be a template for the physical.

Candace Pert, Ph.D., while interfacing with colleagues who are Eastern practitioners at a conference remembers this, "I pulled out a diagram that depicted the two chains of nerve bundles on either side of the spinal cord each rich with the information regarding carrying peptides. An eastern practitioner placed his chakra map over my drawing and we saw how the two systems overlapped."

The Kabbalah, the Jewish mystical path originating around 538 B.C. discusses this mysterious energy as the astral light. When disturbance occurs as mentioned in chapter one, there is a shattering of the "vessel," the auric field and divine sparks are separated from the main source of light in God.

Christians define spiritual energy as the Holy Spirit portrayed by light fields surrounding Jesus and Mother Mary. They call on the Holy Spirit for protection and healing. Jesus of history teachers claim that the Holy spirit is the divine feminine aspect of Christ, the energy of mystical healing. (King 1997)

All of these religions, from ancient to modern, use ritual and ceremony that shift the energy, and create a containment field of energy for all who participate. Calling in the sacred brings in energy from Creator that causes powerful shifts in our internal feelings and external world.

In DEH as you participate in the work and your field becomes free of trauma, you begin to notice what energies of inspiration emerge from within. You may find yourself connected more deeply with the familiar spiritual energies as defined by your tradition, and/or you may find new awarenesses emerging. As we energy test throughout our sessions, we are aware of Source's energy simultaneously with the client's body/energy field. As we tap on the meridian points, we are aware of transpersonal energy flowing in to assist with the healing. We are intentional about using the flow of energy, the divine energies and light that assist us from our various traditions for more rapid efficient healing and change.

I invite you to work in the great mystery now unraveled, to find healing for yours and others' body-mind, in the intersection of science, faith and energy.

Points of interest for discussion from this chapter:

- Energy can be viewed through the lens of science or spirit.
- The purpose of our energy field is to support optimum health.
- The energy field is electromagnetic.
- Quantum science has the most well-developed definitions and concepts regarding energy
- Both Pert and Lipton offer concrete information of cellular change when energy shifts.
- Religions from ancient to modern offer a view of energy as spirit

Chapter Three
The Energy of Medicine, Past to Present

Surrender is the simple but profound wisdom of yielding to rather than opposing the flow of life.

Eckart Tolle

The Mystery of Energy Through the Ages

"Native American shamans have practiced energy medicine for over 5,000 years. They remember stories handed down from grandmother to granddaughter about when the earth was young." (Villiodo, p. 237)

In the old traditions personal healing and care for the earth were closely aligned. Through current energy medicine we are "remembering" that.

Chinese Medicine, also 5000 years old, teaches us that well-being is the purpose of our energy field and when we are injured or ill physically or emotionally, the energy field as well as the body needs treatment.

The Chinese Medicine practitioner moves chi/energy, by administering needles or pressure to specific points on the body, balancing the energy, and facilitating healing of illnesses. In energy psychology we use some of the major pressure points from Chinese medicine and the Chakra centers from the Hindu and other indigenous traditions to balance the energy of thoughts, and emotional, mental, physical and spiritual trauma.

A global view as well as the individual view of energy is described by Harriet Beinfield in *Between Heaven and Earth: A Guide to Chinese Medicine.*

She explains the Chinese view of the human organism as being a microcosm of the macrocosm. The human body, in other words, holds all of the aspects of the universe and interacts with all other aspects of the universe. The individual human energy field has the capacity to hold information from other realms in the universe. Chinese acupuncture and acupressure aligns the body's energy with the universal energy.

This notion of the connectedness with the universal and individual energies is central to DEH®. We call constantly on the universal energy to direct the flow of the individual energy. Through the DEH methods your energy shifts, balancing the energy polarities. This is referred to as yin and yang in Chinese Medicine. When your energy is balanced, an energy flow is created which promotes your healing.

Barbara Brennan in her book, *Hands of Light* (Brennan,1988), traces the many references to the universal energy field throughout history. Brennan notes that the Pythagoreans wrote around 500 B.C. of a luminous field that affected humans in a variety of ways including curing illness. As early as the twelfth century, the scholars Boirac and Liebeault reported that human beings affect one another in either healthful or unhealthful ways, simply by their presence.

Brennan cites that Western medicine and science did not begin to address energy fields until the 1800's. It was then that Mesmer who developed mesmerism and later was credited with developing hypnotism, observed properties of the energy field. He reported that animate and inanimate objects could be charged with this energy and could be influenced at a distance. He proposed this as evidence for the existence of a force field, which he speculated was electromagnetic. Also in the 1800's, Count Wilhelm Von Reichenbach studied energy fields and discovered a minus force field in the left side of the body and a plus force field in the right side of the body, much the same as is present in rock crystals with healing properties. The Chinese yin and yang concept is similar.

Japanese physician Usui sought methods more ancient than Chinese Medicine to replace the barbaric medical treatments available at the turn of the century. Reiki is a hands on model of energy healing developed early in the twentieth century, I learned as I pursued my Reiki Master training. Usui synthesized several ancient models of directing the energy flow for healing, recognizing the interplay of the individual and universal energy system. The Reiki Master, I learned in my Reiki training, calls in divine energy through the top of the head, the crown chakra in Hinduism, and asks that the energy flow down through the heart chakra to one's hands which offer healing to another. In DEH® I call in the divine energy through my body and hands continuously, not to lay on hands but to offer the energy into the session.

Contemporary Energy Models

In the latter half of the twentieth century, there was an explosion of highly academic, thoughtful research regarding energy fields and healing which are rooted in the ancient. Nursing made a major contribution to the understanding and acceptance of working with energy through Therapeutic Touch, widely used in hospitals and developed by Dolores Krieger (1993) which she adapted from the practice of Reiki. Dorothea Hover-Kramer brought a blend of this work to energy psychology with her *Creative Energies* (2002). John Thie, D.C., during this same period developed Touch for Health. Practitioners of these models learn to direct universal energy through their hands and offer that energy to the wound, injury or trauma of the patient.

Deepak Chopra, MD; Larry Dossey, MD; and Bernie Siegel, MD, all document profound physical and mental improvement when working in the energy/spiritual realm. Daniel Benor, MD, produced two volumes documenting research on healing that review hundreds of studies based on using energy and prayer for healing. His more recent book, *Consciousness, Bioenergy and Healing* reviews the energy research on the interface of psychology, the environment and complimentary and alternative medicine.

Energy medicine, which accesses the body and mind primarily through the bio-field, has a longer history of collected research. It is the medicine of the shamans, the Reiki Masters, and the nurses who use healing touch. Energy medicine as a term has been made popular by Donna Eden, LMT, James Oschman, Ph.D., and the Institute of Noetic Sciences, the International Society for the Study of Subtle Energies and Energy Medicine (ISSSEEM), which are all resources for exploring the depth of research on energy and consciousness.

Donna Eden, LMT, and her husband and colleague, David Feinstein, Ph.D., are bringing energy psychology and energy medicine together. (Feinstein, Craig, Eden, 2005) Chakra work is inherent in energy psychology which I studied with local teachers, my friend, Sharon Rommel, LMT, and my editor and partner Ruth Crowley, who also teaches chakra work.

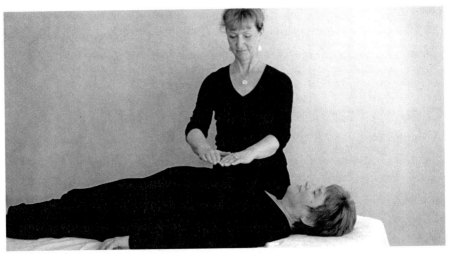

Hands over heart center

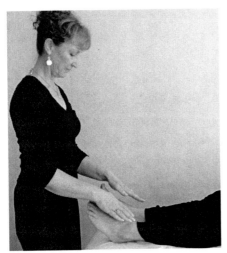

Hands over feet

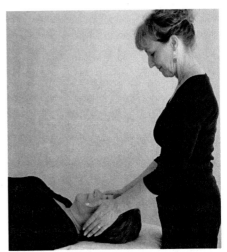

Hands over head

At an International Energy Psychology Conference, I volunteered enthusiastically to be on the table under Donna Eden's magical hands connected to her abilities to see beyond the body. She swirled my chakras and laid on hands with the sacred touch of a master. She sensed darkness and energetic reversal in my womb. This was only months before the diagnosis of the cancer I mentioned in the introduction to this book.

There are several energy psychology models which incorporate working with all aspects of the energy field, the meridians, chakras and biofields,

DEH is one of them.

Healing From the Body Level Up

Helen Tuggy, Ph.D., and her colleague, HBLU developer Judith Swack, Ph.D., became our teachers for several years as we learned to diagnose particular traumas of the energy field and heal their roots. Judith is a botanist and trained in Neurolinguistic Programming (NLP), and Three in One Concepts trainings to bring about HBLU. Helen is a skilled energetic psychologist who enhanced many pieces of HBLU. HBLU works at root causes of energetic problems to collapse illness. As part of our training we were fortunate to study NLP with Seattle trainer, Ragani Michaels, MA, who assisted us in honing our abilities to be sensitive to the many subtle qualities of words and thoughts and their relationship to the conscious and unconscious mind.

Dynamic Energetic Healing®

While Nancy Gordon, LCSW, Howard Brockman, LCSW, (2005) and I experimented with the strategies we learned from the forementioned teachers, we received profound personal healing, and greater access to enhanced intuition. Each week through these growing intuitive abilities we would discover a new level of healing with our clients and one another, and new strategies for our emerging model.

Together, Howard, Nancy and I developed protocols for Creating Sacred Space, a protocol for strengthening the accuracy of Energy Testing, protocols for developing intentions for healing, performance, soul loss, working from the origins, guided imagery particular to DEH, the black hole and other supernatural energies, healing the shattered energy field of chronic physical, mental and emotional illness, combining meridian and chakra work, collecting gifts of the past and communing through the veil to the other side.

We expanded and deepened the trauma work we had learned from Tuggy and Swack. We created a tapestry of many energy and spiritual interventions and processes into an elegant model with endless possibilities for healing and change and living your soul's purpose.

My 10 year clinical project on depression substantiates the power with this model. Over 100 clients remain depression free for two to 10 years after completing an average of seven sessions for major depression or dysthymia.

There is major research regarding energy psychology in general on alleviating phobias, anxiety and pain, post trauma and thousands of anecdotal stories on the wonderful results of energy healing. Research and case reviews can be viewed at www.energypsych.org, and soulmedicine.org.

The research in energy medicine is summarized in the work of James Oschman, Ph.D., and in the journals of the International Society for the Study of Subtle Energy and Energy Medicine (issseem.org), as well as in many scholarly books and demonstrates physical as well as emotional healing when the energy field is adjusted and enhanced.

Points of interest from this chapter:

- The roots of energy medicine are thousands of years old.
- The individual and universal energy is connected.
- Historically all cultures and religions have a view of the energy system.
- Contemporary energy models have been developed throughout the twentieth century and DEH® is a culmination of several models.
- Research is available on various aspects of energy psychology and energy medicine.

Chapter Four
The Energy of Psychology

Energy psychology addresses the relationship of energy systems to emotion, cognition, behavior and health.

Fred Gallo, Ph.D.

It is important that those of us in the profession of Energy Psychology focus not only on the seemingly miraculous energetic strategies, but we also define the work in terms of theory and concepts.

If you are reading this as a layperson to learn to heal yourself and your family, you will still find it interesting to understand the possibilities for theoretical constructs in psychology. You will recall from college or reading what theories you prefer and resonate with you.

I challenge my colleagues and other readers to define their work on two levels by asking, "first, what is your theoretical grounding and second, what are the components of a comprehensive energy psychology?"

Have you read or studied with Ken Wilbur, Ph.D., and colleagues and discovered the psychological links with birth, ancestry and spiritual realms? And therefore are you a Transpersonal Energy Worker/Therapist? Have you immersed yourself in Ericksonian Hypnosis and are you then an Ericksonian Energy Worker/Therapist?

Do you explore the archetypes in dreamtime after reading or studying Carl Jung, MD? Are you then a Jungian energy worker/therapist? Are you interested in the balance of individual optimum health and social responsibility as expressed by Alfred Adler, Ph.D.? Then are you an Adlerian Energy Worker/Therapist?

Do you believe we should only do EP in present time and not return to the past as William Glasser, Ed.D. taught in reality therapy, and so then are you a Reality Energy Worker/Therapist? Are you interested in the client-healer relationship as taught by Carl Rogers in his client-centered approach. Would you consider yourself a Rogerian Energy Worker/Therapist?

Have you immersed yourself in the process-oriented approach of Arnold Mindell? Are you a process-oriented Energy Worker/Therapist? Current psychological research is heavily skewed to cognitve and behavioral work (CBT). Do you use EP to primarily change thinking and then assess changes in behavior? Are you then a CBT Energy Worker/Therapist?

A comprehensive energy psychology includes the psychological theory, and in addition it includes grounding in ancient energy traditions such as qigong, yoga or traditional Chinese Medicine, and an honoring of the client's spiritual path which energy work seems to stimulate.

If you are a professional in energy healing, it is not enough to tap or TAT, two of the major strategies in this book, but to know how you are grounding that psychologically and spiritually.

If you are reading this book to become your own healer, focus primarily on an energetic/spiritual practice, and study psychology as you are interested. If you are a healthcare professional find the links from your paradigm to energy paradigms.

My work is primarily developmental, and client/student centered with a weaving of the transpersonal. If you become my student, you do not have to believe as I do, but eventually I would like you to be able to clarify your psycho-spiritual theoretical stance.

My Human Development Journey

I walked across the campus as a 20-year-old in the sea of brown and black faces feeling oddly self-conscious, glancing at them through my blue eyes. The middle class, white-faced beach city, where I was raised, and West L.A. are only 40 minutes apart, but I had come to another world for my undergraduate education in Human Development at this branch of California State University. I fell in love immediately with the richness of this diverse community; Black Poetry, 1960s politics, and cutting edge professors in Human Development.

Some years later I found myself in another unusual educational setting for a Masters in Human Development at Pacific Oaks College, also in southern California, where classrooms were living rooms and curriculum was designed collaboratively between students and professors.

As my career unfolded in mental health and addictions, and I learned to diagnose illness, I was grateful to have the foundation of wellness—what is normal with people—instead of simply what is pathological, as is common in traditional psychological and mental health training.

Human Development is the study of the natural in human beings, and the organicity of the human process. It implies that all human situations—educational, psychological, medical, religious, and political—need to enfold the whole person: physically, mentally, emotionally, socially, and spiritually. Human Development is also inherently client and student centered.

It is the overriding model that has held all of the therapy modalities that I have practiced over the years; play therapy and child within therapy, addictions therapy, guided imagery and breath work, Transpersonal Psychology, EMDR, and now in Energy Psychology. Human Development guided these therapies with its client-centered, client empowering framework.

By the end of my client's treatment they are empowered with the strategies outlined in this book, and most of the time their personal healing system is capable of being easily activated.

Psychology from all its theories has long explored why we have the tendency to create and recreate similar patterns of dysfunction in relationships, and work. Why are abused children abused as adults? Why does illness run in families? Why does one fail repeatedly in one area while achieving success in others? DEH and other models of energy psychology and quantum sciences would respond with the answer that family patterns, success/failure patterns, abuse, and illness are thought patterns that have a unique energetic structure for each individual.

Tammera came to me due to the trauma that impacted her when a talented teacher with whom she worked made headlines for sexually abusing young female students. She had not had much trauma in her life raised by a loving mother and father in a safe small rural town. Her ancestry, however, was checkered with abuse and addiction accompanied by the predictable thought patterns of denial, fear, and arrogance. With eyes closed she tapped about disgust and fear regarding her colleague, and said, "I feel the energy of my aunt, grandmother and her mother unraveling—I am carrying their fear, their disgust as well as my own. I can't believe he is this bad...they couldn't believe that my great grandfather was that bad either." She tapped on the meridians to neutralize this ancestral energy.

After this experience, Tammera left education for awhile hoping to change the world of her students through politics. After some soul's purpose work, she discovered that her true calling for now is education and returned to this field with new energy and resolution to protect and make a difference for children.

Tammera was able to access the energetic structures in her ancestry and release the fear, disgust and denial of the present through the resonance of her ancestral past. She had a right to feel disgusted, and afraid, but it did not serve her to continue to carry it.

Transpersonal Psychology

My human development perspective was expanded by the work I witnessed in my office in my clients. Children went into trance states as they played, revealing the world of their ancestors. Adults joined me in hypnotic journeys where the body rather than the mind revealed memories of consciously extinguished past events.

Seeking further explanation, I was led to Prague to the International Transpersonal ("beyond the personal") Psychology Association Conference in 1990, the very week that the country split and Czech President Havel, who spoke at our conference, led his beloved Czechoslovakia to a democratic/socialistic way of life. Czech Stanislav Grof, MD, a leader in the transpersonal movement, and developer of Holotropic Breathwork, and close personal friend of President Havel, was returning to his homeland after exile for a quarter of a century. Grof developed breath work after he and Ram Dass, Ph.D., and Timothy Leary were no longer allowed to do the research at Harvard on LSD.

Grof then went on to study how people can achieve the awakened state, the high, naturally, and over the years he developed Holotropic Breathwork. It is Lamaze-like breathing combined with provocative music which activates the chakras to reveal energetic imaged or kinesthetic experiences for healing with the breath. It was my introduction to origins work as we travailed the psyche's landscape of birth, ancestry and karmic memories.

The country celebrated with adolescent frenzy, while our conference cheered on the teachers of the science-spirit-psychology connection. Pioneers like Grof with his simple interplay of music and breath changed the world of therapy.

Through meditation, Guided Imagery and Play/Art therapies in my office I had experienced this natural merging. During this week in Prague I found the constructs to hold my experiences. The word transpersonal speaks to the outer territory of the human experience inaccessible in the current mainstream cognitive/behavioral psychologies.

It is the dream time place of "remembering" the energy and images of our births, our ancestral lessons and karmic connections. I was drawn to the teachings that week of Rupert Sheldrake, the then new biology/botany scientist who studies the morphic fields as plants regenerate into their energetic memory.

For the first time I was introduced to the teachings Fr. Matthew Fox's *Creation Spirituality* which includes as part of his Catholic religion the sacred feminine and social justice, and encourages ministry wherever one works.

The longer I was a therapist the more I sought deeper ways to support people in their healing. My foundation in Human Development served and continues to serve me well in a holistic and client-centered approach to an academic understanding of the psychology of human beings.

Reality, Rogerian, Jungian and cognitive schemas found their way into my paradigm, but all fell short in providing the container to hold the complexity of traumas that plagued my clients. In addition I steeped myself in the expressive therapies—particularly play and art.

I explored Guided Imagery where wake time, dream time images are used for healing. (Whitelight) I explored the depths of Holotropic Breathwork where breathing techniques coupled with provocative music takes one to heal their birth, their family patterns and karmic history. I sat in seminars and learned the magic of Eye Movement Desensitization Reprocessing. EMDR, rapid eye movement to release trauma. (Shapiro, 1995)

All of these models add to the depth of our work with the human energy system, changing emotion and cognition.

Comprehensive Energy Psychology

Components

In developing my own perspectives in energy psychology over the last decade or more it also seemed important to define the framework of EP/DEH that guides my understanding of the journey my clients and I take together. Here are the components I believe make up a comprehensive energy psychology model. Each of these is addressed more thoroughly throughout this book.

A Comprehensive EP model includes:

- An Energetic/Spiritual practice for the practitioner/healer.
- An ability to define one's psycho-spiritual model.
- One or more means of accessing the body's wisdom for diagnosis and on-going assessment.
- A view of trauma, illness, issues, thoughts, and feelings as energy.
- One or more means of accessing the electromagnetic field through the meridians.
- One or more means of accessing the electromagnetic field through the chakras.
- One or more means of accessing the electromagnetic field through the biofield/aura.
- One or more means of accessing energy at the level of the body, personality, ancestry, and soul with an understanding of the interconnectedness of each aspect.
- Practitioner intuitive efficacy.

As you read you will see my bias for the developmental, client-centered approach, and if you take my classes you will be encouraged to strengthen your own psychological and spiritual framework. This book will give you a solid framework toward a comprehensive view of energy psychology.

Points of interest for discussion from this chapter:

- Practitioners can strengthen their work by clearly defining their conceptual framework.
- Human development provides another natural psychological framework through which to view the natural revolution of energy patterns.
- Transpersonal psychology merges the psychological and the spiritual.
- A comprehensive view of energy psychology is necessary.
- Develop and define your own conceptual psycho-spiritual framework as an energy practitioner.

Chapter Five
The Energetics of Trauma

Trauma is about the loss of connection—to the self, to others, to nature....

Peter A. Levine, Ph.D.

Trauma

The hope energy work gives those who are traumatized is that they can now be in control of their brain instead of their brain being in control of them.

In psychology and medicine the effects of trauma on health are now well documented and accepted. We now understand that trauma to the personality or the body underlies most health issues. Energy psychology and energy medicine offer gentle and effective treatments for trauma.

Spirit, science and psychology merge in this model to provide relief for the traumatic roots of illness and many life issues. For the last two decades psychology and medicine have been stunned by the brain and cellular research regarding the effects of trauma on health. This research also has caused us to expand our notion of trauma as we gained evidence that we could not just measure the degree of trauma by the events, but by how an individual's system codes trauma.

Trauma theory has brought together the neurological/biological information with the resulting psychology—thinking and behavior. Energy psychology holds the tools for healing trauma thoroughly. This chapter discusses theories of trauma for theoretical grounding for healing trauma and a later chapter discusses the healing protocols in our trauma model.

Trauma in the body and in the energetic field feels constantly agitating. It originates with physical, sexual, or emotional abuse, neglect, malnourishment, an auto or other accident, near drownings, fires whether there is injury or not, illness, injury, assault, natural disasters, and witnessing violence or a traumatic event. It presents as severe anger, addiction, depression, major illness, and/or the cluster of symptoms we have come to term post-traumatic stress— hypervigilence, startling, flashbacks, numbing, and nightmares. Underlying are the deeper emotional and energetic components.

Also, surgery, chronic illness, and many life disturbances can code as trauma with any given individual and the recurrence of illness can also be re-traumatizing. When the body-emotional system is disturbed, it is usually traumatized, and energy work restores the system to balance naturally.

We currently understand that trauma, grief and loss have a primary impact, at the neurological and energetic level, on the person's ability to heal completely. Trauma weakens the energy field and allows energetic and physical toxins (Radomski, 1999) to accumulate. Trauma at many levels is the primary factor that blocks living one's soul's purpose.

The Energy of Trauma

Trauma is the body-mind's response of stress due to fear. Post trauma is the body-mind responding to current stress as if it were the original traumatic event. Grief and loss or a new traumatic event may be the trigger. On the extreme the body thinks it is in a war zone, whether it is or not. The energy field responds by shattering, holding dark energy and the energy of death, or by splitting into fragments.

One night when Jane's daughter was one, she awakened to the sounds of her young husband, a newly returned vet screaming, "incoming." He jumped out of bed and beat on the floor until his hand was badly bruised. She stealthed down the hall to their crying daughter and held her tightly, briefly wondering about their safety. When all was quiet, she returned to the room where he was on his knees sweaty and tearful. They all returned to bed silently. In the morning she asked him if he was okay and he said "yes" and they never spoke of it again, and there were never any outbursts from him again. They held the trauma of the war within.

This was 1969 during the first year of his return from Vietnam.

They were offered no help and were given no words for this experience.

In the early 1980s in my trainings to be a counselor, I began to hear the others in the domestic and child abuse fields relate what happens to abuse victims to what happens to the survivors of war. (Courtois, 1988) They called it post traumatic stress disorder (PTSD). I teared at the memory of young frightened families like Jane's.

Now we have words for it; now there is help.

Soon after this I became friends with a director of a Vets Center here in Oregon and we talked about our experiences and the feelings that so many never could talk about. I had avoided for all of those years reading about or listening to the horror of the war that forever changed the lives of my generation. My friend had never before heard about the debilitating fears and sleepless nights of Vietnam family members like my friend, Jane.

He gave me books to read on PTSD and the impact on family members and how children of Vietnam vets take on some of the post trauma symptoms. As I learned more about the treatment of PTSD for my caseload of abused and battered women who had lived in their own war zones, I put the personal and the collective Vietnam era to rest for the time being.

Many years later as I studied energy psychology, energy testing indicated that I had some more work to do on this personal and collective trauma in my personal energy work. The Vietnam war had touched us all.

I felt at peace and could let go of how the war trauma had affected a million families at such tender ages. With energy psychology, I was able to clear the vicarious family and collective trauma and put this to rest at a deeper level.

The Biology of Trauma

Trauma has neurological as well as energetic roots. This neurological/energetic symbiosis holds physical pain and illness, disturbed emotion, and irrational limiting thoughts. Trauma, as we understand it in psychology and science today is the interaction of neurology and behavior as the result of being victimized or witnessing a traumatic event. When a current event reminds the person consciously or unconsciously of the original traumatic event(s) the brain gets stuck, so to speak, in the flight or fight response, and reacts to the reemerging fear with anger or isolation.

Animals shake and breathe rapidly, a natural autonomic arousal, after a traumatic event. If they do not do this they die prematurely.

"The human species (unlike other animals) frequently will not discharge this high state of autonomic arousal after a freeze response in the face of perceived trauma, but will suppress the discharge phenomenon, resulting in storage of a high state of autonomic arousal, probably in limbic and procedural memory systems of the brain. Memory mechanisms in trauma probably involve both explicit (conscious, declarative), and implicit (unconscious, non-declarative) memory. Procedural memory is a form of implicit memory involving learned sequences of synchronized motor acts such as athletic, musical or artistic skills. Once learned, these motor sequences are stored with a high degree of recoverability, probably in orbitofrontal and limbic, as well as cerebellar, vestibular and basal ganglia connections of the brain. There is strong evidence that memories of the motor sequences of a traumatic experience may well be stored in this memory system." (Scaer, 2001)

Energy psychology strategies offer access and gentle relief to this debilitating cycle.

In his groundbreaking book, *The Mindful Brain,* Daniel Siegel, MD, reminds us that our focus in any given moment activates the brain's circuitry. (Siegel, 2007)

After the event the traumatized person reorganizes her life responses and often reacts from the place within herself that holds the trauma. For example, fear and panic or an inability to speak may emerge in the extreme when a traumatized person is asked a question at work, triggering the former response of being interrogated by an abuser.

I had worked with clients with trauma in their bodies from sexual and physical abuse for more than a decade prior to my work in energy psychology. I encountered similar post trauma reactions from other developmental traumas such as parental divorce or verbal abuse, or situational trauma such as near drowning, witnessing a crime or surviving an earthquake. Sand tray and art therapy, Eye Movement Desensitization Reprocessing (EMDR Shapiro, 1995), and guided imagery addressed these issues satisfactorily but not as thoroughly as energy psychology.

I often wondered what trauma was exactly that it would show up as physical pain, rashes, and chronic illness decades after the assaults when there seemed to be no residual injury. I trained with and studied the work of Christine Courtois, Ph.D., (1988,1993) and read John Brierre, Ph.D., (2005) experts in the field of abuse, and they had not yet discovered the answers, but clearly saw the relationship with trauma and physical responses.

As I worked with trauma over the years, I greatly expanded my view of the trauma model from the abuse-war-disaster model to an understanding of trauma in a larger scope. People are traumatized by grief and losses, their own and other's illness, addictions, allergies and other intolerances, rejection, betrayals, injury, surgeries and anesthetics. People report anxiety, stress, and many of the forementioned physical symptoms of trauma in these instances, also.

Poignantly clients taught me the subtle differences within and behind the traumas. Abuse survivors, whose homes were like a war zone reminded me that homes were supposed to be safe, while one expected danger in a war zone.

Trauma and the Whole Person

Trauma theory merged well with my whole person, human development model. Trauma affects the whole person.

Energetically, each person's trauma has a unique structure that holds the emotional responses, the thoughts, and behaviors and the neurology in place. Trauma additionally impacts relationships and energy testing indicates that it even affects the soul. In energy psychology we treat the energetic structure of trauma and illness. We have discovered the links that hold trauma in place and how to dissolve them energetically. The core of healing the trauma lies in the energetic connections. There are energetic connections within the trauma and energetic connections between the traumas. For instance, one childhood abuse situation has energetic components described in later chapters that keep it active in the person's system, and these energetic components may be linked to other childhood, ancestral, and karmic events.

Generally speaking, DEH participants are depression and anxiety free within six months and trauma free—all current, ancestral and karmic origins— within three months to a year depending on the length and severity of the trauma. There are a few who take less than this, and there are very few who take more.

The Physical Aspects of Trauma

The terror of trauma sets off a chain of physical reactions that the body and mind continually attempt to adjust to from then on. The frequent flight or fight response activation results in rapid heartbeat, over production of adrenaline and cortisol, sleep disturbance, increased startle response, thyroid malfunction and other endocrine and immune system disorders. If untreated, the generalized long-term stress will exacerbate any predisposed tendency toward illness or injury.

If there is assault then the physical aspects of healing the trauma are more obvious. There may be old injuries or lingering pain. For sexual abuse victims there are often medical problems connected with the sexual organs or pain and trauma with normal adult sexuality. For others, it appears that trauma is held energetically in the body and creates illness. When we treat the trauma, the physical/medical problems disappear except those where there is extreme physical damage, (ie.) a lost limb, some head injuries, plates replacing bone, or extreme nerve damage.

Trauma seems to generalize in the body's system. Pam's story is common.

She was traveling a bit too fast on a country road in Oregon, looked off to the scenic moonlit meadow on her right and when she looked up there were headlights and horns screaming at her. She remembers the horrid sound of crunching metal and then remembers waking up in the hospital after surgery on her crushed right shoulder. All survived this crash except her conscious memories. She received physical therapy, care from family and friends and seemed to go on with life and a new car.

Six months later the nightmares began. She was a child, in bed, and she then would see herself screaming in the recent auto accident. This nightmare recurred to the point that she recognized she would need help for not just the trauma of the auto accident but from the sexual abuse by her brother that she thought she had long ago resolved as she has a "good" relationship as an adult with her brother. The auto accident had literally shaken loose what was energetically still not resolved from the childhood abuse.

We embarked on the intention to heal from the auto accident and the childhood abuse:

We tapped the meridian points focusing on the moment of shock when her head turned toward the headlights and heard the horn. It is that breathless moment of shock, it seems, when trauma locks into the body. We also tapped regarding denial and lost memories, as I always have people do who claim "not to remember" on everything that occurred from the last memory to waking up in the hospital, tapping on, at my suggestion, "everything remembered and not remembered, all that the body and mind is holding, continue tapping on all that was consciously forgotten but that the body remembers."

Then we moved on to tapping the meridian points on the physical pain and the emotional reactions to the auto accident from the time in the hospital to the present; anger, sadness, depression and loss of activity are the themes she released.

She reports no haunting memories of the auto accident since.

In the next session, we began the first of several sessions on the abuse, returning in the tunnel of light to her childhood nightmare. We tapped on the meridian points on her anger at her brother, her sadness at lost innocence, and her ensuing fear of males.

Auto accidents seem to shake the body-energy field to such a degree that unresolved trauma pops out of the blocked pockets for healing. I call it "shaken energy field syndrome." I work with several chiropractors in town who tell me that combining energy work with their chiropractic work for auto accident survivors reduces the frequency of treatments and increases the speed of healing.

The Mental Aspects of Trauma

Trauma results in intense fear, helplessness, a sense of horror, and creates a confused, disorganized, depressed and agitated brain which has trouble then coming up with positive thoughts. Thinking about the possibility of catastrophe for the traumatized brain is a day-to-day occurrence and is rationalized as normal. The mental component of trauma is directly related to the overactive physical and emotional state resulting in negative or catastrophic thinking which in turn further elevates the physical and emotional reactions. Mentally life is difficult to navigate when cynicism and negativity rule life's perspective.

Jenny says, "I worry all the time that my daughter will die while she is still a child." Jenny grew up in a household that was constantly threatening. There was incessant parental fighting and some domestic violence. Her body had taken on her mother's fear and her brain reacted continuously to the impending danger. She married a mild, mellow man so that she would never have to live this way again, and was constantly surprised by her current levels of fear in her "safe" home.

We did the protocol in this book on the obvious childhood traumas but also returned to this past life:

After emerging from the tunnel of light Jenny says,

"I see a woman on the shoreline. I believe that was me. I am playing with a child, my little girl. It seems to be a familiar soul—oh it is my little girl now." Jenny begins to

tear. *"I turn around and she is not there—I am frantic. It seems in an instant a wave washed up and swallowed her."* Jenny is now sobbing, *"My baby, my baby! I let her die."*

We continued tapping and using several other energetic strategies and some of the process in the forthcoming chapters.

Jenny has not had fears of her daughter dying since that session.

The Emotional Aspects of Trauma

Trauma in most people presents as emotion as the neurological reactions result in shock, denial, anxiety and fear, grief, depression, aggression and anger associated with serving in or growing up in a "war" zone or witnessing natural or perpetrated disaster. To a lesser degree with other traumas the body's responses become the war zone continually in attack-defend mode.

There is an altered cellular biochemical response associated with trauma that locks it in the body until it is energetically healed. (Pert, 1994)

Emotionally, PTSD clients tend to avoid strong feelings because the limbic area, the brain's womb for emotions, does not differentiate well and strong feelings trigger the strong feelings of the trauma-terror and panic. This can even be true with positive feelings; closeness, love, intimacy, and joy can trigger the fear of potential loss and the traumatized person will withdraw from close relationships rather than risk devastating feelings.

Thus it is difficult to express one's self and to be in relationship with others at an emotional level when a traumatized emotional system is in charge. Most people with PTSD tell me that they believe that a closed heart is part of survival. On the other end of the scale, there are clients who are so meshed with their traumatic feelings and seem to scream and cry their way through life. Others ride the roller coaster from distancing with their closed heart to exploding to keep people at bay. This is exhausting and physically debilitating and of course wreaks havoc in relationships.

The Social Aspects of Trauma

Socially, because of these mental-emotional patterns, people with traumatic histories or even one major traumatic event tend to act out in relationships or isolate themselves. Both strategies work to keep them at a distance from their emotions and from others. Community and relationships do not come easily even when they deeply desire them. Again, feelings of love and closeness bring up strong feelings and the brain is not always kind. Strong positive feelings bring up the energy field of strong negative feelings, and emotions are taken over by the traumatic responses.

Staci, 8 years old, suffered neglect and abuse for the first six years of her life before child services intervened and had her removed from the home. Her foster Mom adopted her a year before we met. Mom described Staci at first as being loving and receptive, and then one day seemed to turn on her mother and would not receive the love that Mom still offered. Mom was in pain and angry as we talked.

Adopted children will take out their conscious and unconscious feelings about not being protected and about being abandoned particularly on their mothers. Even if it is a carefully planned adoption at birth, adoptees tell me their experience is abandonment.

I always explain to children why they are reacting the way that they are because they feel so badly for not "loving" their new parent. I ask them to imagine how mad and scared they were when they were a baby and their birth parents couldn't take care of them or hurt them. For several months Staci played and drew and tapped the meridian points about her feelings and experiences.

Mom came in and did an intention to "Heal and clear everything that is in the way in her life of Staci attaching fully to her." Not surprising, it is my experience that parents and foster parents of adopted children have attachment issues and these intentions turn out to be very powerful for their growth as a person and a parent and in all of their relationships. Within a short time I asked Staci to initiate five minutes a day of cuddling with her mother, and within a month Mom reported that the cuddling sessions were lengthening. Tapping on the fears and traumas allowed this true closeness for Staci and her Mom.

The Spiritual Aspect of Trauma

Spiritually, trauma may create a crisis of faith or a block to seeking the spiritual—many die with a bitter heart turning away from their faith, or at the very least deeply questioning their spiritual life. The soul's job is to live on beyond this earth-plane experience, and it goes to any length to survive. Pieces of the soul that hold precious positives that the spirit needs to keep intact will split off. Often, joy, happiness or a gift is laying in wait after the healing of trauma.

I should note here also that there are those that may develop illness from their traumas and may suffer horribly from imprisonment, abuse or natural disaster that are spiritually resilient and keep their faith intact. I am reminded of the stories of Nelson Mandela, imprisoned in South Africa during apartheid for 25 years who prayed for and befriended his prison guards.

In 2005 I had the privilege to work for a few weeks in a shelter in Louisiana weeks after Hurricane Katrina hit, including the weekend that Hurricane Rita followed. I was intrigued that most had a story of faith that helped them hold their anguish and their devastating losses. It did not matter at all what their religious or spiritual history was, those that coped best had a story based on their faith and the story became the sacred energetic container that held all that was lost and a future unknown. Whether Baptist or Catholic, they were able to maintain one day at a time with the strength of this story.

Sometimes religion thwarts the creativity and curiosity of childhood and young adults have to abandon the god of their childhood in order to grow.

Greg calls himself a recovering Mormon who came to do energy work reluctantly with his new partner, Barb. He had some mild depression, but mostly they were so excited about this new relationship that they wanted to do this work together to clear baggage from past relationships. When Greg was 17, he decided to break from the church he had been raised in which caused a tremendous amount of tension and guilt on his part regarding his Mom and Dad. He loved his parents, just not their theology.

A number of times in working on origins this "Mormon guilt" came pouring forward and tapping the meridian points was effective in releasing it.

Greg went on to fully embrace his lost creativity and curiosity and his artistic talents as a painter and recently had a show featuring his art in a major city.

Evidence of Energy Healing Trauma

In Energy Psychology and Dynamic Energetic Healing specifically, we have come to realize that trauma, loss and grief underlies most mental-emotional and physical health issues. We have also come to understand that trauma's foundation is energetic and creates bio-energetic disturbance. Most trauma can be completely alleviated and the body and mind restored to physical well being through energetic-spiritual intervention.

our trainings with Swack that we, the DEH development team, first
...ed trauma as energetic. However, it was at a play therapy seminar in
portland, rather than an energy psychology training, that the neurological and
the energetic came together. I sat in awe as Bessel Van der Kolk, an MD from
Harvard first displayed images of the brain taken of single episode rape victims
before and after Shapiro's Eye Movement Desensitization Reprocessing (EMDR).
These images showed remarkable healing in the right hemisphere after only
three sessions of EMDR (Van der Kolk, 1996). EMDR shifts the energy field
which shifts the neurology. As I listened to Bessel van der Kolk at our Play
Therapy Institute in Portland talk about the neurological basis for traumatic
stress, I was impressed by the larger than life brain images he displayed on the
screen of pre and post treatment images of PTSD. He explained that trauma is
typically held in the area of the brain that holds dreams and the unconscious
and that treatment makes the trauma conscious and therefore available for
healing as reflected in his patient's brain images. (Van der Kolk, 1996)

This has been similarly replicated in energy psychology using a digitized
electroencephalogram after tapping on the meridian points with similar results as
van der Kolk's in the reduction of anxiety by Joaquin Andrade, MD, published in
The Energy Psychology Interactive (Feinstein 2005) and summarized at
energypsych.org. We now have physical evidence of healed trauma from
anxiety in the energy field with energetic interventions.

In an earlier clinical study we found nearly complete resolution of PTSD
in 17 DEH clients with that diagnosis. (Brockman, Hammond-Newman Gallo,
ed. 2002).

DEH and other energy psychology models work so well because the core for
healing all illness is trauma. Depression, panic disorder, dissociation, and psychosis all
traumatize the brain and the body. Multiple sclerosis, fibromyalgia, rheumatoid arthritis,
cancer, heart disease and injury all traumatize the brain and the body and have
associated grief and depression which is why patients with chronic physical illness
come to see me. Grief and loss and the resulting fear also traumatize the mind and the
body. Trauma, in what we commonly call mental and physical conditions, can be
accessed and healed from the energetic level by following the steps in this book.

In my practice 95 percent of people who come for treatment or help get
better to their satisfaction or completely heal. The other 5 percent do not want
to pursue energy work, or I do not know enough yet to help them.

A few clients came in when death from cancer was imminent ᴄ
assisted them with clearing unfinished business, their fear of death, and
confusion regarding the possibilities of afterlife. It was too late for their bodies
to heal, but not too late for their spirits to prepare.

*Chad and I had known each other but not seen each other for twenty years.
We had both developed some of the first college chemical dependency programs
in the Northwest. He came in to see if we could heal his cancer which by then
was throughout his body. In the ensuing sessions, however, he needed to talk
about relationships and his children and the harm he had caused in his addictive
years. We tapped about his ancestry and the origins of addiction, and we tapped
regarding guilt and loss in his relationships. We tapped about the hurt that he
had caused for his children.*

*We did TAT about the origins of cancer—the shock and the anger and the
pain. I watched his body go as his heart and spirit were freed.*

We can and often do heal cancer energetically, except when it is very
progressed or it is time for the person to cross over.

Trauma in the energy field and expressed in the body is the basis of illness
and disturbance. Physical, mental, emotional, social-behavioral and spiritual
recovery is possible with the careful application of energy work, and
reconnection with self and others and nature results.

Points of interest for discussion from this chapter:

- Traumatized people can now be in control of their brain function.
- Trauma results from illness, injury, and witnessing traumatic events.
- Trauma has bio-neurological effects.
- Trauma affects the whole person.

SECTION TWO

Preparing the Energy Field

Prelude:

Grounded now in the comprehensive framework in the previous chapters, we are ready to discuss the major preparatory components of energy work. Most energy psychology and energy medicine models begin with strengthening the energy field to contain the healing. We add calling in the sacred to prepare the space and consecrate the energy fields of the individuals.

Chapter Six
Calling In The Sacred

"I saw a brightness so great..."

Hidegard von Bingen

Whether working with energy in people for healing work or soul's purpose we are aware that the surrounding energy needs to resonate with sacred frequencies. In an individual or group session we begin by calling in the sacred to protect the room, the practitioner, the client, and the objects and process of healing. We find healing to be deeper and more profound with this emphasis on the sacred.

The Room as Sacred Space

My new found friends and colleagues in energy psychology had anticipated this weekend for months—an advanced training in working with trauma with energy work. My clients were anticipating this also as they had been deeply comforted by simply tapping on the thymus and meridian points which I had learned in the basic training.

I got to our classroom early the next morning and found Allie, another student, circling the room with a smudge stick, and Jane, also a student, chanting. Allie, walking counter clockwise in the shamanic fashion, explained she was clearing the room of unwanted energies from yesterday. Then, walking clockwise, she invited in Creator's protection for us as we worked. Jane and Allie were assisting in raising and strengthening the vibrations of the energy of the room. They were creating sacred space which allows for greater healing.

There are many ways to create sacred space, preparing the room for the healing session. We may call in a visualization of colors or nature. We may ring a Tibetan bell, or the crystal bowls with their pallet.

We may call in the energy of love, or the essence of soul.

To create sacred space before a DEH session, draw on the universal energy that is available at every moment and invoke this energy to infuse the rituals that are a part of your path already. Invoke the universal energy and pray, invoke the universal energy and smudge, invoke the universal energy and rattle or drum, invoke the universal energy and chant or meditate, or read from sacred texts, draw a tarot or an angel card and meditate on the message from the forces behind the text or the card.

We prepare the space daily to clear negative energies and strengthen the sacred space throughout the day. We pay attention to the colors, the sounds, the scents, and the essence of the room. We make the space and its furnishings safe for our energetic exploration.

Sacred space makes a distinctive difference in allowing for the energy strategies presented in this book to work more fully and efficiently. Sacred space offers protection to the body and the spirit of the practitioner and the client.

Creating the space as sacred also offers the protection of the spiritual realm as you are working on a difficult trauma or on healing disease or illness or injury.

Doubting the Sacred

If you picked up this book you are interested in healing or energy work, soul's purpose or all three. But some of you do not consider yourself spiritually inclined, so calling in the sacred may seem antithetical to your nature. Spiritual or religious language may conjure up images of pious church ladies, abusive priests or outdated ideologies. Inherent in DEH are opportunities to heal the limitations, misuse or abuse of the religions of our past.

I want to pause for a moment here to acknowledge that the sacred is not initially comforting for all participants.

Ginny deeply desired the healing she knew she would attain from attending a DEH group, but she was also very frightened as we drummed and chanted to call in the sacred. She curled up in a corner, did the tapping intervention you will learn later in the book, and soon rejoined the circle. She later told her story of being 12 in her parents' charismatic church and being taken to "healings" with no explanations of the practices, but worse yet conducted by a minister who unbeknownst to her parents had sexually abused her.

With guidance she used the energy interventions described in this book to clear her religious trauma.

In this circle her 12-year-old within found her voice and made steps in reclaiming her religion and her spiritual center free of the abuse.

I generally do not invoke the rituals that create sacred space when clients are present unless they are trained in spiritual or energy psychology, and would like to participate in this. I add the spiritual components more overtly as trust builds with a person and I get to know the person's spiritual point of view. DEH is at its strongest when combined with the client's spiritual or religious traditions. If the client is not interested in the spiritual, I then ask what inspires them? Generally, their answer will be love for family and children, or nature. Love and nature hold powerful healing energy. I simply use those words when calling in the sacred, as necessary, during a session for deeply imbedded trauma or other negative energies.

I met Sam when I was fairly new in my energy psychology training and was eager to try my newfound tools on his depression and addictions.

He made great progress in spite of the fact that he claimed to have no spiritual life. He had had a bitter break as an employee of the Mormon church years before and turned his back on God. To help him refocus on his spirituality, I asked him what inspired him? He replied, "The willow tree in my neighbor's yard." For months as he worked through his issues we called in the sacred space with the power of the willow tree.

The divine is ever so generous.

The sacred in DEH is organic to the process. Healing strengthens the individual connection with the universal energy field. If there are blocks to spiritual language, simply focus on what you love, what inspires you, what you long for and what your passions are. In this lies the energy of the divine—our personal soul connection.

Sacred Space and the Practitioner

The practitioner also must resonate with sacred energy frequencies. Healing and self-healing practitioners are best protected and most effective if they have a spiritual practice and a daily energy routine. Development of both unfolds as you follow the steps to healing in these pages. The spiritual practice may include meditation, prayer, qigong, yoga, or many other practices.

DEH guides you to become aware of and to adjust to your body's energy field to make healing possible. The first step in adjusting the energy field is to create sacred space. Please create your space as sacred as you read this book, intending that whatever healing or unblocking you wish will begin as you read. I offer healing ahead of time to all who read this book with the intention that as millions of people throughout the world heal, the positive energy will in turn heal those around them, their communities, the planet and bring peace in all of our relations.

Ritual and The Sacred Space

Somewhere along the way, for many, ritual lost its place and its meaning in modern cultures, and became a rote, mechanical process. In DEH work we recapture this practice of creating sacred space and ritual, and encourage you to do so as you embark on your DEH journey. As you learn energy testing and the meridian and chakra clearings, think of them as rituals as well as strategies for release and relief. When you work with the imagery and trance states in DEH, imagine the acupressure tapping as tapping into the collective rhythm of our ancestors, and the collective beat of the ancient drummers drawing in the Goddesses and Gods to promote health, wealth and healing. Imagine the bells and bowls as ancient temple or church bells ringing in Creator for healing.

Here is a ritual for creating sacred space beforehand or when you and the person wishing a healing experience agree to do it in session.

Light a candle or two or three, and incense if fragrance enhances your healing experience.

Say to yourself or to your client or your healing circle:

Close your eyes with me for a few moments, calling on your connection with the Divine. You may call that divine connection God, Great Spirit, Universal Light, Divine Mother, Goddess, Higher Power or whatever you wish. You may feel, see or hear the whisper of Her/His presence. Ask for blessings upon the room, the space. Call in the colors of Divine Light to seal the space as sacred and protected from malign influence. Ask your Guides and Ancestors that will assist us today to be present. Ask for protection and guidance for the person who requests healing and for the practitioner/healer. Ask to be fully connected with your inner healer. Use sound—ring a crystal bowl, or a sacred Tibetan bell, or drum to increase the vibrations in the room. Sing a song or chant to enhance the sacred space. Thank all of the Beings from the other side for their presence.

If the person you are working with has a special prayer from their tradition invite them to add this to the creation of sacred space.

In creating sacred space we sometimes use a ritual, as stated here, to call on the Divine to create the spiritual container for healing. Since the beginning of human existence we have used ritual and ceremony for transformation and change. In ancient times, ritual was alive and understood to be a natural, essential component in daily life. Indigenous people all over the planet still have a vital relationship to ritual. Ritual is a conscious act of recognizing transition and change.

Ritual was very important in the ancient divine feminine cultures. Ritual had deep meaning because the women connected with the universal energy and channeled it through their hands, projecting that energy into ritual objects to make them sacred. The sacred objects would then be drawn on for spiritual ceremony or used to invoke physical healing. The objects were sacred and held their place because of the intention the women held to create them as sacred. The objects had meaning because of the lore that built up as the healer and the priestess worked with them in the community. All women in these early communities had healing gifts and used them day to day for healing, to bless the food, enhance the crops, and care for their children.

Prayer, visualization, movement, chanting, and other sacred sound are examples of rituals. Nancy Gordon guided me to the work of Allan Combs and Mark Holland, _Synchronicity—Science, Myth_ where they explain that the word "ritual" comes from the Indo-European root which means "to energetically fit together." In DEH we use ritual to energetically fit together or link the energy of Spirit and the practitioner, the client, the problem to be addressed, and the environment in which you are working, to enhance healing.

While working on healing we treat the energy strategies, the use of sound, and the use of imagery throughout the session as ritual, thus linking spirit and energy with the practitioner and the client. Throughout the DEH process, spiritual energy threads through ritual in sacred intention, in our use of sacred objects, and in the act of witnessing the healing. In DEH we treat each step of the process as ritual, as sacred.

Ritual
by Ruth Crowley

Ritual is a door.
Walk through it,
you will find
the multitudes who have
said the same words,
danced the same dance,
lit the same candle,
drawn down the same moon.
They have been waiting for you.
They reach out their hands.
Join the circle,
dance with the ancestors.

And when you have danced—
turn back to the door
and open it
to invite
the multitudes who will
dance the future.

The Healing Field

DEH seems to be most efficient and effective when contained by universal energy, which many would call Spirit or God or its thousand other names. Picture, if you will, a bubble of sacred energy surrounding the space you are in creating a container of light and love for your healing. In addition picture an energetic container that surrounds the individual and contains the healing. When people have continued failed attempts to overcome a problem or an issue, it is often because their spiritual container or energetic vessel is not strong enough to hold the healing of the illness, issue or the problem. In other words their depression or their addictions, for example, are larger than their spiritual life or practice.

To illustrate this container I often draw concentric circles for people to see what it looks like to have a problem, issue or illness larger than one's spiritual container rather than having a large enough spiritual vessel to hold the healing of the problem, issue or illness.

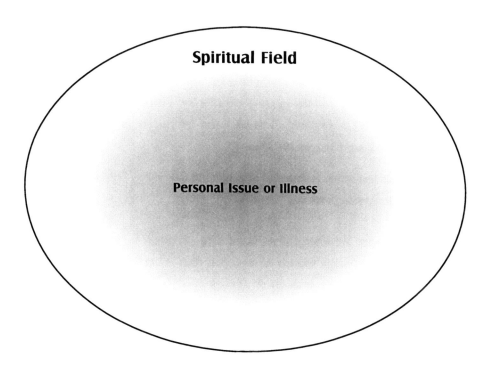

Thus in DEH we continually call in the sacred energy to assist in creating a spiritual vessel for healing that is not only larger but also stronger than what is available to the individual without spiritual aid.

Creating sacred space results in an energy field for healing. When you call in the divine, the call creates a vibrating field of energy that resonates with your particular needs for healing. This energy field continues to attract the divine energy, which recaptures the everyday sacred and protects the individuals. The sacred healing field allows you to work alone or with a practitioner, deepen your connection with Spirit, and bring the magic of the mystic to your work as a healer.

There are as many stories of healing as I have had clients over the last decade. Here is one of my favorites as we take this written journey together.

Roy brought his young girls in to see me after they revealed that they had been abused while they were not in his custody. They were in terrible pain and he was wracked with guilt for not being there to protect them. He had gone to a Christian Bible college and was active in his town in his evangelical faith. I taught them the energy tapping in the first session. The next week he told me that he had tapped every day, focusing on his grief and his guilt, and was amazed by the results. I suggested that he also combine tapping with familiar prayers, and to think about what he was experiencing as the Holy Spirit, or the Christian version of chi.

He grew to trust me as his girls recovered and began to find normal lives, and a couple of months later he said, grinning, "The truth is in that first session I thought you were crazy and the tapping was silly, so I tapped every day to prove that it wouldn't work and I could come back and tell you so! But it did work and along with God, it has changed our lives!"

Creating sacred space is essential in preparing the energy field for energy testing and energy interventions.

Points of interest for discussion from this chapter:

- DEH® and some energy models recommend reinforcing the energy field of the room and the people with divine energy.
- Some people have life experiences that cause them to doubt the support of anything sacred and energy work can help heal their doubts.
- The practitioner is advised to do a daily energetic practice.
- Energy work returns or enhances ritual in our lives.
- Then sacred space contains the illness and issues that present for healing.
- Practitioners are encouraged to be ever mindful and respectful of the spiritual orientation that each client embraces.

Chapter Seven
The Body's Energetic Wisdom

"The body heals itself in a sure, sensible, practical, reasonable, observable, predictable manner. The healer within can be approached from without and possesses a potential for recovery through the innate intelligence or the physiological homeostasis of the human structure."

George Goodheart, D.C.

Assessing the Body's Energy Field

In this sacred space, energy can be put to our highest use for our health and well-being. This chapter describes methods for assessing our body's energy field.

In 1982 my friend Daryl Thomas, with whom I worked at an alcohol and drug treatment center, asked me to stick out my arm. Surprised but curious, I extended my arm and she pressed on it as she asked me yes or no questions about my life and health. When the answer was yes, my arm would remain strong and straight; when it was no, the arm would fall, seemingly without my conscious input. We did this muscle testing several times, and I found it interesting but just too strange to accept. It ran counter to my intellect and my need for control that my body could be giving answers on its own. Besides, the muscle testing came from my wonderful but strange new age friend. But times change. Daryl and I dance in and out of one another's lives at pivotal times, and now I am considered stranger than she in our community, I am sure. She is now a professor of Mind-Body Health at Western Oregon University, and making a difference for many in Oregon communities with her interest in integrative health; she recently became a DEH practitioner.

Over a decade later, in my initial Energy Psychology trainings, I learned manual muscle testing, which I also term energy testing because it more accurately describes what we are testing. We are testing the body's energy through the muscle. We are not testing the muscle, however, the strength of the muscle indicates the strength of the energy rather than muscular robustness.

It still felt strange and may be strange to new people using it. By the time I was re-introduced to testing the body's wisdom, I had spent a decade or more playing in the realm of the sub-conscious and working with subtle energies and now readily accept that what we know at the conscious level is just the tip of the iceberg.

I was told again to hold my arm out steadily while my partner asked yes or no questions placing light pressure just above my wrist regarding what was best for my healing intention. I was no longer resistant, and more than curious. It has since become one of the most useful tools in my Energy Psychology practice. Most DEH practitioners use a combination of energy testing (ET) and intuition. ET is used by some but not by all Energy Psychology practitioners. Those that use it extensively emphasize the science of it (Gallo, 2000). Those that do not use it emphasize the importance of the practitioner's intuitive abilities. (Craig, 1998)

Soon after my time in Prague, where I first heard Sheldrake speak, I experienced a great deal of personal and professional angst. Always a seeker, I looked for teachers and was led to this budding field, Energy Psychology. I spent several years in hotel conference rooms in Seattle, Portland, San Francisco, San Diego and Las Vegas learning the strategies that guide the body's wisdom in Healing from the Body Level Up with Judith Swack; Thought Field Therapy with Helen Tuggy; EFT with Gary Craig; Touch and Breathe with John Diepold; Tapas Acupuncture Technique with Tapas Fleming; and Be Set Free Fast with Larry Nims. These trainings opened the way to DEH.

The Thought Field Therapy seminar taught by Helen Tuggy was abuzz with the conversation of about 30 seasoned therapists, many of whom I recognized, as we anticipated the experience of learning Roger Callahan's methods from psychologist Helen Tuggy, Ph.D.

We not only tapped with two fingers on meridian points for specific mental/emotional issues, but also learned how to assess the body/energy field from the body's own wisdom. I have to admit, we were all fascinated by the process and somewhat self-conscious about tapping on ourselves and pressing on one another's arms as we muscle tested. We alternated between asking scientific questions from our academic minds, and giggling like children with a new game.

Energy (Muscle) Testing

We witnessed demonstrations of the body's wisdom with Energy Testing, also called muscle testing and energy checking was first developed by physical therapists Florence and Henry Kendall to test the function and strength of the body's systems (Kendall & Kendall, 1949). Later, in 1964, Dr. George Goodheart, chiropractor, observed that a weak muscle could be treated and the strength immediately improved. From this simple observation he began a lifelong search for the treatment methods that could improve muscle strength, viewing muscle strength as an indicator of health holding the body's energy. Along the way he discovered many factors, physical, emotional and mental, that could positively or negatively affect muscle strength. He named this area of investigation and discovery "Applied Kinesiology." He chose to use the term "kinesiology," as this implies the study of motion, movement, and muscle function. He added the term "applied" because what he was doing was not the discipline of standard kinesiology. (Goodheart, Frost, 2002)

Dr. Goodheart and his colleagues discovered that when the practitioner puts the correct quantity of needed herbal supplements in a person's hand, the person's arm strengthens when muscle tested. If the practitioner places the wrong kind or amount of supplements, or toxic substances such as sugar, in the person's hand, the arm would weaken when muscle tested. Applied kinesiologists went on to develop a complex system of using different muscles in the body to assess the function of the organ systems in the body.

Energy (Muscle) Testing

Psychiatrist John Diamond, MD, studied Goodheart's methods with particular interest and discovered that the arm weakens with distressing thoughts and strengthens with positive thoughts. He elaborates on this research in his books, *The Body Doesn't Lie* and *Life Energy*. Gradually, through the work of Diamond, Callahan, and others such as Fred Gallo, Ph.D., we have come to understand that during muscle testing, the arm will strengthen on statements that are true for the person and weaken on statements that are not true.

Sharon suffered for years from chronic depression, and was on many medications over a couple of decades. She had arthritis, and fibromyalgia as well. She had to leave a job working for a legislator which she was good at, although her real love was art. Using the process in this book, we detected the origins of her seemingly debilitating depression with energy/ muscle testing, and with DEH treatment it completely disappeared. She has been free of depression for 10 years. A few years later she consulted me again because of an underlying anxiety and compulsivity that was creating discomfort. Again we used manual muscle testing to track the energetic structure of her anxiety and within a few sessions the extremes of her compulsivity disappeared. Although she did not return to the legislature to her old job, she attended a soul's purpose group and began living her dream of pursuing art for both pleasure and income.

Manual muscle and energy testing are the generic terms used by those outside the chiropractic field for assessing a person's symptoms and issues by means of indicator muscles. In the chiropractic field it is called Applied Kinesiology. Energy testing (ET) reflects the assumption in energy psychology, derived from psychiatrist John Diamond's work with George Goodheart, that "the indicator muscle is reflective of specific information within thought fields when a psychological problem is attuned..." (Gallo, 2000)

The developers of muscle testing found that there could be interferences or problems that distort the results of muscle testing. In DEH, we have found that we can mitigate these interferences by teaching the practitioner to connect with Universal Sources. However, problems still occur. Later in this chapter energy strategies are described to correct them.

John Diamond, an Australian psychiatrist, developed Behavioral Kinesiology after studying Applied Kinesiology in the 1970s.

"In 1979, Diamond's model began to integrate aspects of psychiatry, psychosomatic medicine, kinesiology, preventive medicine, and humanities... Diamond's earlier approach involved the use of affirmations, the thymus thump, homing thoughts, imagery, and elements of the Alexander Method, a posture therapy, to balance the life energy of Chi after a meridian imbalance was detected through kinesiological tests...Diamond's work represents the first attempt to integrate Applied Kinesiology and psychotherapy." (Gallo, 2000, p.68)

Dynamic Energetic Healing Style of Energy Testing

I have always enjoyed the detective work of being a healthcare practitioner—asking the carefully formulated questions to determine the differences between mental health problems and spiritual crisis. Or to determine the patterns of emotion and thought that accompany physical pain or illness. Or the client and I may unravel denial or discover the early origins of trauma so that they might heal. This makes my day to day work interesting and extremely satisfying. Discovering the art and science of energy/muscle testing to do the detective work makes it more thorough, exact and much less tedious than previous assessment models. Let us consider energy/muscle testing in several related ways: physically, mentally, intuitively, spiritually and, of course, energetically.

Physically, energy testing uses the anatomy to read the energy field. In forward, face-to-face muscle testing using one or two arms, we attend to the locking of the deltoid muscle in the shoulder to determine strength and accuracy. We also pay attention to the difference in the strength and weakness as each person that is tested; some people test very strong on true answers, others less strong even though the deltoid muscle locks. Some people's arms drop on a weak or a "no" answer, while others move a few inches down.

Mentally, people report both a tremendous increase in focus and awareness as they clear their energy field and consistent reinforcement of this increased intuition through ET. They also describe changed thinking about themselves as energy testing affirms positive change.

Energy testing is the body's register for intuition. What is unconscious becomes conscious as the fingertips of the practitioner meet the energy of the one being tested. Intuition straddles the categories of mental and spiritual, since intuitive information comes through the subconscious mind and is felt in the body or seen in visions. Energy seems to have a spiritual connection to our

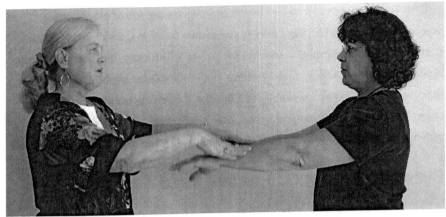

DEH Energy testing, face-to-face

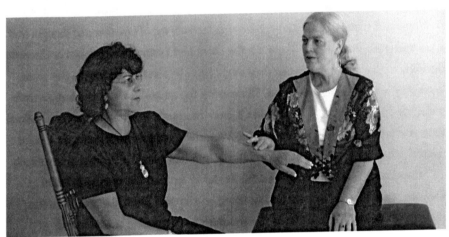

DEH Energy testing, side

highest self and guides, and comes forth in images, body sensations, or words. Information from the subconscious mind can be ascertained with energy testing. We ask questions whose answers are stored in the body's cellular and genetic memory, and receive answers about what to heal.

Spiritually, we intend in DEH that the testing, as well as the entire session, is guided by a Universal Source. Energy testing is enhanced by creating sacred space. You may call it "Source" or you may call it by a divine name of your choice. The practitioner's and client's spiritual practice in DEH is important, and we consider ET to be one of the sacred rituals in which both participate. Spiritual practice alleviates the frequency and the need for many of the corrections that follow in this chapter as a standard part of energy work.

Energetically, we pay attention to all of the attributes of energy-strength, balance, reversal and the person's relationship to the practitioner's energy, and to their relationship to the room and the surroundings.

In DEH we use face-to-face muscle testing, either standing or sitting. Most energy healing models that incorporate energy testing stand to the side and behind or in front of the client to muscle test.

However, we have experimented with both styles and find no difference in efficiency or accuracy. We prefer the overlap of the practitioner's energy field with the client's, both to develop rapport and to strengthen the client's healing field. The overlap of fields also allows for greater sensitivity on the practitioner's part to the client's field. The face-to-face position creates an energetic interface where one energy field can "read" the other. The face-to-face position is also more comfortable and less stressful on the arms during longer sessions.

Energy testing is perfectly safe for anyone to use; however, as with any new skill, practice brings ease, proficiency, and accuracy. The body's wisdom seems to access a power greater than ourselves, a guiding force, or "Source."

How We Energy Test in DEH

Stand or sit face to face with the other person's arms outstretched, angled slightly downward from the shoulders. The practitioner places gentle but firm pressure about halfway between the wrist and the elbow on the person's forearm while the person resists slightly. The arm will remain strong on answers that are true for the individual and weak on answers not true for the individual—unless some of the correctable problems exist as described in the next section. Say, "Hold against my fingers," or "Meet my pressure," when you begin to press. A strong, firmly held arm position is a yes answer; a yielding or weak arm is a no answer.

Additionally, as I test a person I say the word "neutral," silently to myself, to dispel any preconceived notions of mine that may interfere.

We combine our sense of intuition and scientific evidence in DEH. We have found it to be useful and trustworthy and efficient in assessing directly what we should work on for the client's progress.

Manual Muscle testing and Applied Kinesiology in general have built a large body of physical science behind the use of testing muscles for diagnosis. However, our experience of Energy testing is that it simultaneously builds

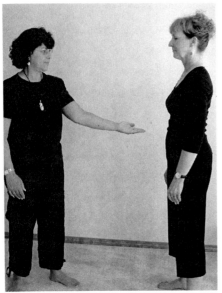

Zip up   *Zip down*

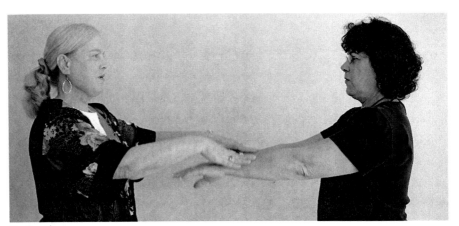

Testing the arm

intuition and checks intuition. So the more we use ET as practitioners the less we need it. The more we use it for our clients, the greater the expansion of their intuition which is why we continue to use it.

Although karmic work reveals that female healers used ET in ancient times, energy psychology adapted muscle testing from the chiropractic field, which originated in physical therapy. (Kendall and Kendall, 1949) The chiropractor Dr. George Goodheart, Jr. developed manual muscle testing (MMT) as part of a larger field in chiropractic medicine, Applied Kinesiology. Chiropractors determined that the body/energy field could be read by isolating what they called the "indicator muscle." The deltoid muscle used in energy psychology is one of the muscles used by chiropractors. We use the deltoid or shoulder muscle as the indicator muscle while the client holds her/his arm straight out to the side or in front parallel to the floor. Saying, "Meet my pressure," and holding firmly, the practitioner places gentle but firm pressure above the wrist on the person's forearm while the person resists slightly with about 10 percent of strength.

In DEH the emphasis on creating sacred space seems to alleviate many of the usual problems that muscle testing may otherwise present. Our intention is to have energy testing divinely guided. Thus we experience less difficulty in achieving accurate, reliable energy testing.

However, other energy testing problems can occur in addition to psycho-energetic reversal that need to be corrected before the assessment and answers will be accurate. Let us review some of them.

Dehydration

Humans are 70 percent water, and the energy field is electromagnetic. Therefore, the body-energy field must be well hydrated to operate effectively. Sometimes the simplest correction for difficulties with energy testing is to provide adequate water. Both practitioner and client need to drink water throughout the session. We always provide a pitcher or a bottle of filtered water to drink during the sessions. Recently I have been blessing the water that we drink with love and gratitude, as Emoto found in his work, *New Messages from Water* that water responds to loving words by forming beautiful, exquisite crystals, the holiest of water.

Switching of Energy Polarities

In contrast to energy reversal which is your energy flowing backwards on the meridian lines (see diagram page 82) switching of the energy polarities is a problem with the auric field.

Instead of being open, the client's responses may indicate that the energy system is closed to muscle testing and the healing process. To detect switching:

Zip up and Zip down

1. Practitioner slowly sweeps her hand up the center of the client's body from the pelvic bone to the chin without touching the body. Arm should test strong. Switching is detected when the arm tests weak.

Cook's balance standing   *Cook's balance sitting*

Triangle at heart center

2. Practitioner slowly sweeps her hand down the center of the client's body from the chin to the pelvic bone without touching the body. Arm should test weak. Switching is detected when the arm tests strong.
3. Always end with number one, and add energetic boundary work from this book to keep the auric field strong.

Strong Arm Problem

Another indication is continuously strong arm responses to all questions. correct for non-polarization with the deep breathing and/or the thymus thump, and check for a clear intention to access the body's wisdom. The person may be switched in general or in relationship to a specific issue.

The ET problems may reflect that the person is not ready to reveal their personal thoughts and feelings to the practitioner, or as Nancy Gordon determined with several clients, they were not allowed or able to make clear decisions, to say yes or no, in their daily lives.

Corrections: Create an intention to be able to clearly say yes or no in your life, or an intention to have full access to your body's wisdom, and proceed with the protocols outlined in *Energetic Origins,* or do Cooks' balance from *Touch for Health* and adapted in *Energy Medicine.*

Cook's Balance

This is an excellent general posture for correction of any energy imbalance, as well as excessive energy or deficient energy. This balance is used in *Touch for Health* (Thie, 1977) and in *Energy Medicine* (Eden, 1999).
1. Stand or sit with feet crossed at ankles.
2. Cross arms across chest and grasp hands with little fingers resting on chest.
3. Stare forward at spot on the wall until there is no sway.
4. Then stand with feet apart about two and a half feet.
5. Create a diamond with index fingers and thumbs over heart center, palms facing outward.
6. Stand in this position until centered—1-3 min.
7. Retest and the client's energy should be in proper balance.

Sometimes problems can arise due to the condition of your energy field. Problems with energy testing are always correctable with the following solutions. These are some of the problems that you need to be aware of when you do manual muscle testing. Strengthening the sacred space may prevent problems that arise with energy testing.

The body's wisdom becomes a guide for the healing path.

Energy Testing Yourself

There are several ways to energy test yourself, but most of us find it awkward to use the arm method on ourselves. Here is one method that works well for me and my clients and students.

The "O" Ring

Look at the picture below and follow these steps:

1. With your non-dominant hand make an "O," and hold it strongly.
2. Place your forefinger in the "O" and pull, stating "yes." The "O" should remain strong.
3. Pull again and say "no." Your "O" should come apart.

If your energy field reverses easily or you often have testing problems, it may be hard to use energy testing on yourself. In that case, it is best to work with someone who is skilled in energy testing and energy psychology to correct the problems. After you work on your initial intentions and use tapping and

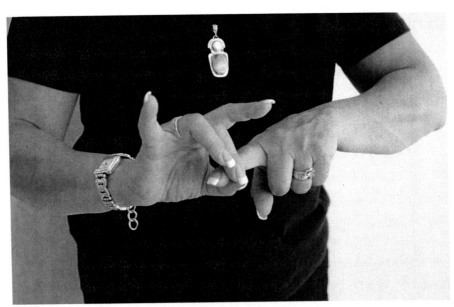

The "O" ring

chakra balancing for several months you will likely be able to test yourself.

To Energy Test or Not?

People frequently ask me to muscle test them on whether they should take a job, date or marry a person or wonder if we can pick lottery numbers! I explain that this is not the appropriate use of energy testing, and if we could pick lottery numbers my office would be more plush!

Tabitha came in for a session very excited about a new job prospect. She stuck out her arm and said, "Will you test if I should take this job or not?"

"Well," I said, "muscle testing is not a good fortune teller, so how about if we develop an intention, "To clarify whether I should make this career move."

Then we will check for origins and do energy clearings, and you will be clear to use common sense, discernment and your intuition to determine whether this job is right for you.

She agreed. The major part of the energy work was clearing a family pattern of fear of changing jobs or career paths for several generations.

In the end she took the job to work in government, and we never muscle tested if that was okay or not.

Energy testing tests the body's wisdom about the present and about present knowledge of the past, and assists in developing your own intuitive and discernment abilities. However, it is less reliable as a future predictor.

Discernment

Over a decade ago I felt "guided" to sell a business and move to another state. Within six months my employment fell apart and I had to give up and move back to Oregon. In the process I had hurt co-workers who were dear friends, and embarrassed myself greatly. This resulted in a crisis of faith and as I visited with a spiritual teacher I said, "I don't think I trust myself to meditate and so I am not going to anymore."

She said, "Don't stop; just meditate more often and more deeply."

During that same time period I attended a conference in Portland called Spirituality and Mental Health. I needed both! I attended a workshop on spiritual discernment taught by a Quaker. Much is written about spiritual discernment among Quakers. It is a merging of the group mind to "hear God's calling." There is focus and centering over a period of time, hours or months, depending on the complexity of the issue, and the following kinds of questions are asked:

1. What do your elders say?
2. What do your peers say?
3. What does your heart say?
4. What does your head say?
5. What does your whispering voice say?
6. What kind of music do you hear when you think about this?

From my single devastating experience I strongly urge using a combination of intuitive and discernment processes. We all make mistakes in life when risks are taken, but this gentler approach creates greater success in decision making.

Body or Intuition or Spirit?

Energy testing merges the mystery and the science of energy work. One can feel the muscle lock or go weak when testing, but how does the body know the information stored in the body's wisdom and the unconscious mind? Is it intuition or spirit, or is it the body's unique quantum energetic system?

It is all three.

Points of interest for discussion from this chapter:

- Energy testing is commonly called muscle testing and originates with applied kinesiology in the chiropractic field in recent times.
- There are several styles of energy testing.
- There are sometimes problems that call for correction before energy testing is accurate.
- Clarification and discernment are sometimes better tools than energy testing for major life decisions.

Chapter Eight
The Energetic Blocks

Psycho-energetic Reversal

Resistant clients and clients in denial have long been challenging to mental health professionals. I used to wonder why some clients would come to sessions and pay me only to dwell on what wasn't working and why what I had in mind for them would not work in the future—and then continued to come back and pay me again!

We would spend an inordinate amount of time as I carefully directed them to what was right in their life and what possibly could work. This took a good part of each session before we finally got down to the work that was more significant for the changes that they desired. I understood resistance then as fear, anger, distrust, and stubbornness. We addressed resistance at the emotional level and painstakingly got through it.

Clients in denial also provided particular challenges. When clients say they do not have an illness or a problem that is obvious to the practitioner, then what? Denial is a defensive pattern that plays out when life is too painful to face.

The problems these clients first bring to a session usually relate to important relationships in their lives with partners, spouses, or children.

Their view of the world was that if they could just get their child or their partner to act differently, or treat them better, then they would feel fine; never mind that they were so depressed they could barely function, having occasional suicidal thoughts, or drinking a six pack in an evening. Generally, people with strong denial systems have developed them through childhood where denial was required for survival of parental addiction, dysfunction, or abuse.

Denial also has ancestral patterns because the parental addiction, dysfunction, or abuse has gone on in the family for generations. In addition to encouraging abstinence from addictions, I would do careful written assessments with them, and have them log their moods and the interplay of their moods with their significant relationships. Gradually they would get through denial and see the need to focus their treatment on their own issues. Again, the process was long and painful.

It was such a relief to hear from Helen Tuggy Ph.D, in one of our energy psychology trainings say that "Reversal of the electromagnetic energy field accounts for most of what we have referred to as resistance or denial." In energy psychology we have simple energy tests and simple solutions for this problem.

Energy testing often reveals that the energy field is blocked and this chapter deals with the most common block, energy running backwards which is called psychological (Gallo, 2000) reversal or psycho-energetic reversal (Brockman, 2005).

John Diamond discovered what he calls "the reversal of the body morality." Roger Callahan went on to call this Psychological Reversal (Gallo, 2000) and currently we are calling psycho-energetic reversal. It is the interplay of thoughts, feelings, and energy that cause reversal so this term seems a more accurate description. At times when the electromagnetic field is not working properly, it behaves like magnets do when placed end to end. The energy is stopped or more likely is running backwards. When the energy flow is aligned, the chi should flow up the left side of the body and down the right side. When you are reversed, your energy runs backwards and otherwise true statements will test false with ET. Now the standard term is psycho-energetic reversal; the interplay of psychological disturbance with energetic underpinnings.

Interventions on your intention for healing may not work until the reversal is addressed. For instance, even if a person is perfectly willing at the conscious level to do this work, if we ask the person to state, "From the Source and the body/energy field's deepest wisdom, I want to heal my illness," the arms may test weak. That would indicate reversal of the body/energy field.

Toxins seem to cause reversal. Toxins from food and environmental allergic reactions can cause reversal (Radomski,1999), and toxins from emotional reactions and negative thinking patterns such as fear and anger stored at the cellular level can cause reversal. Additionally, we find reversal as a reaction to drugs that have been prescribed to help.

We tend to exhibit this toxic reaction to our own emotions and thoughts as resistance and denial but also as irritability, spaciness, and lack of coordination. People who have chronic illness often have chronic reversal and need to do the energetic reversal correction daily until they have done the origins work described later in this book, and collapsed the energetic structure of their illness.

Celia came to me after suffering for several years with fibromyalgia, chronic fatigue, depression, anxiety, and debilitating chronic pain. She was on many medications for depression and pain, which only gave mild relief.

While doing the origins work on her intention to "100 percent heal my depression, anxiety and fibromyalgia and chronic pain and fatigue, to be active, and full of energy without fatigue," she constantly tested weak on "I want to get well." Celia did the reversal correction every morning and afternoon. Within a month she noticed an increase in functional hours and a decrease in pain even while we were continuing to treat her accompanying issues. More often she would test strong on "I want to get well."

Assessing Psych-energetic Reversal

There are several standard ways to check for psycho-energetic reversal:

Energy test each of the following statements, filling in the blanks with you or your client's desired change. If there is energy reversal the arm will be weak. Use either "heal" or "change," whichever fits the intention or issue.

A. I want to heal/change_____, get well.
B. It's safe for me to heal/change_____.
C. I deserve to heal/change___ _____.
D. It will benefit myself and others for me to heal/change_____.
E. It is possible for me to heal/change_____.
F. I will heal/change this.

The client is reversed if the arm tests weak on any of the above statements.

Another energy test for polarity reversal is as follows:

A. Palm of hand up above crown, should test weak.
B. Palm of hand down above crown should test strong.
   (See photos on following page.)

Palm of hand up above crown.   Palm of hand down above crown.

Correcting Energetic Reversal on Wellness and Purpose

Although some EP systems would suggest using energy testing to choose an intervention for correcting reversal, I find that because of the reversal, energy testing is difficult, and thus I will intuit which one to use. It may be any of the interventions in the chapter, or the sacred energetic tools, but most of the time rubbing the neurovascular points above the breasts will clear it. Among EFT practitioners tapping the karate chop point is used for reversal correction.

In addition to being reversed on wanting to get well as described, one may also be reversed more deeply at the level of soul's purpose. Using the format above try energy testing and stating one at a time:

"I want to live my soul's purpose as an individual,"

"In relationships, in family, in career,"

"In my community," and

"In the world."

It is an enormous block to one's well-being and work in the world to have energy reversal on soul's purpose issues. Reversal can interfere with major life decisions such as marriage, divorce, parenting, or deciding on a career course. Follow the same procedures below for clearing this reversal as for other reversals.

Those in energy psychology and energy medicine call these points, located directly above the breasts, the "psychological reversal points" (PR points), or "reversal points." If intervention is indicated, the client should rub the points in a circular fashion while repeating:

72

1. "Even though I don't want to heal/change/live my soul's purpose in _____, I absolutely love, honor and respect myself."

2. "Even though I don't deserve to heal/change/ live my soul's purpose _____, I absolutely love, honor and respect myself."

3. "Even though I don't feel like it is safe to heal/change _____, I absolutely love, honor and respect myself."

4. "Even though I don't deserve to heal/change/ live my soul's purpose _____, I absolutely love, honor and respect myself."

5. "Even though I don't believe I will heal/change/live my soul's purpose _____, I absolutely love, honor and respect myself."

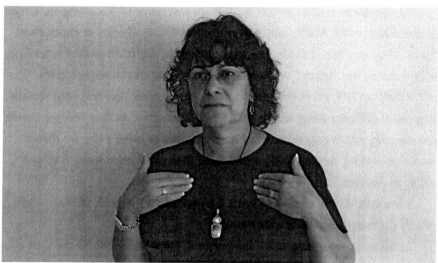

Neurovascular points

Each statement is repeated for one to three minutes or until the reversal statements test strong—that is, until each statement is repeated and manual muscle tests strong. Once in a while chronic reversal persists. If this is the case, you can create an intention with your client to heal the chronic reversal and follow the Energetic Origins protocol.

Correcting psycho-energetic reversal may be the single most important component that energy psychology and energy medicine offer to make wellness possible and living one's purpose plausible.

Energetic Disorganization

"These exercises changed my life and my health."

Client with chronic fatigue and learning challenges

Sometimes people have an energetic problem that impacts the energy system even more dramatically than psycho-energetic reversal. If the person is homolateral, energy is moving up and down on each side of the body and not crossing over the mid-line, resulting in 50 percent less energetic efficiency. Neurological Disorganization is the lack of communication between left and right brain.

The homolateral problem (Eden, 1999) is defined at the energetic level and neurological disorganization (Gallo, 2000) is defined at the physical level.

This condition is often present in children and adults with learning challenges or disabilities, ADD, ADHD, depression, chronic illness, allergies or exposure to toxins. They may have trouble focusing, reading, solving math problems, spelling, with memory, feel "spacy," lack coordination, or have speech impediments.

If they are ND, when they do the following exercise, they will have varying degrees of difficulty doing one or both types of marches. As they continue to do the exercise, which only takes a few minutes, once or twice a day for several weeks or months, they gradually make more than usual improvement in their ability to perform.

It is a safe, simple exercise. Give it a try for yourself or with your child to greatly decrease frustrations with learning.

To proceed, we energy test if the person is homolateral/ND: Draw X on a large piece of paper, energy test while the person is looking at the X, s/he should test strong if not ND or homolateral. And s/he will test weak, if s/he is homolateral/ND.

Correcting the ND/ Homolateral Problem

1. Tap on collarbone points, thymus gland, and spleen neurovascular points, (under breast and over two inches). Tap about 20 times each—a series of three times.
2. Do 12 lateral (soldier) marches—right arm and right leg together, then left arm and left leg together.
3. Do 12 cross crawl marches with the tapping routine interspersed between. Repeat three times.

Tapping under collarbone

Tapping the thymus gland

Tapping or holding the spleen points

4. Do one more series of 12 cross crawl marches, swinging the right arm across the left leg while raising the leg, and then repeat with the opposite arm and leg.
5. Check again with MMT.
6. If still homolateral or ND, check for further interventions.
7. If client is chronically ND, energy test how many times per day or week the ND correction should be performed.

Lateral marching   *Cross-crawl marching*

People who are chronically ND usually have a long term chronic illness or toxin or trauma exposure.

Both adults and children report life-changing results as a result of repeatedly doing the ND correction.

When my daughter Amber was in the fourth grade I visited her classroom every Friday and after the flag salute we did the three thumps and the marches, and also heart center tapping to take care of emotional upsets. They would count to twenty and 12 out loud to make sure I got it right. The first time we did it the teachers' eyes widened and she reported to me quietly after the exercise that all of the children who had trouble with the marches also had trouble with reading and math.

I encouraged them all to do this daily, but especially if they had trouble with reading, math or remembering things.

We began in October and in January one of the little guys came to me in the hall with tears in his eyes and said, "At the beginning of the school year I couldn't read, and I did the tapping and marching everyday and over Christmas vacation I read Harry Potter."

Often times if you clear reversal ND/homolateral clears and vice-versa.

It is difficult to get well from anything let alone live a life of purpose and passion, if your energy is running backwards, or your energy is disorganized. If you take care of these two things all of your healing work will go more smoothly and efficiently. In addition, when reversal and disorganization are corrected then the future healing for the individual will be more lasting and thorough.

Points of interest for discussion from this chapter:

- Energetic reversal presents itself as resistance, denial, and negativity.
- Toxicity from negative emotions, foods, substances or the environment seem to cause reversal.
- Energetic reversal refers to the energy running backwards which impedes our ability to heal.
- Energetic reversal can be easily assessed and corrected.
- Energetic reversal on soul's purpose is a major block to one's well-being.
- Energetic disorganization refers to the energy and the brain communication not crossing over the mid-line.

Chapter Nine
The Sacred Energy Tools

"My life is in my hands, not in the control of heaven and earth."

Lao Tzu, Tao Te Ching

Pressure Points

While studying Chinese medicine, Goodheart discovered that it was possible to substitute pressure for needles in touching acupuncture points, as well as percussing or tapping on the points. The interconnection of glands, organs, and meridians is inherent to acupuncture. By bringing knowledge of muscle testing to the arena, Goodheart and his colleagues discovered a relationship between the various organs and the meridian pathways outlined in Chinese medicine.

By using our hands for self healing our lives are returned to us—fully and responsibly, "in our hands," metaphorically and actually.

In 1979, clinical psychologist Roger J. Callahan began studying Applied Kinesiology with John Diamond. As his interest grew, he went on to attend the 100-hour Applied Kinesiology course and became certified by the International College of Applied Kinesiology. Soon afterwards he developed what was perhaps the first widespread energy psychology methodology initially referred to as the Callahan Techniques™ or Thought Field Therapy (TFT). Callahan's model uses ET to determine exactly which acupressure points will heal a certain mental/emotional issue, and each client is muscle tested for the specific point for his/her particular symptoms.

Callahan chooses to keep Thought Field Therapy or Callahan Techniques™ separate from the mainstream that has become Energy Psychology. Callahan's students and their protegees became the teachers to the world regarding Energy Psychology. From 1990 to the present, however, there has been a surge of developments in this field. Fred Gallo, Ph.D., developed Energy Diagnostic and Treatment Methods (EDxTM). He is thus far the major academic author, with *Energy Psychology* published in 1998, *Energy Diagnostic and Treatment Methods* published in 2000, and *Energy Psychotherapy in Energy Psychology* published in 2002, in which DEH was featured.

Gary Craig, a retired engineer and motivational speaker, has popularized a grass roots movement, tapping for healing with his simple model, Emotional Freedom Techniques (EFT). Larry Nims, Ph.D., also developed some simple techniques, which he keeps simplifying, with his model, Be Set Free Fast, that tailors his techniques to thinking the points with similar results with clients as tapping or holding the points.

Tapas Fleming, acupuncturist, discovered the energetic link between trauma and allergies, and was given her technique, Tapas Acupressure Technique (TAT), in a dream. Judith Swack, Ph.D., developed Healing from the Body Level Up (HBLU, 1995), combining Neurolinguistic Programming (Grinder & Bandler, 1975) with energy work.

John Diepold, Ph.D., developed a gentle offshoot of EFT and TFT with his Touch and Breathe (TAB) methods where one holds the points and breathes deeply for release.

All of the energetic tools have ancient sacred roots. Tapping, spinning or brushing the energy field not only adjusts the individual energy field but taps into a dreamtime, sacred connection with the mystical origins of energy work, and a connection with our individual internal healer. This is their power.

Thus far in this writing we have introduced energy testing for diagnosis and assessment, rubbing the neurovascular points for psycho-energetic reversal, Cook's balance for general balancing of the energy field, and tapping on the heart center for strengthening the energy field. Now we will discuss in the next few chapters using energy interventions to create intention, clear trauma, negative or limiting thoughts, and general disturbances of the energy field. It is possible to adapt any healing intervention to DEH. Therefore, we provide an example of the combined interventions that many DEH practitioners use to show the richness that is possible.

For now we will discuss the primary interventions that most DEH practitioners use. In addition to what is mentioned above, we use strategies from the energy traditions; meridian points such as Emotional Freedom Techniques (EFT), Be Set Free Fast, Tapas Acupressure Technique (TAT), Frontal Occipital

Holding, tapping the temporal curve, and chakra balancing and clearing.

We also use accompanying spiritual interventions such as prayer, drumming, sacred bells, and crystal bowls. We use the interventions separately and in combination as intuition or muscle testing indicates.

The Meridian Therapies

Thought Field Therapy

One of my first experiences in the TFT training parallels the field of Energy Psychology that first gained fame and criticism with Callahan's book *The Five Minute Phobia Cure,* by reducing simple phobias quickly. I found that simple phobias could truly be alleviated quickly.

I had been afraid of dogs all of my life and it was getting to the point that I could not walk in my neighborhood without being afraid and returning home prematurely. So when our instructor said, think of something you are phobic about and tap gently on the meridian points, I chose this fear. She asked me to rate this fear on a scale of I-10. It was an easy 10. I tapped for three to four minutes with the guidance of my partner in the training on Callahan's points for phobias. At the end of the tapping, I rated my fear level at zero. I remembered that I had been afraid, but I was no longer afraid. But, I thought, I was not at my home walking in my neighborhood either. We'll see, I thought.

Later that week I walked my usual path and saw the usual dogs. I was not afraid as I had been previously. I have remained free of dog phobia for over a decade.

There are pathways of energy that run the length of the body that when activated become your inner healer. They were used naturally in indigenous cultures, but the information survived through Chinese medicine to be brought to the western world. In Energy Psychology we use 14 points where meridians are layered, and thus are major points that can be accessed easily. By tapping or percussing the points below you can heal the trauma and other disturbances of the energy field that impede your soul's purpose path.

I have placed the points on Kwan Yin, the feminine aspect of Buddha, because she encompasess the energy of compassion to offer this healing process.

Kwan Yin, the feminine aspect of Buddah.

Meridian Points

Eb **Eyebrow—BLADDER meridian**

Where: Slightly off center above bridge of nose.

For: Inner Direction, peace and harmony

Corrects: Fear, Anxiety, Dread, impatience, frustration, restlessness, trauma, miffed

Affirmations: I have a sense of perfect order. I am in harmony. I am at peace.

OE **Outer Eye—TRIPLE WARMER meridian/GALL BLADDER meridian**

Where: Outside Corner of the eye at the temple. Harmony, adoration

Corrects: Rage, fury, wrath, fear of self growth and issues of growth and change, resentment, rage, muddled thinking

Affirmation: I reach out with love.

E **Eye—STOMACH meridian**

Where: Lower edge of eye socket, in the midline of each eye.

For: Contentment, tranquility

Corrects: disgust, greed, emptiness, deprivation, nausea, hunger, fear, disappointment, bitterness, nervousness, disgust

Affirmations: I am content. I am tranquil.

UN **Under Nose—GOVERNING VESSEL meridian**

Where: Midway between the upper lip and the base of the nose.

For: Inner connection

Corrects: embarrassment, grief, physical disturbance, guilt, fear of failure, success

Affirmation: I have joy. I have happiness.

UL **Under Lip—CENTRAL or CONCEPTION or CONTROLLING VESSEL meridian**

Where: Midway between the lower lip and the point of the chin.

For: Self

Corrects: shame, embarrassment

Affirmations: I honor my being. I uphold my being. I respect my being. I glorify my being.

Cb Collarbone—KIDNEY meridian

Where: About one inch below the depression where clavicles meet in the upper chest, about one inch to either side of centerline, between upper two ribs.

For: Gentle spirit energy, sexual assuredness

Corrects: fear, anxiety, craving, sexual indecision, paranoia, worry,

Affirmations: I am fearless. I am calm. I am addiction free. My sexual energies are balanced.

A Arm—SPLEEN meridian

Where: Midline on either side, about four inches under armpit, on the bra line or on a line just below male nipple line.

For: Choice making, confidence, empathy, centeredness

Corrects: Realistic anxieties about the future, obsession, hopelessness, insecurity, low esteem

Affirmations: I have faith and confidence in my future. I am secure.

R Rib—LIVER meridian

Where: Just beneath the rib cage on both sides, down from the nipples.

For: Transformation, happiness, forgiveness, self-esteem, respect

Corrects: Anger, unhappiness, complaining, frustration, bitterness

Affirmations: I am happy. I have good fortune. I am cheerful.

T Thumbnail—LUNG meridian

Where: Corner of the base of the thumbnail, toward your body.

For: Worth, humility, correctness, feeling good about oneself

Corrects: Negative thinking, disdain, scorn, contempt, false pride, prejudiced, intolerance

Affirmations: I am humble. I am tolerant. I am modest.

IF Index Finger—LARGE INTESTINE meridian

Where: Corner of the base of the fingernail, thumb side.

For: Letting go, self-worth

Corrects: guilt, grief, lack of initiative, and openness, forgiveness, dogma

Affirmations: I am clean/I am good. I am worthy of being loved.

MF Middle Finger—CIRCULATION/SEX meridian

Where: Corner of the base of the fingernail, thumb side.

For: Bonding, relaxation, generosity, and abjuration

Corrects: Regret, remorse, jealousy, stubbornness, sexual tension, painful memories that are kept out of awareness, unhappiness, insatiability, jealousy, regret

Affirmations: I renounce the past. I am generous. I am relaxed.

LF Little Finger—HEART meridian

Where: Corner of the base of the fingernail, ring finger side.

For: Unconditional love, forgiveness, compassion, care for one's self

Corrects: Anger, over excitement, over achievement

Affirmations: I have forgiveness in my heart.

H Hand—SMALL INTESTINE meridian

Where: Middle of the fleshy side of either hand

For: Joy

Corrects: Sadness, loss, sorrow, worry, obsession, compulsiveness, vulnerability

Affirmation: I am jumping with joy.

G Gamut Spot—TRIPLE WARMER (thyroid) meridian

Where: Back of the hand, about one inch toward the wrist from the knuckles, between the carpals of the little finger and ring finger.

For: Hope

Corrects: Depression, despair, grief, hopelessness, despondency, loneliness, solitude

Affirmations: I am floating with hope. I am light and buoyant.

Mary's Brief Client-Centered Emotional Freedom Techniques Recipe
The steps to immediate relief are:

1. The energetic reversal protocol is used each time without ET.
   Even though I have this problem (of fear, anger, sadness, describe)
   I absolutely love, honor and respect myself. Tap karate chop point,
   also known as the mini reversal point.

Karate chop or mini reversal point

2. Focus on the feeling, thought or the problem, such as, "I am afraid." or
   "I deserve this." "I can change him." "It will be different this time."
   Keep it client centered, use the client's words.
3. On a scale of 1-10, 10 being high, rate the intensity of your issue.
4. Tap gently on the points 5-10 times in the order below focusing on the
   statement you intend to release such as, "I am afraid" until your
   disturbance neutralizes and is at a zero.
5. The treatment may be complete or another aspect, thought, feeling, or
   issue may come up for clearing. If so repeat the process.
6. Tap gently on the points on the positive statement that usually comes
   up naturally as the negative clears.

Focus your mind back to the problem and see if it remains at zero.
Focus your mind back to the positive.

EFT activates your internal healing system as all energy interventions do and sends the chi to the fear, or the disturbance much as the acupuncturist's needles send the chi to the pain in the body.

Zoe's Addicition to Worry

At a workshop in Denver, Zoe's hand shot up when I asked for someone to help me demonstrate client-centered EFT.

Zoe explained that she was addicted to "worry."

I said, "It is unusual to describe worry as an addiction."

She said, "Well I do it all the time just like an addict."

I guide, "Tap on your karate chop point, and state,"

Zoe: "Even though I worry all the time, I absolutely love and respect myself."

Repeats several times.

Mary: "What do you worry about?"

Zoe: "I can't sleep at night, I worry my daughter will die."

Mary: "Tap on all the points and repeat that."

Zoe: "I can't sleep at night, I worry my daughter will die."

Repeats several times.

Zoe: "When I can't sleep at night I worry my husband will die too."

Keeps tapping

Zoe: Crying. "I worry that I can't save my daughter. I feel guilty. I feel guilty a lot."

Zoe: "Now I am thinking about being in Germany—we are German and I am feeling guilty for my family being Nazi's and killing the Jews."

Mary: "You are feeling guilty for all who died."

Zoe: "Yes, this is crazy, but I do." Still crying.

Mary: Keep tapping.

Zoe: "I'm worried, no one could sleep. So many died."

Mary: "So many died, and you are worried and guilty."

Taps on "worried" and "guilty."

Zoe: "Worried and guilty." Repeats

Mary: "The halocaust is your fault and your family's fault."

Zoe: "It's my fault and my family's fault."

The intensity for Zoe reduces...she says,

"It's everbody's fault." She repeats and the intensity dissipates.

Mary: "Return in your mind to the present. Are you still worried about your daughter and your husband dying?"

Zoe: "No!"

Mary: "Can you imagine yourself sleeping?"

Zoe: "Yes!"

A month later I got this message from Zoe:

Thanks so much for the session wherein I was the demo last month. The next day, I felt a real difference in my nervous system, and I had a quiet calm feeling that I haven't had for a long time. It's still there. I also appreciated seeing and experiencing your specific way of doing EFT, which I'm going to try with clients who are able to "run with it."   www.zoez-therapy.com

Tapas Acupressure Technique

Tapas Fleming Lac., was given the pieces of TAT in a daydream, from a friend, and while contemplating healing for her patients.

I experience a depth of work for myself and with my clients that moves us to a place that is beyond technique. The pose, as we call it, while touching points on our face and holding the back of our heads touches those places within us that hold points of view that no longer serve us. In the shift that occurs while holding the pose and doing the steps, we take on a new point of view that now serves us, our families, our ancestors and our collectives.

It is one of the simplest of the strategies presented here, and frequently the most powerful.

The Steps of TAT for Healing a Trauma

© 2007, TATLifeTM. All rights reserved.

Tapas Fleming, the TAT developer has given me permission to reproduce her protocol here.

Intention

The healing I am about to do will also benefit all of my ancestors, my family, everyone involved, all parts of myself and all points of view I have ever held.

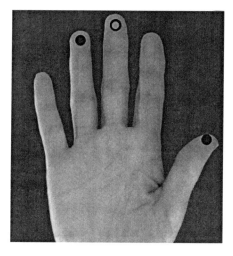

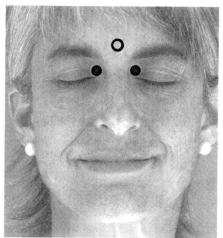

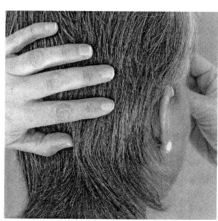

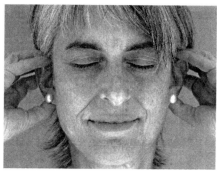

Step 1

The Problem

"This happened."

Step 2

The Opposite of the Problem

"This happened, it's over, I'm okay and I can relax now."

Step 3

The Places

"All the places in my mind, body and life where this has been stored are healing now." You do not need to know what all the places are; just make the intention that they're healing now

and/or

"God (whatever name you use), thank you for healing all the places in my mind, body and life where this has been stored."

Step 4

The Origins

"All the origins of this are healing now." You do not need to know what all the origins are; just make the intention that they're healing now

and/or

"God, thank you for healing all the origins of this."

Step 5

Forgiveness

"I apologize to everyone I hurt related to this and wish them love, happiness and peace." It is not necessary to think of each person involved; just make the intention of forgiveness with your heart.

"I forgive everyone who hurt me related to this and wish them love, happiness and peace."

"I forgive everyone I blamed for this, including God and myself."

Step 6

Parts

"All the parts of me that got something from this are healing now."

Step 7

Whatever's Left

"Whatever's left about this is healing now."

Review the original problem to see if there is any aspect that still has an emotional charge for you. If there is something, do TAT about that before proceeding.

Step 8

Choosing

"I choose (whatever positive outcome you want related to this)."

Step 9

Integration

"This healing is completely integrated now."

and/or

"God (or whatever name you use for God), thank You for completely integrating this healing now."

Move whichever hand was in the front position to the back and vice versa and put your attention on: "This healing is completely integrated now." Encircle your right ear with your right fingertips and your left ear with your left fingertips and put your attention on: "This healing is completely integrated now."

Lastly, I recommend that you give thanks to whomever or whatever you feel did the healing for you—God, Mother Nature, Holy Spirit, Divine Love, etc.

A client of mine who has illnesses resistant to healing because of her compromised immune disorder got to step three in this process about healing "all of the places in my mind, body and life," and found an energetic film that surrounded her blocking her healing. In the process she cleared her emotional resistance to healing also!

Touch and Breathe (TAB)

Touch and Breathe was developed by John Diepold, Ph.D., he uses the same points as EFT and has the client hold each point and breathe in and out while focusing on the problem for a very gentle release.

This method of clearing is highly preferred by clients affected by domestic violence and others with trauma to the face and upper body. Tapping tends to retraumatize the person battered by a mate or an accident, while TAB calms the abuse trauma.

Be Set Free Fast (BSFF)

Be Set Free Fast was developed by Larry Nims, Ph.D., simultaneously along side EFT. At first Dr. Nims used the following protocol with tapping and achieved positive results.

1. Energy test: I can use this simple procedure to correct any problem I ever want to clear. If yes, proceed. If not rub the neurovascular points for the psycho-energetic reversal spots, "I have this problem, and I accept myself."

2. Instruct the subconscious to include in every clearing the culmination of all of the roots and the belief system, anything that would make me keep the problem, ever take it back or ever be receptive to it coming back.

3. Clear:

   Eyebrow   all of the sadness (repeat)

   Under eye   all of the fear

   Little finger (outside by nail) all of the anger

   Eyebrow   all of the trauma

4. Index finger   forgive self for having this problem,
                                        I know I was doing my best

I forgive others for having this problem. I know you were doing your best. I Forgive God/Spirit for having this problem I know you always do the best and right thing for me.

After a few years of tapping with clients Dr. Nims began to experiment with clients "thinking" the points and found equally positive results. It seems our inner healing system simply needs to be asked to flow for our healing purposes.

Now in BSFF they choose a key word such as "faith" or forgiveness and repeat the word while thinking about the problem while the practitioner works with the subconscious mind and it clears.

My experience is that some clients still resonate with the versions that Nims has put behind him in his work.

Energy Medicine

Energy medicine includes some work with the meridians, but is more associated with hands on by the practitioner. Here is our favorite energy medicine procedure, from Touch for Health.

Frontal Occipital Holding

Again my guides assure me that Frontal Occipital Holding is not new to this century but returned to those for healing through Touch for Health and Three-in-One Concepts for alleviating stress and pain. We learned this from Helen Tuggy, Ph.D., and Judith Swack, Ph.D., in the HBLU trainings and find that it is profoundly nurturing to clients who are ready for direct touch and not generally indicated with energy testing when they are not ready for touch. Tapas fleming calls this the child pose. I find that it is most often called for

Frontal Occipital Holding

when clients are working on an early childhood trauma where the inner child needs nurturing or when there is much shattering and fragmentation in the energy field.

1. First establish energetic boundaries with touching clients, client's energy, strong emotions/trauma, and physical pain.
2. Focus on your heart center throughout the holding experience as your energy entrains with the client.
3. The practitioner places the palm of one hand over the forehead, while the other hand is placed over the occipital bone at the back of the head.
4. While the practitioner's hands are being held in place, the client focuses attention on the problem or issue particularly where it is located in the body. In a relatively short time, the emotional energy that was keeping the problem in place will dissipate.

Crystal bowls

Tibetan bell

As the client's issues dissipate, the practitioner may pick up knowings and visions during this process which are helpful, and usually are shared with the client.

Brushing the Biofield with Sound

Many of us are attracted to sound

Drum

for adjusting the biofield, the aura that surrounds our body from eight to 20 feet, and connects us with the universal field. We use crystal bowls, Tibetan bells and bowls, drums, guitars, and CD's. We energy test for what will clear or balance the energy and sound often accompanies the meridian or chakra interventions. There are other interventions for adjusting the auric field such as Eden's Fluff, where you use your hands to scoop your energy field upward (Eden, 1999) and smudging with smoking cedar or sage.

Practitioner Resonance

We began to notice among the DEH practitioners that we would often energy test different interventions for similar issues. Howard Brockman, LCSW, would call for FO holding more frequently, and I would frequently energy test for TAT or EFT. Nancy Gordon, LCSW, would call for rattles and drums, Deborah Jones, MA, and Marybeth Carden for heart center tapping, Holly Williams, LPC, and Eileen Foster-Sakai, LMT, for the crystal bowls, Scott Johnson and Howard for the Tibetan bowls, Ruth Crowley and Nancy Link for the Tibetan bells.

Through discussion, intuition and energy testing confirmation we determined that some energy interventions resonate through the practitioner for a particular client and situation at a certain time.

Honoring All

When there has been research on great teaching or healing methods, what has held up is the teacher or healer's passion and commitment to the process rather than one technique or model being superior. In DEH it is our intent to honor all of the strategies that we have learned and developed and to determine which is superior in each particular moment to the healing experience for the person before the practitioner for optimum wellness. In the world of energy all is equal over time. It is in the moment that a tap or a hold, a spin or a swish, a ring or another sound will restore the energy of illness or misaligned purpose to balance.

Points of interest for discussion from this chapter:
- Pressure points on the Chinese meridians are a central tool in this work.
- There are several meridian therapies in energy psychology.
- Although each person's energy field is as unique as a finger print, general techniques seem to work for most people.
- All current energetic tools have ancient, sacred, powerful roots.
- Generally speaking energy medicine and energy psychology overlap.
- Sound and prayer and sacred ritual also change, enhance and heal the energy field.
- Different practitioners resonate and offer more intense healing with different energetic or sacred tools.

Chapter Ten
The Chakra Path to Soul's Purpose

Contributed by Ruth Crowley, Ph.D.

About Ruth by Mary

Ruth attended a dream group of mine 10 years ago. Through her dreams she identified her alcoholism and got sober through the dream group, and DEH sessions. I explained to her that no one stays sober in dream group alone, and that she would need to do some traditional forms of support and treatment also. She attempted this but just kept dreaming dreams of recovery and stayed sober. When we ended the dream group, I said to her, "You are really better at this than I am, and I want you to lead the dream group from now on," which she did for several years. She did deepen her spiritual life to stay sober and she teaches classes on Goddesses and on the chakras.

She has steeped herself in the essence of the chakras intellectually and spiritually. She leads an e-mail group regarding the relationship of the chakras and the cycles of the moon with some of the meditations included in this chapter. E-mail her to join or schedule one of her classes in your area at r.a.crowley@worldnet.att.net.

The Way of the Chakras

The chakras are seven energy centers situated from the tailbone to the top of the skull in mammals. They correspond to seven central nerve ganglia located along the spinal column. They were identified centuries ago by the ancient Indian sages. Other ancient cultures also identified energy centers in the body; Egyptians, Mayans,

The seven chakras.

other Native Americans all had some sort of energy system. Traditional Chinese medicine uses energy meridians, for instance, and the Sumerians may have had a chakra system similar to the Indian system (see the description of Inanna's descent to the underworld, in which she is required to strip away her divine and human attributes one by one, in seven stages roughly corresponding to the seven chakras; Sylvia Brinton Perera, *Descent to the Goddess: A Way of Initiation for Women*, Inner City Books, Toronto CN, 1981). Our knowledge of these other systems is limited, however. For the Indian system we have centuries of texts and tradition.

The Indian chakra system is very detailed and uses yoga as well as visual and aural aids to meditation and a system of animal correspondences for each chakra. For a detailed discussion of the Indian system see Susan G. Shumsky, *Exploring Chakras: Awaken Your Untapped Energy* (Career Press, Franklin Lakes NJ, 2003). Recent works on chakras in our culture have also set up correspondences that sometimes vary from the Indian lore and may include colors, gemstones, archetypes, music, aromas, and foods for each chakra. Because our culture differs from that of ancient (or contemporary) India, I am not troubled by variance from the Indian system. The correspondences for this culture work well to address the chakras.

In our culture, for instance, the chakras have been associated with the colors of the rainbow: red for the first chakra, orange for the second, yellow for the third, green for the fourth, blue for the fifth, indigo for the sixth, and violet for the seventh. The ancient Indian culture had different color associations with the chakras. The association with rainbow colors seems to work well, however, and use of color is an easy way to activate chakra energy.

Some chakra workers have identified more than the traditional seven chakras. Certainly there are energy centers in the hands and feet as well as along the spine, but those along the spine are the major centers and the subject of our study here.

In Sanskrit, the language of the Indian culture that developed the chakra system, chakra (pronounce the "ch" as in church) means disk or wheel, and the chakras are envisioned as spinning wheels of energy radiating outward from the central column, or nadi, of the spine. Energy from each chakra moves to the front as well as the back of the spine. When we pat someone on the back, we are instinctively touching the back of the heart chakra, for instance. Some of the DEH interventions focus on touching the back of the chakras; this location is as effective as touching the front of the energy field and is less intrusive.

Each chakra holds and conveys information about our development and our current state of being. The chakras develop in ascending order as the human matures. The lower chakras develop and hold our sense of self as body, family, tribe, cultural group, self identity; the upper chakras hold and express what Jung calls our individuation, our becoming unique and self-determining psychological, emotional, and spiritual beings. Thus each chakra contains a wealth of information about the phase of development it governs, the course of that development, and the functioning of that aspect of the personality overall and in the present moment.

Chakras as an Energy System

Literature on the chakras usually discusses each individually, and this approach is useful in acquainting the reader with the chakras. It is important to remember, however, that the chakras form a system. While a current life or past life or ancestral problem—say a family pattern of sexual abuse—may be lodged in the second chakra, an energy blockage in that chakra will affect other chakras as well. Since the second chakra governs our experience of the flow of universal energy and the matrix of all creativity, blocked energy here will directly affect the fifth chakra, which governs our expression of experience and creativity. Or an overactive seventh chakra, which governs our sense of being part of the universal energy, may steal energy from the lower chakras and keep us from experiencing our life in and of the body. So while we discuss the chakras here one by one, bear in mind that they do not function alone but interact in ways you will discern as you study them.

Because they form a system, the key to healthy chakras is balance. Each one is important. We draw energy up from the earth and down from the cosmos. We are embodied spirits and inspirited bodies and each chakra, functioning well, helps us in realizing our task on the planet.

I began studying the chakras with Sharon Rommel and Cheryl Gribskov in Salem, Oregon as did Mary, and wish to thank them for a wonderful introduction to this rich field of experience. Authors whose works I have found particularly helpful are Anodea Judith, who also has an institute for chakra study in northern California (see www.sacredcenters.com) and who has written extremely useful works such as *Wheels of Life*, Llewellyn, 1987, 1999; *The Sevenfold Journey*, Crossing Press, 1993; the boxed kit *Chakra Balancing*, 2003. See also Liz Simpson, *The Book of Chakra Healing*, Sterling, NY, 1999, which has wonderful illustrations of chakra altars and of the correspondences; Brenda Davies, *The 7 Healing Chakras*, Ulysses Press, Berkeley, 2000, which chronicles the work of a psychiatrist using the chakras; and Carolyn Myss, *Sacred Contracts*, Harmony, NY, 2001, which consolidates the chakras with the author's system of archetypes to create a reading of the spirit's purpose.

Here is a diagram of the chakra system and an introduction to the chakras from lowest to highest.

For each chakra I have included affirmations and a meditation as well as a description of the chakra's role in our overall development and the functions, characteristics, and qualities it governs. Imbalances in each chakra can be caused by over activity or underactivity.

Using chakra holding, chakra tapping or chakra spinning with the meditations may be the way to create a clearing, and the affirmations coupled with the chakra work may also be a way to clear.

The ancient Indians envisioned the individual's energy as a serpent that initially lies coiled and sleeping in the root chakra at the base of the spine. As the individual moves toward animation of all the chakras the serpent awakes and rises up the spine, through each chakra's energy field. When the individual awakens and energizes all seven chakras, the serpent is said to be risen. The serpent, called kundalini, represents the awakening of human potential. As you read through the chakras and begin to work with them, picture the serpent of your energy rising through the spinal chakras and becoming fully awake at the crown chakra.

First Chakra:
Root (Sanskrit Muladhara, meaning root support)

This chakra, found at the base of the spine, is associated with the color red. The element associated with the first chakra is earth. The first chakra houses our sense of belonging on the earth, in our bodies, in our families of origin. A healthy first chakra is important to give us a sense of security and comfort in the most basic areas of our life. Its principle is groundedness: having a firm sense of belonging, believing that our physical selves will be nourished and nurtured and sheltered. The sense associated with the first chakra is smell.

Imbalances in the first chakra can manifest in fear, overeating (to give a false sense of grounding), general insecurity, inability to be alone, physical disorder in the personal sphere, generalized distrust, or distaste for the physical. In addition to the interventions described after Chakra Seven below, we can balance the energy of the first chakra by meditating on or wearing the color red (or, if the first chakra is too active, brown), by walking, gardening, or preparing food for our loved ones. Anything that brings us into immediate contact with the earth and its fruits can balance the first chakra.

First Chakra Meditation:

Sit with your bare feet flat on the floor, in a comfortable chair. Make sure you will not be disturbed for 20 minutes. Begin by breathing in full, deep breaths until you feel that the air you take in and expel is cleansing you of stress, daily concerns, and the trivial monkey mind energy that drives so much of our days.

Close your eyes. Picture yourself in a calm landscape, a place that makes you feel both safe and joyful. Spend a few moments relaxing into this landscape. Bring your focus softly to the root chakra, bathed in red energy.

Now, as you breathe out, imagine roots emerging from your tailbone and from your feet. With each breath they grow larger and stronger and find their way deeper into the earth. Make yourself completely rooted in the earth. You are not stuck but you are anchored.

When you have grounded yourself with these roots, with each breath in imagine you are drawing energy from the earth. Pull this red energy up into your body. Let it fill your feet and calves, your thighs, your pelvic basin, your core, your arms, chest, neck, head. Let the red energy of earth fill you completely.

The earth nurtures and sustains you. She is bountiful and shares her abundance gladly. Imagine your body filled with the gifts of earth—the feeling of being grounded and secure, of enjoying what she produces. Imagine your body as part of the earth, as a great spreading tree. Enjoy the feeling of belonging to the earth. Breathe with this feeling for several moments.

When you are ready, breathe your roots back in, but retain the earth's energy in your body. Come back to your daily reality slowly. Open your eyes and when you are ready, practice the affirmations for the first chakra, either those given here or those you create yourself.

First Chakra Affirmations

The earth is bountiful. I am part of the earth.

My needs are simple. My needs are met.

I am at home in my body. My body is at home on the earth.

I belong here. I am rooted and secure.

Second Chakra:

Sacral (Sanskrit Svadhisthana, meaning sweetness or one's own place)

The second chakra is located in the upper part of the sacrum, just below the navel. The second chakra is associated with the color orange and the element water. As the first chakra stands for stability and groundedness, the second stands for fluidity and change. The second chakra taps into the flow of universal energy and is therefore the source of much of our body knowledge of the universe we live in. Although we process this knowledge with the sixth chakra, our third eye, the second chakra is its source. This chakra is also the source of creativity in the individual, bringing universal energy to individual expression via the fifth chakra.

The principle of the second chakra is pleasure. After our basic needs are met, we evolve toward gratification, sensual and sexual. We enjoy the ebb and flow of desire. The sense associated with this chakra is taste.

Imbalances in the second chakra may manifest as guilt, addiction to alcohol (which gives a false sense of flow, as overeating gives a false sense of being grounded for the first chakra), overindulgence in sexuality, alienation from the body and sexual expression, rigidity and fear of change, poor or overly developed boundaries. Walking with a swing to the pelvis or riding horseback or swimming or dancing, especially belly dancing, help to balance this chakra's energy. Meditating on orange or wearing it can address the second chakra as well.

Second Chakra Meditation:

In a quiet place where you can sit comfortably without being disturbed for 20 minutes, put your feet flat on the floor and breathe deeply in and out to quiet your mind and center your spirit.

When you have come into the moment and are fully present, close your eyes. Bring your focus softly to the area of the second chakra, just below your navel. Allow the feeling of fluid orange calm to fill you.

Imagine a waterscape in which you are comfortable and at home—a pool under a waterfall or a swimming hole in the woods, where you are safe and can experience water everywhere on your body. Imagine yourself in the water, embraced by it, held afloat gently, rocked with its small movements. Imagine floating on your back and seeing the trees sway overhead as you scull your hands through the water and slowly move around the pool.

When you are comfortable in your water environment, allow your body to dissolve into the water. Become the water in its fluidity. The water has depths that the sun doesn't reach; imagine yourself flowing into those depths, shadowed and secret. These depths, the unconscious, contain treasures—take a moment to explore them. They could be pearls, or rare words, music, or the pleasures of the senses. Stay in the depths, breathing calmly, until you have found and claimed a treasure.

Now bring your energy back into your physical body, but hold on to the sense of liquid movement you discovered as water. Bring your body to the surface of the pool, sun dappled and peaceful. Contemplate what you brought back from the depths. Memorize the feeling of being water.

When you are ready, open your eyes and make second chakra affirmations. Here are some suggestions:

Second Chakra Affirmations

I welcome change and flow with the energy of the universe.
My body deserves pleasure. I take joy in the pleasures of my body.
As the universe creates me, I create it.
I respect myself and others as deserving pleasure.
My senses are gateways to delight. I open them wide.

Third Chakra:

Solar Plexus (Sanskrit Manipura, meaning lustrous gem)

The third chakra is the engine of the body. Located below the breastbone, this chakra is the seat of will and personal power. The color associated with it is yellow or gold and its sense is physical sight. The element associated with this chakra is fire. This is the chakra of self assertion, of finding and claiming our place in the world. It is also the chakra that brings our creative force into being and creates prosperity for ourselves and others. Fire transforms the matter of the lower chakras into energy. Because of the transformative aspect of the third chakra, its principle is growth. The sense associated with it is physical sight.

As with all the chakras, the third chakra itself is not negative. It drives our beings into the world and makes achievement possible. It provides our sense of self. On a body level it is responsible for our efficient digestion of nourishment. However, in excess it leads to aggressive behavior and hierarchy based on power. Some aspects of contemporary culture encourage males to develop an overly active third chakra and females to damp down their third chakra energy.

In *Waking the Global Heart* (Elite Books, Santa Rosa, CA, 2006), Anodea Judith states that an overdeveloped third chakra in the nations of the world has led to incessant war and a sense of us/them instead of peace and an understanding that we are all connected. As with society, so with the individual: we need to temper the third chakra's fire with the compassion of the fourth, or heart, chakra.

Third chakra imbalances might be indicated by feelings of shame, subservience to authority, challenging authority, riding roughshod over others' feelings or expression, lack of empathy, aggressiveness, or passivity. Digestive troubles can be a third chakra issue, as can obesity, when the metabolism is slowed and holding energy (often anger) instead of releasing it.

Ways of bringing your third chakra into balance include meditation on a candle flame, wearing or carrying bright yellow, and monitoring of our behavior with others. One way to address third chakra issues is to devise a plan for acting on the world around us. A friend developed the intention to state clearly and without judgment what she wants from others. Figuring out what we want is a third chakra function, where wants and self esteem and self actualization are forged.

Third Chakra: Meditation

Make yourself comfortable in a place where you won't be disturbed for about 20 minutes. Sit comfortably with your feet flat on the floor. Breathe deeply and rhythmically until you settle into the place where your body is.

When you are fully present, close your eyes and bring your inner focus softly to your solar plexus. Picture this area filled with a glowing yellow light. Experience the warmth of this light. This is your own sun, the sun of your person.

Imagine this light and warmth spreading throughout your body. As your legs fill with light and warmth they become stronger. As your chest and belly fill with light and warmth, they grow stronger. As your arms, throat, and head fill with light and warmth, they increase in strength. Enjoy this feeling of strength throughout your body.

Now imagine your light, warmth, and strength flowing outward and touching the people you are closest to. Your strength is real but gentle, not overwhelming. Picture your light enfolding those you care about, holding them in its glow. You are adding to their lives, not imposing your power on them. Hold the image of this gentle power.

Now let your light and power shine out over the earth. What you touch prospers in the light of your sun. Your light is a blessing to all it touches. Your power is benign and nurturing. Experience how this gentle flow of light and power warms you as well as all it touches.

Ask this power to help heal old anger and old hurt. Release those old feelings into the glow you are experiencing, and let them dissolve in the light.

When you are ready, fold your light, power, and warmth back into your body, into your solar plexus. You will be able to carry this glow with you wherever you go. Your breath fans it into life. Breathe and experience the yellow glow of your third chakra. Slowly open your eyes and prepare yourself for affirmations.

Third Chakra Affirmations:
I am a source of light and power.

I am a blessing to those around me.

My power is gentle and strong.

I know my wants and needs and express them clearly.

I am sure of myself and have nothing to prove.

I respect the authentic strength and power of others.

Fourth Chakra: Heart
(Sanskrit Anahata, meaning unstruck, sounding on its own)

The fourth chakra is located at the center of the chest. It is the balancing point between the upper and lower chakras, as between our bodily and spiritual aspects. When we tap the heart center in DEH we are activating the heart chakra. What is tempered by the heart chakra is an expression of the fully human.

The color associated with the fourth chakra is green and its element is air. Its body sense is touch; the heart chakra's energy flows out through the hands.

The principle associated with this chakra is compassion. In terms of our development, the heart chakra represents the turn from self and family of origin and immediate community to a global perspective. The heart chakra transmutes our personal energy into universal compassion and infuses the energy from the universe with individuality.

If the heart chakra is out of balance, you might experience apathy, codependency, issues with controlling the behavior of others, grief, feelings of abandonment and loss, and trouble with the immune system. Ways to bring the heart chakra into balance are to wear green, to tap the heart center (sternum) to strengthen your boundaries and open the heart, and practice love with detachment—not indifference, but allowing the loved one autonomy. Physically, you can open the heart chakra by bringing your arms together behind your back and stretching your chest wide.

Fourth Chakra Meditation:

In a safe and comfortable space, where you can count on 20 minutes of uninterrupted peace, sit in a chair with your feet flat on the floor and breathe yourself into your body. Take calming and cleansing breaths until you feel fully present.

When you are centered, close your eyes. Imagine a green planet, bursting with life and growing energy. Find a secluded spot in the abundant nature of the planet and imagine yourself there, surrounded by benign growth and green energy. Breathe in the sunlight filtered through leaves and the fertile smell of earth. Enjoy these moments of pure peace.

Now imagine yourself becoming a part of this landscape, turning into a tree with roots deep in the earth and a crown of luxuriant green leaves. Your arms become branches, outstretched and green at the tips. You sway in the breeze but are firmly rooted in the earth. You draw energy and nourishment up from the earth and transform it into your beautiful growth. You take energy from the sun and turn it into the green of your leaves. You are perfectly balanced between earth and sky. Give yourself a few moments of being in tree form.

When you are ready, draw your spirit back into your body and picture your heart, in the center of your chest, as two great ancient doors slowly opening to receive light from the cosmos. The light floods into your heart as love and compassion for all of life. Let this divine light flow throughout your body, enlivening your limbs and organs, suffusing your sense with the certainty that all life is connected and that your are a significant part of life. Breathe this certainty in until you are a vessel of light and love.

Now, pick just one resentment or grudge from your past. Hold on to it for a moment and look at it from all sides in the light illuminating you. And let it go. Just let it go. Let it dissolve in the light, lose all form and substance, and become an undifferentiated part of the glow around you. You are learning forgiveness, which is part of learning love.

When you are ready, let the doors of your heart close softly, keeping the light within. Know that you can open them at any time to receive more light from the universe. Breathe yourself back into your present moment and open your eyes.

Fourth Chakra Affirmations:

I am in the light of Spirit, and the light is in me.

Everything that lives is holy.

My touch conveys love.

Compassion and gratitude fill my heart.

I freely give and receive forgiveness.

Fifth Chakra: Throat
(Sanskrit Vishuddha, meaning purification)

The fifth chakra is located at the base of the throat. The color associated with it is sky blue or turquoise. Its element is ether and its associated body sense is hearing. The fifth chakra governs our powers of expression. It is the chakra through which we speak our truth, the truth we learn from our bodies and the truth we gain from insight and intuition about the universe.

The principle of the fifth chakra is resonance: when we find our voice and speak our truth we resonate with cosmic principles of compassion, justice, and harmony. This chakra embodies the ideal of the communicator, who can create a bridge between the individual and the universal as well as mediating between opposing viewpoints to find common ground.

The fifth chakra is also key for our sense of self and our interaction with the world, since it governs the shape of our creativity. The second chakra is the source of creativity, but the fifth makes our creativity intersubjective, shared with others. Sound, and therefore voice, is the characteristic of the fifth chakra, we can express creativity through any medium—dance, song, speaking, writing, painting, sculpture, gardening, cooking. All that matters is the expression.

Imbalance in this chakra can manifest as babbling, speaking meaninglessly, dishonesty; cracking voice, tight throat, tight shoulders. Silence about things that matter or keeping secrets, voluntarily or not, often signals a lack of fifth chakra energy. You can open the fifth chakra by doing gentle, slow neck rolls. Start with your head to one side, as far toward your shoulder as you can bring it; roll it slowly back to the midpoint of your back, but not beyond, then back to the starting point; then move your head to the other side. While the throat is stretched open at the midpoint, chant "om." Other ways to activate the fifth chakra include wearing blue, practicing any form of creative expression, journaling, and singing.

Fifth Chakra Meditation:

Find a safe place where you will be undisturbed for 20 minutes. Put a journal and writing instrument close by. Center yourself by breathing deeply and evenly until you are calm and feel ready to begin a meditation. Close your eyes.

With feet flat on the floor, imagine a sphere of clear blue light glowing at your throat. Imagine bringing up energy from the root chakra, the sacral chakra, the solar plexus chakra, and the heart chakra—red, orange, yellow, and green energy flowing into the blue sphere, swirling and moving within it. Imagine that each chakra has a message for you, for the world, or for someone you care about. Listen to the energy of each chakra.

Now send the energy of each chakra out into the world in a beam of shining light. Let the wisdom of your body shine out in clear expression.

Concentrate now on the green heart energy. With this energy swirling in your sphere of blue light, think of people you love or have loved. Send them messages from the heart, clothed in the blue light of clear expression. Your messages are not bounded by time or space. Send messages to people from your past; imagine people in your future and send them your truth and your love.

Ask your guides and higher powers to protect you now as you ask for wisdom from the universe about your highest truth, the truth of your purpose on the planet. Open yourself to receive this wisdom. Allow as much time as it takes for a message to come to you.

When you have received a message, breathe yourself into your present moment and record the message.

Fifth Chakra Affirmations:

I speak my truth without blame or judgment.

I am open to hearing others' truth spoken with love.

I listen with empathy and understanding.

I take joy in expressing myself in any medium.

Sixth Chakra: Brow

(Sanskrit Ajna, meaning to perceive or command)

The brow chakra is located in the center of the forehead, at the third eye. The color associated with this chakra is indigo, a deep dark blue. Its element is light and its principle is knowing—about self and the universe, things seen and unseen. Its sense is vision, second sight, intuition—seeing with the eyes of the spirit.

This is the chakra in charge of personal knowledge, which can scan and evaluate information from all the other chakras. This is also the chakra that perceives both obvious and subtle messages from the body and the universe. Clairvoyance is associated with the sixth chakra.

An overactive sixth chakra can lead to atrophy of the lower chakras' functions and result in the negative archetype of the intellectual or rationalist (often the third chakra, will or ego, is overactive in these archetypes as well). An underactive sixth chakra denies you access to your personal truth and makes you the victim of received opinion. A balanced sixth chakra allows you insight, intuition, knowledge about yourself an the world, and perhaps psychic powers as well. In the body, an imbalance in the sixth chakra can result in eye problems, sinus trouble, pressure headaches, migraines, or problems in the endocrine system. The headaches may be the result of denying things that need to be seen.

You can balance the sixth chakra by wearing or being around the color indigo; by trusting your senses beyond the merely rational, by trusting your intuition when you receive subtle messages. You can also exercise your visionary powers by exercising your eyes, rolling them in circles, stretching the muscles by looking far to each side, then far up and far down.

Sixth Chakra Meditation:

In a safe and quiet place where you will be undisturbed, sit with a journal and writing instrument close by. Breathe yourself into a place of peace. Center your energy. Sit straight with eyes forward, feet flat, shoulders and neck relaxed.

When you are ready to begin, close your eyes. Focus your closed eyes on the middle of your brow, the site of the third eye. Allow the idea of indigo light to flood into your third eye, saturating your spirit with its presence. This light is as old as the universe and brings you insight into what you already know implicitly. Use the power of this light to scan your lower chakras. Ask each one whether it is active or blocked, and whether it has a message for you. If you receive messages from your chakras, write them down, then return to your scan.

Once you have scanned your chakras, return to your position, eyes closed and focused slightly upward toward the third eye. Allow the indigo light, calming and invigorating at the same time, to suffuse you. Aim your beam of indigo light softly into the cosmos. Ask the universe if it has any messages for you. Sit still while you receive them, then write them down.

Finally, send your indigo light out into the future. Allow its forms to move toward you, unknown but welcome. Make yourself ready to receive the gifts they are bringing you. Thank them for their gifts; allow yourself to feel gratitude.

When you are ready, bring yourself back into your body in the present moment, slowly open your eyes and prepare to make affirmations.

Sixth Chakra Affirmations:

I know and accept myself.

The answers to all my questions lie within me.

I love the questions and trust that answers will come to me.

I embrace silence and stillness as time for reflection.

I trust the eyes of the spirit and pay attention to my intuition.

I accept the gifts of understanding and wisdom.

I infuse the chakras below with intuition and insight.

Seventh Chakra:

Crown (Sanskrit Sahasrara, meaning thousandfold, because the ancient Indian symbol for this chakra is a thousand-petaled lotus)

The seventh chakra is found at the top of the head. Its associated color is violet or white or gold, and there is no element associated with it. This chakra brings us to the realm of universal spirit. Like the sixth chakra, its issue is knowing, but where the sixth chakra deals with personal knowledge and knowledge of our place within the cosmos, the seventh deals with transcendence and universal consciousness. Opening this chakra allows our energy to flow into and merge with divine energy.

Imbalances in the seventh chakra may manifest as overemphasis on the spiritual at the expense of the body, depression, mental confusion, alienation from our sense of self, too great an attachment to the body, hostile atheism, or a spiritual practice with too great an attachment to being right.

Awakening and nurturing this chakra requires meditation and reflection. Even five minutes a day of meditation can place you in touch with the spiritual energy that wants to flow through you. Always work to ensure that your boundaries are strong before you invite universal energy, however; heart centered tapping for a minute or two will work.

Seventh Chakra Meditation:

In a quiet and secure place, where you will be undisturbed, breathe yourself into your center and sit relaxed on a chair with feet flat on the floor. Tap your heart center for a minute or two before beginning this meditation.

When you are ready, imagine a beautiful flower emerging from the crown of your head. Its petals are softly folded, open enough to allow air in but not wide open. Open the petals wide now and invite universal light and energy to flow into the flower. Breathe this divine energy in.

When your crown chakra flower is suffused with divine energy, draw the energy down through each chakra. Visualize the sixth chakra as an indigo flower gently opening to receive the divine energy. When the sixth chakra is fully open and receptive, visualize the beautiful sky blue flower of the throat chakra, then the green flower of the heart, the yellow flower of the solar plexus, the orange flower of the sacral, and the red flower of the root chakra. Open each in turn and let divine energy flow into it. Take your time with this meditation and visualize each flower individually.

When all your chakras are open to divine energy, enjoy the feeling of being part of the cosmic whole. When you are ready, move your attention to the root chakra and gently fold the petals of the red flower inward—not closed, but protected from being too open. Then close the petals of the orange, yellow, green, blue, indigo flowers in the same manner. Finally, draw in the petals of the violet flower of the crown chakra so that they receive light and air but are protectively folded.

Slowly breathe yourself back into your body and open your eyes.

Seventh Chakra Affirmations:

I am aligned with the universe and with my own desires.

I experience deep inner peace and a daily connection with the divine.

My spirit connects me to the source of all knowledge.

I am a unique, radiant, loving being.

I release all limited thoughts and lift myself up to ever higher levels of awareness.

Energy Psychology/DEH Chakra Interventions

When a person's body wisdom tells us, through energy testing, that a chakra balancing is called for, we energy test (ET) with the following questions:

1. Do all seven chakras need balancing? If not, ET to determine which ones are out of balance.

2. Do we balance the chakras going from the lower root chakra to the crown chakra?

3. Do we balance the chakras going from crown to root?

4. Do we hold the chakras with the palm? One or two at a time? Hold, crown/up, root/down.

5. Do we tap the chakras?

6. Do we spin the chakras? Always spin counter clockwise to release, for overactive chakras, and clockwise to hold the positive energies for underactive chakras.

When the client and the practitioner intuit that the balancing is complete, double check this intuition with energy testing.

Heart Center Tapping

Mary was walking around the Oregon State Fair with her children and it was getting very crowded and hot. She was feeling a bit irritable and ready to leave when she looked up and walking by her was a woman, whom she did not recognize, with a very intense look on her face tapping on her heart center. "One of my people," she thought!

The heart center is the governing center for the entire human energy system. Innovators such as Christine Page N.D., President of Holos University, and the The Heart Math Institute have studied and teach how bio-chemically and energetically the heart actually rules the brain. The Heart Math Institute has developed a program that measures the electromagnetic effects of the heart on the physical and energetic system. We find that simply tapping on the heart center activates the chakra and meridian system for healing. Some of our practitioners use this exclusively with remarkable results. We use it for clearing negative emotional states, and for strengthening positive states and for establishing energetic boundaries which the next chapter talks about.

Tapping the thymus gland and the heart center.

Points of interest for discussion from this chapter:

- Chakra systems were identified by many ancient indigenous cultures.
- There is a wide variety of literature on the chakras.
- Meditating on each chakra enhances one's relationship with this system.
- There are several ways to balance the chakras.
- The heart center may be a stand alone intervention.
- The heart center is the governing energy center.

Chapter Eleven
Energetic Boundaries

Like the human cell, strong energy boundaries keep toxins out and allow in that which nourishes the energy field.

Judith Swack, Ph.D.

Conventional wisdom teaches that if you are uncomfortable with a person or a situation, you should set a boundary. But what does that look like and what does it mean? Many of our most educated clients are unable to grasp this seemingly simple concept regarding clear boundaries in relationships until they learn that boundaries are not only relational, but also energetic. When this conceptual framework shifts, it becomes easy for them to achieve healthy boundaries in relationships. Strong energetic boundaries are also essential for finding alignment with one's soul's purpose

In our first Healing from the Body Level Up training, where we learned to work with the energy field for boundaries, I doubted that tapping on the chest could improve my career, my health, and my relationships—let alone with men!

As I worked with this concept over time, however, I was amazed at the subtle but powerful results. Imagine being enclosed in your own pulsating, translucent bubble that allows you to communicate effectively with anyone you choose and to be comfortable with intimacy, assists you in emotional and intellectual discernment, filters the cultural assault of noise, lights and toxins, and enables, if you choose, a relaxed, safe connection with the spiritual world. These possibilities are realized with effective, strong energetic boundaries, which result from strengthening and balancing the energetic aura.

In DEH, we usually balance the energetic aura by tapping on the heart center chakra for two to four minutes with the intention of strengthening boundaries in relationship to people, emotions, qualities, our bodies, spiritual matters, or situations. As throughout DEH, however, we use ET to determine which intervention will create the strengthened boundaries, and sometimes a different intervention is indicated.

When our energetic boundaries are not at 100 percent, negative emotions, qualities, or situations may invade our field with unwanted toxic energy. Internal toxins held at the cellular level may attack us. The ability to assert ourselves may be compromised. We may be unable to fully experience love, joy, or compassion. To have appropriate boundaries is to be present and not threatened in relationships, to identify and express emotions appropriately, to experience well-being at work, at home, and out in the world. Establishing appropriate energetic boundaries maintains our wholeness and our choices. Strong boundaries are an essential precursor to the energetic origins work we will get to soon.

Boundary Concepts Through The Decades

In the 1970s, many of us eagerly signed up for assertiveness training workshops. In the 1980s we immersed ourselves in classes and books, on codependency. In the 1990s we breathed and imaged our way to strong boundaries and had many conscious energy experiences. With each book and each training we came closer to achieving the boundary skills these methods promised; however, it continued to be difficult to know when and with whom to care, give, or share our intimate feelings, and with whom to state our strong opinions.

There was a missing piece: the energetic level.

Many of you are familiar with the term boundaries from your experience with assertiveness or codependency classes. Both in the literature and in the clinical setting, the codependent is the one who ends up enabling the ill or maladjusted person, often an addict or chronically mentally or physically ill person who requires everyone else to adjust to her/his needs. I refer to this person as the intimidator.

The co-dependent/intimidator relationship provides the extreme example for the need for boundary work, along with the treatment of the codependence and the source of the intimidator's behavior. The energetic level gives us the tools we have needed to successfully treat the participants in this relationship.

The codependent often has an energy field disturbed by trauma that is collapsed and unable to hold the light, causing her/him to shrink from confrontation and suffer from deflated self-esteem. As codependency is treated, ongoing energetic boundary work insures the success of the person's recovery.

We also immediately and continually do energetic boundary work with the intimidating person and all other family members. The ill or intimidating person—whether addicted, volatile, bipolar, or suffering from some other debilitating condition—also needs boundary work. The intimidator's energy field is traumatized, toxic, brittle, and dark, and treatment that includes energetic boundary work is an effective addition to treatment for this population.

In DEH work everyone does boundary work from time to time no matter what the reasons are for seeking healing.

Establishing Healthy Boundaries

In DEH, the relationship is central for establishing healthy boundaries: the relationship with yourself, with others, and with your environment. In the initial phases of healing we encourage people to begin establishing stronger boundaries, energetically, with all people and in all situations in their life. Heart center tapping is one of the energy strategies taught in the first few sessions.

To establish healthy boundaries for yourself, tap on your heart center to deal with many of your life's issues, be it grief, an auto accident, chronic physical or mental illness, abuse, or negative emotions. Tapping the heart center stimulates the thymus gland, which governs the strength of the immune system. The immune system is compromised when the body is traumatized or boundaries are compromised. Heart center tapping stimulates the immune system, which assists healing.

Encourage others to tap the heart center as well. This is the simplest, most direct technique for bringing initial relief, regardless of the degree of disturbance the client experiences.

Energy fields are contextual, ever changing from person to person and situation to situation. This fluctuation speaks clearly to our interconnectedness, and the need for a strengthened energy field in as many contexts as possible. Tap, tap, tap on your heart center!

When people are at 100 percent boundaries in relationships, they experience a greater ability to tolerate other's shortcomings and a greater ability to speak their truth. When they are at 100 percent boundaries with a situation, optimum communication or performance results. When they are at 100 percent boundaries with a quality, such as compassion, they can give it and receive it more easily.

Jenny went from an empty, unfulfilling relationship in her 20s and 30s to a seemingly exciting, passionate relationship in her forties. Soon, unfortunately, this relationship became abusive and the whole family entered treatment. We worked on the grief and trauma for all, on the anger and trauma patterns for the abuser, and on the fear and confusion for Jenny and her children. With boundary work, Jenny was able to move out with her children within a month. Continued DEH treatment did eliminate the physical abuse, but did not eliminate the verbal or emotional abuse. Within six months, after trauma therapy and continued boundary work, Jenny ended the relationship. As often happens, the abusive partner did not continue treatment for much longer, but with boundary work did enter a conventional anger treatment program for abuse.

Establishing energetic boundaries is simple but powerful work. Generally, when boundaries are established, they are permanent. Trauma, however, can disrupt the boundaries. This can be detected with ET and then boundaries can be reestablished. People with a history of severe trauma are more susceptible to having boundaries disrupted. Healing the shattered energy field (Chapter 21) in Energetic Origins work will eventually stabilize the energetic boundaries so they will not be easily disrupted. This is true even for highly traumatized people who have experienced ongoing abuse, war, or hostage situations.

The diagrams below show the difference between a disturbed energy field and a healthy field. Within a few minutes we can lead ourselves and our clients from one state to the other with heart center tapping.

Energy Fields

Imagine the Possibilities with Energetic Boundaries

There are endless possibilities for energy boundaries, because our energy fields change in each context. We want to get to 100 percent strong energetic boundaries in all contexts. Our energy fields are different with each person, each situation, and each inner quality. Think about people who give you a lift and people who seem to drain your energy. In one situation your energy is strengthened, in the other your energy is weakened. Imagine yourself at your most loving moment with your children or your spouse, and then imagine your angriest moment with them. Love strengthens the energy field and anger weakens it.

In DEH work, our first step is to establish boundaries between the practitioner and the client. This allows the DEH work to flow more smoothly and the client to feel safer. In each early session we spend a few minutes establishing energetic boundaries with family members: our mates, children, parents, grandparents and siblings, perhaps aunts, uncles, cousins, nieces and nephews. We are usually able to establish general family boundaries with the first few rounds of tapping while concentrating on a few key family members. Establishing 100 percent energetic boundaries with all family members allows us to handle conflict and let go of resentments more easily, speak up for ourselves, and share feelings more appropriately. People report much more ease with difficult family members just from this simple exercise.

Next we establish general boundaries with two to four minutes of heart center tapping. The intention here is to have a generally stronger energy field in all contexts. Then we establish boundaries with our physical being to prevent illness, maintain health, and establish healthy attitudes regarding self-care as well as to protect against sensitivity. Some clients need to establish boundaries with the visual to be less sensitive to visual stimuli, or with auditory boundaries to be less sensitive to sound and noise.

We also apply energetic boundary work to our place of employment, establishing 100 percent boundaries with our bosses, authority figures, employees, coworkers, and the office environment. As a result, practitioners and clients report more effective relationships with colleagues and greater comfort with the noise, air conditioning, heat, or colors on the wall that may not be our favorite.

In drafting their intentions, clients often include a desire to develop more effective strategies for dealing with money and finances. Part of that work is establishing clear and strong boundaries with money. Tap on your heart center on the way to becoming debt-free and to creating abundance! Tapping relieves the anxiety many of us feel in dealing with money issues.

People come to a DEH practitioner for three basic reasons. Often they are desperately ill and are hopeful that DEH can help, usually on the advice of a friend or family member who has experienced DEH. Others come because they have difficulties in their relationships with their mate or their child. Another group comes because they are spiritual seekers and have heard or read that DEH assists with personal growth. Many come for all three reasons. In the first month of my work with clients we establish boundaries with the problems or issues they describe when they first come in: physical pain, depression, a difficult relationship at home or at work, addictions, or limiting or negative thinking.

Gradually throughout the process of DEH we establish boundaries with both positive and negative emotions. We clear anger at the origins and establish 100 percent energetic boundaries. We also clear fear, grief, sadness, at the origins and establish 100 percent energetic boundaries with these emotions. We establish boundaries with love, gratitude, joy, and happiness; in doing so we are more able to give and receive and hold the positive.

We also establish 100 percent energetic boundaries with other inner qualities such as honesty, compassion, integrity, intuition, and patience to hold the positive in a strengthened energy field.

As we work with the ancestors and clear the energy through the generations we clear at the ancestral origins and then establish boundaries with our ancestry, genetics and DNA, and our family history. We establish strong energetic boundaries with our ancestors so that we can work with them as guides where it is appropriate.

When we work more deeply with DEH and establish a trauma-free energy field, spiritual longings surface or deepen, and our personal communication with the spiritual world is enhanced. It is then necessary for those participating in this work to establish 100 percent energetic boundaries with some or all of the following: intuition, spirit guides, Creator/God, the chakras, energy healing with others, the supernatural, channeling, mediumship, past lives, karma, visions, voices, soul, telepathy, and intuitive abilities.

Energetic Boundaries Process

Establishing energetic boundaries may be a stand-alone process or it also may weave into the energetic origins work. Either way, this is the process:

To Establish Energetic Boundaries:

1. ET, "Are you at 100 percent energetic boundaries with
   _____"
2. ET if tapping on the heart center is the priority intervention?
3. ET if another energy intervention is indicated to establish 100 percent energetic boundaries? EFT? Tibetan bell, crystal bowl?
4. ET or intuit the number of minutes, usually two to four minutes.
5. After intervention is complete, ET if each boundary is at 100 percent at the body, soul, conscious, unconscious, auric field, and chakra levels.

Gradually we want all people to be at 100 percent energetic boundaries with all people in all situations. This process, straightforward and simple as it is, changes your relationships, your health, and your life; it has mine and countless others.

Knowledge of and practice with the interventions and some established boundaries with this work, with your healing abilities, or with your practitioner, and with the universal energy prepares you for the rest of the wellness and purpose process.

Points of interest for discussion from this chapter:

- Boundaries, traditionally written about and spoken about as psychological are also energetic.
- Codependency and intimidation are two examples of relationship boundaries that are out of balance.
- Disturbance in the energy field requiring energetic boundary work is common.

Chapter Twelve
Energetic Intention

"Every intention sets energy into motion."

Zukav

Strong energetic boundaries now allow us to choose the priority intention for healing.

Just out of consciousness in the realm that connects our sub-conscious mind and our auric field lies the heart material of intention where change takes place. According to Eckhart Tolle in *The Power of Now,* choice or intention requires consciousness, deep consciousness (Tolle, p. 224). There is an unfolding of the intention in DEH from consciousness to deeper consciousness. Dyer (2002) teaches that intention is an ever present energy field that holds inspiration, and that consciousness about the possibilities for this intentional field is our work in life. Deep consciousness that inspires calls up that which needs to change or grow.

In life intentional living is determined by what we attend to consciously. In DEH healing and change occur by attending for awhile to what has gone wrong, what we are afraid of or what hurts, and then gradually shifting that to what is right, where we are brave and courageous, and where we are loved and healthy. Our tool for guiding consciousness from negative to positive we call intention which creates the thought fields of energy that need healing.

In DEH the client and practitioner work together to develop an intention regarding the client's symptoms or issues. It is more typical in the general counseling and teaching profession, as it is in many professions, to talk about goals or outcomes rather than intentions. We were challenged in our work with clients to recognize the power of the connection of energy and language to keep us stuck or to free us.

We used the principles of energy psychology not only for our own healing and our clients' healing but to create our own model for change.

We stopped setting goals and started setting intentions, tapping into the language of the ancient that Wayne Dyer has thoroughly researched in his book *The Power of Intention.* (2003)

Whether a client is recovering from depression, or a student is learning DEH, the outcome is always down the road, in the future, and once the destination of relieved depression or energy strategies mastered is reached, it seems that more goals come to the surface. That is the nature of humans, to seek, to strive.

As developers of DEH, and ever curious, we became as interested in the process as the outcomes, and therefore required language to match this viewpoint that the process is the treasure. What happens along the way as people are healing or learning? Our style with clients attends to the process of the relationship, as we learned in various models of client-centered therapies. The energy strategies open people's personal process, and intuition and energy testing assesses and guides the process.

Intention as Process

Thus, we departed from the standard language of "goal" in mental health and in the energy psychology trainings we had completed, and decided on the term "intention" because it encompasses the entire process of a person's work instead of just the end result.

You are encouraged as a practitioner of DEH or in your self-healing to attend to the entire process in your energy work.

Some of our students wondered about the energy or "thought field" connected with this word, so we looked it up in the dictionary. "Intent" according to Webster is:

"1) The act of stretching out... 2) purpose 3) The state of with which an act is done, volition...meaning...significance...clearly formulated 4) Directed with strained or eager attention: concentrated having the mind, attention or will focused on some end or purpose."

An "intention," again according to Webster is:

"1) a determination to act in a certain way, resolve 2) what one intends to do or bring about 3) The object for which a prayer, mass or pious act is

offered 4) A process or manner of healing incised wounds. 5) A concept considered as the product of attention directed to an object of knowledge. 6) Purpose with respect to marriage. 7) Design, aim, objective..."

We used this word for several years in this work before we looked it up in the dictionary. It was exciting and validating when we did look it up to note the texture and richness implicit in this word, and how it melded with the depth of the results when we set an intention for healing. People report that as soon as the intention is written things related to their intention begin to shift in their lives. Or they report that issues or origins will begin to come up between sessions that they are compelled to work on.

You do stretch, and find meaning, as blocks to desired health in your life clear energetically. Stretching, of course, is not always comfortable—there are inevitable periods of pain, grief, confusion, and anger as the past is revisited for healing. Intention brings up everything that it is and everything that is its opposite, in other words everything that is to heal. Meaning comes slowly as unknown history is revealed and healed and the problems of the present are explained by the child within, the ancestors, or karma of the past.

Cassandra, a very beautiful 53-year-old, came to me to find answers regarding her inability to find success in her marriage or other primary relationships while at the same time experiencing success in all other areas of her life. She has a successful business, is financially secure, and has very close relationships with her children and with her friends. She talked at length about the longing she felt to talk more intimately with her husband of 25 years. They had lost time together as she was busy raising their blended family and he was building a major business in southern Washington. Workaholism and alcoholism also fogged their ability to connect emotionally. Apparently, she revealed as we visited, her mother had been rather business like and matter of fact and not emotionally available. She would have loved, she said, to have had close conversations with her mother like she has with her daughters. We determined that these past issues blocked her abilities to be intimate, and we developed the following.

Intention,

"Heal my intimacy issues and find success in my marriage."

The crux of the energy in her family that led to this distance came to light vividly in this healing experience.

Eyes closed, and with my guidance, Cassandra traveled in her mind in a tunnel of light to the cellular, dreamtime memory of her mother's childhood. My mother is three, she is swooped up and taken out of her southeastern flooding house. Her mother is there, screaming... "My babies, my babies!" Mom's siblings perished in the flood.

Cassandra was, of course, upset during this session, shedding tears for herself, her relatives and the sisters her mother never knew. As Cassandra used the Emotional Freedom Techniques tapping and the Tapas Acupressure Technique intervention she said, "Oh, Mom made a decision that day along with her mother not to feel, not to be close."

We continued the tapping to clear that pattern.

Cassandra's intention quickly took her to the answer to her question about why she had difficulty with intimacy in close relationships. The energy of the ancestors gets passed on through the generations and settles in the family's energy field.

The written intention then leads to the origins work which is described in the following chapters to heal grief, trauma and to realize our soul's purpose. Energy testing along with the intention help clarify as people report daily with statements like, "The fog is lifting or the cloud is clearing," that the intent of their work is unfolding.

To begin to be clear about the issues that have stopped us from reaching our potential is as another client Sheila said, "Amazing!"

Sheila came in three years after she escaped domestic violence and as happens all too often in these cases the husband had the financial means, the home and the job that looked more desirable to the courts and she lost her children. She had resumed her habit from her younger adult years and found herself drinking alcoholic beverages to excess everyday. She was depressed, agitated and had recurrent nightmares regarding her ex-husband. Although she wanted to emphasize her depression in our treatment, I gently explained to her that it is difficult to recover from depression when you are putting large doses of a depressant drug into your body every evening. We were able to confirm that with energy testing that her body's wisdom advised us to write "recovery from alcoholism" as well as "depression" in her intention.

In addition I also assessed with questions that she had many of the symptoms of post traumatic stress disorder (PTSD) due to the violence in her

*former marriage and the ensuing loss of her children. We further clarified with
energy testing that we would write in the intention to heal PTSD.*

*I then asked her how she would want to feel if all of these issues were healed. She
replied, "Oh I would feel free and at peace!" We added this to complete her intention.
We then muscle tested to check for the completion and accuracy of this intention.*

Her intention then read,

*"To 100 percent heal depression, alcoholism and PTSD, and to feel free and
at peace."*

This process also minimizes the initial tension between the practitioner and the
client's denial system. Energy testing touches the deeper wisdom within that the client
may doubt to begin with, but is generally inarguable, and trusted then over time.

Once the intention is written and confirmed with this deeper wisdom, there
is an eagerness to move forward, the stated and written words have set the
energy in motion. People are disappointed if they cannot make another
appointment very soon to work on their health problem or emotional issue that
is so vital to them. This eagerness is the life force, the energy which drives the
intention and the healing such as Melinda's.

Melinda reported that the week following writing an Intention,

"To heal from the impact of her mother's abuse,"

*…she had dreams that brought up feelings and memories and she began to
do energy tapping at home preparing her for the next session.*

No one is ever really eager or anxious to face the devastation of abuse. So,
it is very touching and encouraging to feel the person's healing system jump start
the healing process.

Webster added "determined" also in defining intention. I am often struck by
the bravery of my clients who come to my private office, tucked away in a small
city in Oregon, to face what they have been most afraid to face, or feel hopeless
to heal. Some have sought healing for years, and some have hidden the need to
heal for just as long.

*Mark, the friend of a DEH practitioner, called from Wisconsin to see if I could
help. He said he was desperate, that his life and his relationship were falling
apart due to a long history of affairs and alcohol abuse. We spent a couple of
sessions tapping the meridian points while I encouraged him to seek local*

addictions treatment. He went to intensive addictions treatment, and pursued work with a Christian 12 step group, a Reiki master and a psychic. He called about six months later. He had remained in recovery, his relationship was healing, and he wanted to come back to Oregon to do some deeper work with me. DEH.

This is determination.

There has never been a time since I was a young therapist that I didn't think of my work with clients as sacred. Webster's next definition of intention relates it as "sacred, as a prayer." Thus if I didn't sense the presence of the divine in our work it would be daunting to have people like Teri come in and say tentatively that she would like her intention to be,

"Heal my lifelong depression, recover from divorce after 30 years of marriage and to be joyful and contented with clear direction for her life."

Teri is assistant to the CEO in a major corporation whose days are filled with the stress of one who sees her job not as work but as a mission to make the world a better place. It is three years later and we are still in touch, although treatment was completed in a year. She says she will be my poster child for being 100 percent recovered from depression. She has a full, vibrant single life and she is full of joy and contented.

The dictionary definition also stated that, "intention is the manner of healing incised wounds." Very shortly after the beginning of my career as a counselor I witnessed in my clients the body-mind connections as people came to me for "mental-emotional" issues. Physical pain would sometimes get worse as we went more deeply into grief, and then would dissipate as grief lifted. It seemed random and unpredictable with the other strategies I used prior to energy psychology. In DEH we pay particular attention to where the limiting thought or emotions are stored in the body, as we use an intervention to clear it. As intentions unfold then, the negative energy is incised from the body with energy strategies, just as the surgeon creates an "incised wound" in surgery. This energetic incision with the intention and interventions followed by the energetic healing holds the seeming miracles of this work.

Rainey, was one of my first DEH clients. She came in with serious depression and anxiety with a long history of abuse and co-dependency. She also had debilitating pain, arthritis, and fibromyalgia. She had only a few functional hours per day and could not walk up and down stairs. She was angry, irritable, felt hopeless, and alone even though she was married and had a family. She looked forward to each time I was away for further trainings because she knew that when I returned, she would receive further healing. Over time she became anxiety and depression free, managed her co-dependency well in her relationships and tripled her functional hours per day, as well as reducing her pain on an average, she said, by 70 percent.

Not only did she attend DEH sessions several times a month, she developed a routine of meditation and tapping daily which kept her pain level down and her functional hours up.

Writing an intention to,

"Heal my depression, anxiety, pain, arthritis, and fibromyalgia, to be free of anger, and happy with my life," was the driving force of intention that aligned with Rainey's deep wishes and commitment to be well. This is a dramatic story of intentional healing.

We come into this world and grow up with patterns of thought, experience and behavior that create an energy field that we become accustomed to like an old, well-worn but familiar home. In an odd way the old home becomes comfortable, even if it is painful. We develop coping skills to dwell in the home that holds danger, fear, grief, and loss. In doing so we strengthen a less than functional energy pattern. The written intention in DEH lays the foundation for the new energetic home in which we will reside. The DEH strategies will gently and gradually collapse the old structure as the intention guides the building of the new structure.

A well-formed intention creates a new design, a new framework for our life and our well-being. Soon we are able to dwell comfortably in this new home, and with time and strengthening of the energy field claim this improved energetic architecture, and create healthy, happy, vibrant, successful lives.

The intention in DEH determines the energetic origins to visit or re-visit and heal—those current life, ancestral and karmic energies that need to be healed in order to actualize the intention. Then various energetic and spiritual strategies are used to heal these origins so the intention is realized. The intention may be to heal relationships with partners, parents, or children. It may be to recover fully from addictions, eating disorders, depression, anxiety, panic attacks, or other chronic pain or illness. The intention may be to heal abuse, trauma, family dysfunction, or birth trauma. It may be to heal infertility or reduce the impact of peri-menopause and menopause. It may be to heal diabetes, cancer, hypertension or injury.

The intention could be to increase success in business, or performance in sports or as an artist.

Intentions should be well thought out and well formed. We find that as with affirmations, intentions are most powerfully focused when stated in the present tense. They also seem to hold greater potential for healing the whole issue when the specific issues are listed. Also, to insure lasting results we add a phrase regarding what a person wants once the healing is achieved. For example:

"I heal post traumatic stress disorder due to my war experience, and function free of nightmares and am able to live in the present with gratitude and peace."

Thus intentions have two parts—what you want to heal, and the results you would like. In DEH an individual develops an intention, in the form of a statement or multiple statements, which determines the energetic origins that need to be healed in order to attain the intention. Then various energetic and spiritual strategies are used to heal these origins so that the intention is realized.

When clients list multiple intentions we energy test if it is in the client's highest and best interest to do them all at one time.

After creating sacred space, and listening to the sacred stories that people bring to me, in the second session we begin to write the carefully stated intention that will shape a new and improved future.

Steps to a well formed intention
1. Create sacred space.
2. Identify the major issues that concern you or the person you are working with.
3. Prepare the energy field of the person with energetic boundaries.
4. Write what needs healing, and how the person will feel when healed in the present tense.
5. Check for specific energetic reversal.
6. Check for completion and accuracy with ET.

Here are some further examples of intentions:
9-year-old female experiencing grief and depression
My anger is gone. I feel more comfortable in my new home, and have more friends. I sleep all night and feel happy.

12-year-old female
To mend the parts of my heart that were hurt when my Mom was using drugs. I feel happy and confident.

25-year-old female state worker, artist, healer

I 100 percent heal my acute anxiety and depression. I am in alignment with my soul's purpose regarding my relationships and my work.

38-year-old female abuse survivor

I heal my past relationships with my former husband and with my mom—especially the abuse and trauma that led to my depression and which now weighs heavily on the present, and holds me back from being true to myself. I feel lighter, more peaceful and create a healthy relationship with a partner.

39-year-old female recovering from childhood abuse, domestic violence lasting 17 years, approaching a new marriage

I heal my PTSD and depression including flashbacks, hypervigilance, sleep disturbance, fear/anxiety, nightmares and fatigue. I have healthy boundaries. I have a healthy understanding of my duties and responsibilities in a healthy relationship. I heal from the past in order to be ready to share a home in the present.

55-year-old female

I heal from depression, carpal tunnel, fibromyalgia, and sjogrens syndrome. I have a satisfying job that fills my emotional, physical and financial needs.

Intention and the Law of Attraction

I also came upon another way to think about intentions as I studied the law of attraction in the Abraham-Hicks work and in the movie, *The Secret*.

There is so much beyond healing the wound.

Addressing a client's attraction to unavailable men we created an intention for her to heal from that. We cleared the origins and she felt at peace with her history and the future possibilities.

It then occurred to me to create an intention to work with her to heal whenever she was unavailable to love others. The law of attraction "mirror" I call it. This is the solution to the question, "How am I attracting that?"

She then found real peace, and many more opportunities to love others after addressing an intention, "To heal being unavailable to others." Availability is core to a loving relationship, and she was not lacking after all.

Creating intentions for healing and living becomes a way of life for those who continue on-going work with energy psychology and DEH. Intentional living is conscious, and co-creative with the divine. It is simultaneously challenging and refreshing.

Inner Objections

About 50 percent of the time, we energy test that there is an inner objection from the subconscious mind that is blocking the integrity of completing the intention. When this is present we ask that the person go to their subconscious internally and discover the objection. For instance on the above intention,

"To heal being unavailable to others."

Jane found that her objection was, "If I am available then I will have to get really close to a man."

We did the TAT hold and cleared the inner objection.

Soul's Purpose Intention

As this healing work deepened and my soul's purpose clarified, the aspects of working on soul's purpose emerged.

Living Your Soul's Purpose Intention

After the healing is complete for the presenting issues that people come in with, then I energy test, "Is it in your highest and best interest to do the soul's purpose intention?"

The intention is, "I live my soul's purpose as an individual, in all relationships, family, in my career, in my community, and in the world."

If the answer is yes, then I energy test, "Is it in your highest and best interest to work on your soul's purpose ___as an individual? ___in relationship? ___family? ___in career? ___in community? ___in the world?"

My soul's purpose, as yours will, changes and unfolds. I do an intention for the next step in my soul's purpose every six months or so.

Intentional living and the tremendous stamina that daily energy work gives me allowed me to serve Katrina/Rita evacuees in Louisiana. It was both devastating and miraculous to be with these folks who never intended to be brave. Writing, naturally, was an outlet for me to process this experience, and the last stanza from the poem that follows expresses my soul's purpose intent with DEH and energy psychology following Katrina and Rita. I was changed at the core in these days in Louisiana.

Returning from Rita

I said, "I have to go."
He said, "I know."
Called to Katrina,
Arriving to Rita
Long days spent
Listening to stories of
Devastation, quickly
Revised to stories of
Faith by the
Resilient ancestors of
Slavery and the
Great White Hope.
Returning from Rita,
Soul rearranged,
Making sense of
Teaching the Seekers to
Seek more deeply,
Listening to the daily stories of
People who have homes and
Know the whereabouts of
Family, their photographs, and
Important papers, and rarely
Wonder how they will
Make their way,

Only makes sense if
When healed they
Find a stronger,
Compassionate
Voice to
See all as
One and join the
Cultural soul
Rearrangement.

My intention in writing this book is to create widespread interest in the possibilities for energy psychology in general and Dynamic Energetic Healing® specifically, and to create a culture where people attend to and care for their personal energy field as just another aspect of personal hygiene and health. My further intention is to inspire people to wellness and to the highest level of health so that they are able to make a difference for people and our planet.

Points of interest for discussion from this chapter:

- Intention is the heart of energy psychology healing.
- The language in the intention creates the energy field for healing specific issues.
- Intention implies process.
- Positive intention supports the law of attraction.
- Problems are a mirror for the attraction law.
- Inner objections are sub-conscious blocks.
- Soul's Purpose intentions are life-changing

Section Three

The Sacred Energetic Origins

Prelude

Annie, a hard working client, came in one day having just read Brian Weiss'
book on hypnosis and past lives, Through Time Into Healing, *and said, "I want to*
find the past life that will cure my eating disorder!" Using ET, I asked, as I had been
trained to ask, "Is there a 'root cause' past life that needed healing?" She tested, no.
Immediately the voice of a guide whispered, "ask for the origin." I explained to my
client that I was receiving this guidance I then asked with ET, "Is there an energetic
origin related to Annie's eating disorder that needs healing?" She tested, yes. We
healed this past life. Although it was not the immediate cure for Annie's eating
disorder, it was the beginning of the Dynamic Energetic Healing origins model.

I shared the experience with Howard and Nancy and we began to
experiment with this wording. We wrestled in discussion with what the
difference was between root cause and origins. We began to use ET to
determine how many origins needed healing. We energy tested with our
clients and determined that "origins" was a larger energetic field than the
term "root cause" we had learned in earlier training.

*We had discovered a way to heal a larger energetic field.

We soon began energy testing with each intention.

"How many divine separation, womb/birth, current life, ancestral, and past life energetic origins require healing with each intention?" Generally speaking we only have to revisit 30 to 60 percent of the origins indicated to clear the intention, since energy fields overlap and cluster. So when we clear one ancestral origin, for instance, a couple of current life and past life origins clear also, not because the circumstances were exactly the same, but because the energy is the same.

Healing Divine Separation is the origin right before birth. Current life origins are events that have occurred since birth. Birth-womb origins often hold trauma that occur at conception, in utero, in the birth canal, or during the actual birth. Ancestral origins hold the energy of our parents, grandparents, great grandparents, and on through the generations. Karmic origins hold the energy that comes in with the soul as archetype or from prior soul beings.

DNA origins are a combination of ancestral and karmic energy residing at the DNA level. Bardo origins tap into the realm that some believe exist between soul incarnations. The Buddhists call it the bardo state, and Christians call it heaven.

In the bardo state amends and forgiveness can occur between souls that may not be possible due to death, bitterness or trauma. This origin is usually connected with karmic work. Some soul-to-soul dialogue needs to occur with specific individuals or with the whole community, as indicated with ET. The practitioner asks that the souls dialogue, make necessary amends, and forgive or seek forgiveness as needed. Practitioners then ask that all dialogue necessary to heal both the individual and the collective occur. Compliance at a soul level usually occurs.

Origins are a magical place held by our body-mind-spirit to access healing and change. You will be amazed how simple and easy it is to access the memory of the past that holds the energy connected with the healing intention. What follows is a description of the kinds of material we revisit for healing with energy psychology and DEH® strategies in the energetic origins.

Chapter Thirteen
Current Life Energetic Origins

*When it's over, I want to say: all my life I was a bride married to
amazement. I was a bridegroom, taking the world into my arms.
When it's over, I don't want to wonder if I have made of my life
something particular, and real. I don't want to find myself sighing
and frightened or full of argument. I don't want to end up simply
having visited this world.*

Mary Oliver, Poet

My dear Daddy was bi-polar, although we did not have a name for it until I
was 33. He died the year before I published this book, but he always told me to
tell our story of hope. His hope came from life-saving medication in the 1970s
and mine came from this blessed work. I had developed behavior patterns to
cope with Dad's illness. I avoided other people's anger at all cost, and I had an
unconscious expectation that men would be unavailable. The pictures that
accompanied my patterns were always there—Dad's out of the blue rages that
went on and on, or Dad sitting in a chair behind a newspaper depressed for
months. Over time with energy psychology I visited these pictures and
memories and cried and tapped and healed the energies of death and darkness
and the shattered energy fields until my child was finally whole and integrated.

From the beginning of my career as a therapist the material of our childhoods,
adolescence and adult lives was the bulk of my work with people who had grown
up with alcoholism, abuse, parental mental illness, and other family dysfunction.
The childhood, adolescent, and adult events are those that we have worked with

in other models of therapy for decades. We visited our inner children, dissected our family patterns, sculpted and acted out our family roles hoping to release the emotion and resolve the conflict generated by our family patterns.

We use similar regression techniques to access the inner child material that was popular therapy in the 1980s and early 1990s. Janet Woititz, Ed.D., Claudia Black, Ph.D., Sharon Wegscheider, and John Bradshaw were some of the pioneers that took us within to meet our "kids" at various ages and stages. With eyes closed we would imagine ourselves conversing with and nurturing our five-year-old or 10-year-old to heal the trauma or neglect suffered at that time.

We wrote volumes about our childhoods to let go of the intrusions from the past on the present. This work at its best did not blame our parents, but empowered us to let go of intimidator, perfectionist or victim patterns to live with more freedom and joy as adults. It was both satisfying and grueling work. Much healing occurred, but it was slow and highly re-traumatizing, and for some did not bring the desired results for their issues. In addition to the imagery and dialogue from the old model, we add the energy strategies that clear and heal the trauma and/or neglect rapidly, efficiently and thoroughly without re-traumatization.

Severe Childhood Trauma and Major Depression

Prior to my energy psychology training, a dear client, Joyce, worked with me for years treating the trauma of abuse from her mother and the ensuing depression. Every couple of years she cycled into suicidal thinking. She would resume or up her medication and we would revisit the inner kids. Their trauma seemed endless. One time she was so serious about suicide, I called the police to intervene. I thought she would never speak to me again after that! She did not, for awhile, but then returned. She got better but never fully well. When she heard about my new work, she called and wanted to try again.

Over several DEH sessions we established strong energetic boundaries with her past and her mother and healed the energy of generations of abuse on both sides of the family. She visited many past lives which held the karmic energy connected to the intense early abuse. A pivotal healing occurred when we muscle tested to return to a recurring event that we had worked with in guided imagery, EMDR, inner child work, and cognitive work. We both rolled our eyes and exclaimed, "Oh, no," when it came up again.

Please tap or TAT as you read this and any other disturbing material in this book.

There were six children in the family and when one would do something against mother's irrational rules they would not tell who it was. So she would take them single file down the stairs to the basement and have them face the walk and beat them all with a belt. She could still hear the crack of the belt and the screams of her siblings as we worked. She felt pangs of guilt for not being able to protect the younger ones, after all she is the oldest, and she felt utter hate for her mother.

We tapped on meridians and chakras, to heal these feelings. We healed the family trauma and her individual and her family's shattered energy field from this experience. We prayed and rang a sacred Tibetan bell to release the death wish and the dark energy connected to her hate. We released the grief and judgments about her sick mother. We cleared the connection of this trauma with her addictions, and released her negative thinking about her mother and her thoughts of absolute worthlessness about herself. She began to find peace and forgiveness. We have never had to roll our eyes again and face this scene.

Her energy was now free to help others. She pursued her nursing career, and supported her four children's healing from the affects of her PTSD and addictions. She has a healthy, happy marriage albeit her fourth, to a smart and handsome man who sends poetic monthly journals to their community, which I am blessed to be a part of, as they have traveled and are now settled in the southwestern US. She maintains her recovery with a strong spiritual life. She recently wrote to thank me for the years of joy since our final DEH session in 1997, and to report on the productive and healthy lives of her now grown children, and her joy at being very involved in her grandchildren's lives.

Joyce is one of the clients who led to my despair as a therapist, and to my resolve to seek energy psychology training. I knew that she was trying as hard as she could to work on herself and I knew that I was trying as hard as I could with all the skills and spiritual connection that we could muster. It is just unacceptable to me when people do not get well. This is not a comment about Joyce or my clients but rather a comment about my determination.

I have learned to balance this point of view as I work with more and more severe illnesses, but it is still my basic stance that spirit and energy can heal anything if we access it effectively!

DEH developers and students all approach the energy interventions by what resonates for them. What follows in the next chapters is how I work with trauma, grief and soul's purpose.

Current life energetic origins include those events that occur right after birth to the present in their lives. By now we have created the space as sacred, written an intention, corrected reversal and objections and established energetic boundaries with one another and the work. We then use energy testing to determine the number of current life ancestral and karmic origins to heal. We clear reversal, neurological disorganization and inner sub-conscious objections.

We then use energy testing to determine if a current life, ancestral or past life origin is the priority for healing. We then travel in the tunnel of light or use another induction to get to the origin to heal the energetic structure of the trauma.

We determine which interventions to use: tapping the meridians, TAT, FO holding, prayer, sound with energy testing. We then tap, for instance until the emotions are neutral, and the body pain is at zero on a scale of zero to 10 as we did with Joyce's horrific childhood memory. It is not that Joyce does not remember that this happened, rather there is no emotional charge left because there is no energy holding it. People describe these memories after energy work as faded or distant memory.

Many of my clients have been in therapy for years or decades before they find me and energy psychology. They often resolve those things that they have been working on for a long while in weeks, or months.

Points of interest for discussion from this chapter:

- Current life energetic origins are events that hold energy that require healing from infancy to the present.
- Healing the child within has been a therapeutic process for several decades, now we accomplish that energetically.
- Depression and trauma are often imbedded in the current life energetic origins.

Chapter Fourteen
Energetic Origins:

Divine Separation—Conception, Womb and Birth

Andrew Hahn, Ph.D., and Judith Swack, Ph.D., have brought the Ennegram, a spiritually based system of personality assessment dating back to ancient cultures, to energy psychology. This system has become popularized throughout the latter part of the twentieth century by many including Helen Palmer. The Ennegram defines nine personality types that come into form at the point that the soul separates from its divine source. The Ennegram theories put much emphasis on how the soul interprets this separation and the impact on later life. Hahn and Swack have developed a very complex system called the Essence Process designed to heal these soul wounds.

Once again, one of our clients provided the guidance to a greatly simplified process. I was energy testing, and tested that this particular client had a current life origin related to her healing intention that was not adult, adolescent, childhood, birth, or womb. I then asked with ET if it was conception, and the answer was no. I then asked with ET if it was when the soul separated from God, and the answer was yes.

I then guided this person to when her soul was with Spirit/God/Creator right before this life. I suggested that she bask in this Oneness and report the accompanying feelings.

She reported feeling "peaceful, totally loved and at one with God."

I then guided her to create the illusion of separation from God/Creator/Goddess by imagining moving away from Creator toward her mother's womb. I then asked her to notice the thoughts and feelings that accompany this experience. Tears filled her eyes, and she said, "I'm not sure I want to do this earth life again." I guided her to tap on the meridian points until this thought was neutral. She then said, "What if I can't accomplish what I am supposed to do?" Tapping once again cleared this. "This family will be too difficult. I am afraid of what will happen to me." There were several other expressions of loss or fear that were cleared with the energy strategies. In the end she said, "I accept that I have chosen this."

This process generally brings up soul wounds, or layers of the Ennegram as described in that body of work.

Some other expressions of soul wounds by other clients are:

"I don't want to go."

"Why doesn't God want me anymore?"

"I don't want to do this again."

"I am reluctant."

"This is going to hurt."

"I will have to make them love me."

"Pain dictates all of my decisions and relationships."

Soul wounds go to the core of our being and become life patterns that direct our decisions, relationships, work, leadership roles, whether we have children or not, our educational status, our self-esteem, our spiritual paths, our values and behaviors.

After basking in the Light of Oneness at the divine separation origin, while working on a soul's purpose intention, I became aware of a limiting thought:

"I have taken on too much for this lifetime!"

Since clearing this I am much more able to be less overwhelmed, and prioritize and complete projects.

Misdirected soul's purpose is also another result of the unconscious power of soul wound material guiding our lives. Wounds always want protection and safety, so to go after your soul's purpose to be creating abundance, right relationship, a prominent business, or a name for yourself involves moving beyond one's safety zone or comfort level. Sometimes while the soul wounds are in place, they simply will not allow you to go beyond them. Clearing the soul wounds will open up new possibilities.

Energetic Origin at Conception

When conception is indicated with energy testing, which in my experience is rare, usually there was conflict between the parents at the time of conception, or the mother was raped, or one or both were drunk or using drugs at the moment of the sperm-egg merge. Negative or traumatic energy then is attached to the forming fetus.

In the soul's purpose work it appears because conceiving a new family, relationship, career or community is blocked by negative energy regarding "conceiving." When positive conception energy is released, a powerful stream of creative healing energy is unleashed.

Lori had come to therapy to resolve a history of abuse by her parents, a physician, and a couple of men in her life. She is a lovely 40-something professional who after several months of tapping on these traumas moved to her soul's purpose intention. She longed to develop a career cut short as a singer and the soul's purpose work began to open doors for her.

She was having trouble getting started and following up as the doors opened for singing opportunities. When we were guided to her origin of conception, she discovered that her father had been abusing her mother the night she was conceived. We cleared the trauma in her energy field and a death energy pattern as well as her mother's thought field that she was "trapped and unhappy."

She did a combination of chakra balancing and tapping and ended with saying, "I am free and happy!"

She went on to develop her career as a singer.

Energetic Origins in the Womb and at Birth

Daryl Thomas, MA, introduced me to rebirthing ala Sondra Ray style 25 years ago. Over several sessions she gently guided me through some Lamaze like breathing to the story in my womb. I was the first born post WW II baby in my family. My mother was a first year P.E. teacher and my father was finishing up engineering school at Cal Berkley. There were no signs of his bi-polar disease until I was five. I was born "early" before Mom was finished with school and in the middle of Dad's finals. This origin held the tension of their anxiety and excitement, and I had been rushing into things ever since.

In another session we went to the womb experience the day I was born in a crowded Navy hospital. Mom was drugged, the staff was not available and Dads were not allowed into the birthing room in those days. I was coming into the world alone. I too then was drugged and I recalled liking the feeling…

In a later session we returned to the struggle in the birth canal and the feeling of loneliness, and a determined thought that, "I will do it on my own!"

With breath work and imagery we resolved some of these feelings and messages.

As I progressed through healing intentions with energy psychology I eventually have revisited all of these scenarios and energy tested that there was additional energetic trauma to clear. And Daryl has become a DEH practitioner!

Womb and birth issues are reminiscent of what Leonard Orr, MD, brought to the Western world 35 years ago. He had learned from a Hindu teacher about how to create an altered state with Lamaze-like breath work in which one can return to heal issues in the womb and to heal the experience of birth. He taught this process to Sondra Ray who travels the western world teaching therapists, healers, and OB/GYN's the importance of healing womb/birth issues, and at the same time the importance of creating birth as a nurturing, non-traumatizing experience for the newborn children of generations to come.

During this same period Stanislaf Grof, MD, a psychiatrist, was also developing Holotropic Breathwork. He was part of the original Timothy Leary team who studied altered states with L.S.D., and then went on to study natural altered states resulting in Holotropic Breathwork. Grof also found that many of the "breathworkers" spontaneously entered the womb/birth realm for healing.

I participated for about 10 years in rebirthing sessions and breathwork sessions and had profound experiences. There is some negative literature on both of these models as some have misused them or created dangerous situations for clients. Be assured that the structure of DEH®, the careful training of practitioners and the use of energy interventions keep this womb/birth work gentle and safe.

We identify with energy testing whether conception, womb, birth or all three need healing. Energy testing then guides us for in utero-trauma to the trimester that holds the issue for healing. Sometimes it is one, sometimes all three.

Healing of the womb/birth issues are identified and the person is guided with gentle language to experience the physical and sensory experiences of the womb as well as the thoughts, knowings, and emotions. Often the fetus is carrying toxins from alcohol, drugs or medication used during pregnancy, or toxins due to the overproduction of cortisol by the mother during a stressful event. Research by Bruce Perry, MD, Ph.D., (childtrauma.org) has determined that maternal anxiety and stress during pregnancy result in overproduction of cortisol by the mother and child which causes a range of attachment issues as the child develops—from acting-out to obsessive-compulsive behaviors. The mothers' and the fetus' energy are one and the same in utero. The core of the physical responses are cleared while simultaneously using the energy strategies, for example, "I feel sick…" "I feel nauseated…" "I feel scared…" while tapping.

The person may not have received adequate nutrition due to parental neglect or ignorance, or because of an organic problem that keeps them from absorbing nutrients. Or they may have been surrogate victim to assault on their mother. These circumstances can result in death energy that is imperative to clear, for example one might feel "I feel like I'm starving…" "I think I'm going to die…" Thus, we guide the person to tap or do TAT, or energy test another intervention to use on this trauma.

They may be carrying parental messages of being unwanted, or stressors in the parent's life. They may be carrying emotions such as fear about leaving the womb, mother/father anger regarding a life circumstance, or fears of the parents about their ability to parent. It is important to be aware that the energetic vulnerability in the perinatal (womb) stage can cause the slightest physical or emotional disturbance to code as trauma for the fetus. In the present something may seem minor; to the fetus it was very traumatizing.

Interestingly, independently Howard Brockman, LCSW, and I both discovered a specific time of vulnerability for the fetus is at the threshold of the second trimester. Howard noted with energy testing that many of the origins that required healing were at that point.

I had the unusual experience of having eight pregnant clients over several years prior to this writing. This was a larger number of pregnant clients than I had worked with in the last twenty years! I energy tested that these little beings were seeking pre-birth healing through their mothers. The pregnant women also had consistent ET indicating that dark energy work could not be done after the first trimester. It is interesting to note that in Buddhism they believe the soul enters the body at the fourth month of pregnancy, and our laws make it more difficult for abortion at this stage of pregnancy.

When the actual birth needs healing, the client will often experience movement through the birth canal and pressure on the shoulders and head during the reliving of the crowning. They may need to heal moving too quickly or slowly through the birth canal. They may experience the bright lights and harshness of technological birth. They often remember the exact words that are spoken by their mother, others who are present, and the medical staff.

In Orr and Ray's work they noted that the birth canal experience, how one enters the world—slowly, laboriously, quickly, with the work of travel in the canal or passively as in caesarian births—are precursors of patterns to how one operates in the world. These are your original belief energy patterns. Energy work will, of course, shift the energy of this original patterning.

The womb/birth healing in our work ends with recreating the birth experience as the client would like her/his birth to be. Have the client imagine soft lights and an attentive midwife or physician, where all the caring, nurturing people from this lifetime are present, welcoming him/her into the world with love and the exact words s/he needs to hear. The practitioner may chime in with some of the words, "You are wanted so much...we love you...look at this precious child...oh, it's a girl, how lucky we are to have a baby girl...what a beauty!"

Healing current life, birth, and soul wounds with the tools of energy psychology and DEH also often clears ancestral and karmic energetic material, but not all and the following chapters reveal how to work with those origins.

Points of interest for discussion from this chapter:
• Divine Separation is rooted conceptually in the Ennegram work.
• Divine Separation holds the negative energetic patterns; thoughts and feelings from the moment our soul moves towards our mother's womb.
• These soul wounds go to the core of our being and become life patterns that direct our decisions.
• Misdirected soul's purpose is also another result of the unconscious power of soul wound material guiding our lives.

Chapter Fifteen
Ancestral Energetic Origins

When we are deeply in touch with the present moment we can see all of our ancestors and all future generations are present in us. Seeing this we will know what to do and what not to do—for ourselves, our ancestors, our children and their children.

Tich Nhat Hanh

The Hammond family owned the successful Crystal Refrigerator Company in the early 20th century up until the time that Hotpoint went from iceboxes to electric. Apparently, Crystal refrigerators were of higher quality than Hotpoint and according to family lore could have outsold them a thousand to one.

My great grandfather was by that time somewhat senile and one day out of foolishness or fear sold the business out from under his sons. My dear grandfather, Earl, tells of years of working on anger and forgiveness. By the time I got to working on my soul's purpose intentions and attracting abundance, energy testing indicated that some of the energy of loss, grief, betrayal, and anger was still left in my field. With the gift of identifying the origins and energy work I eventually have cleared this situation from the family field.

There has long been theory and evidence in the family therapy field that children seem to absorb or take on their parent's emotions or issues, and that family members will even hold the past issues of their ancestors (Satir,1967 and Bowen, 1990). Such is the phenomenon of ancestral energy. So the bad news is that we not only get illnesses and other negative traits passed on at the genetic and cellular level, but also at the energetic level. The good news is that we can heal the negative energy at the energetic and the genetic/cellular/DNA levels. Our energy fields are eight to twenty feet around us. If a child grows up in the depressed field of a parent who inherited depression from a great grandparent, that energetic as well as neurological tendency may get passed on. This work can heal both. Dawson Church, Ph.D., has elegantly traced the research regarding consciousness and energy changing DNA in his book, *The Genie in Your Genes*.

In a few years will our research demonstrate that when we do ancestral energetic work that we change family patterns at the level of DNA? Could it be that that family disease and mutation will not be passed on?

Ancestral Origins are the genetic/cellular energetic lineage passed on through our families. The potential for healing illness by following the family lineage is extensive. We determine with energy testing if there is an ancestral lineage and then if it is maternal or paternal and whether it is biological or adoptive, if that applies.

Energy testing indicates that ancestral origins are targeting deep and broad lineages. After we energy test which lineage and how many generations ago the origin is that needs healing, we then follow the process unfolding in this book, and we go to the origin to heal this aspect of our intention.

Soul Talk: Working with the Ancestors

When I had done this work for about six years and my abilities as a healer and as an intuitive increased, I became aware of the ancestors visiting the sessions, thanking us for offering them healing also. The ancestors let us know that as we do this work we are assisting the healing of their souls on the other side. Sometimes the ancestors give me messages to pass on to the client, and sometimes the client gets messages directly from their ancestor, which I term "soul talk."

Karen, an ancestor of Marlene's, often visits sessions giving encouragement and love as Marlene does her healing work from the events of the past two years. One of us will hear her say, "Go on with your life…" "It will be okay."

Over time, as trauma clears with energy work our ability to be in touch with other realms increases.

Sometimes there is an overlap of ancestral and past life origins. For example, one of my clients is the same soul as her deceased grandfather who died before she was born and inherited his alcoholism as well as his intellectual gifts. I have grown to know this because the person working will become the soul being who is also an ancestor and say "I." The client will always say "they" when witnessing the events of an ancestor who is not also their prior soul being. Some clients request that we double check this with ET. In spite of the overlap these origins will generally test ancestral or past life, depending where the primary energy for healing exists. These ideas are substantiated by Carol Bowman in *Children's Past Lives* (1998) and *Return from Heaven* (2001) regarding our soul's tendency to be born again into the same families.

When we arrive at the origin of the ancestors, sometimes we have first hand knowledge of the family story, and sometimes family secrets are revealed. Many ancestral stories that are unknown by the client have been corroborated by living relatives.

Allison came in to grieve the fact that she could not have children due to multiple miscarriages. She said the doctor could not determine any physical reason she could not get pregnant, but she was devastated by her experiences. It was causing depression, strains in her marriage and touched the very core of her womanhood. She felt incomplete and inadequate. I suggested that as well as working on her grief, we also intend that she strengthen and heal so she could become pregnant. She was both amazed and cautious at my suggestion. Besides clearing her trauma due to the miscarriages, we also worked with her great-great grandmother's stillbirth trauma when her great grandmother nearly died. Through the gentle DEH® process we worked through and cleared Allison's ancestral energy that held imminent death for the mother, and death for the baby should she become pregnant.

Ten month's later Allison gave birth to a healthy baby girl!

Seven Generations

Another interesting original source of healing is the seventh generation. Historically and biologically seven is a restorative number. Our bodies' cells regenerate every seven years, and personal change, according to some, has seven year cycles. It seemed to me and energy testing confirmed that when people returned to the seventh generation on either side of their family that they had reached the core origin for change. Perhaps from then on they or their children's children would no longer suffer from the family malady.

Linda is a healer extroadinaire in Oregon and her recent soul leap through cancer and divorce brought her to me for healing. Surgery and many other complementary medicines had put her cancer on hold for the time being, but I am strongly in favor of preventing it forever so we embarked on that intention, "Healing all emotional, mental and physical blocks to preventing cancer through all time and all dimensions."

Nancy Gordon came up with the... "through all time and all dimensions"... phrase. It is tremendously thorough and powerful.

One evening as Linda and I were working she energy tested to return to seven generations ago on her mother's side of the family to work on this continuing healing. When she energetically tuned into seven maternal generations ago she said simply, "Cancer runs in my family." She held meridian points on this limiting belief pattern, which is usually her preference for clearing, and soon reached neutrality. She received insights in her soul messages, "I am clean." "I am part of a generational line, and I am not." "I am not guilty for not being able to keep myself well." "I can feel and know myself as a being of light."

DNA/Cellular

Before I discovered Bruce Lipton's wonderful work *The Biology of Belief* on cellular genetic change connected with emotion and consciousness, it occurred to me that all illness or disturbance of the energetic field had to start somewhere. What we call origins are defined as the origins of the trauma that energetically hold the illness or disturbance in place. I then started asking in addition if there was an origin at the level of DNA that held the origin of the illness. The DNA energy field seems to come up most frequently with physical illness or neurologically hard-wired mental illness such as bi-polar disease.

Working at the level of DNA we often find ourselves pre-seven generations ago—perhaps the set-up for the seven generation cycles? Yes, science confirms, "DNA represents the cell's long-term memory, passed from generation to generation." (Lipton, p. 63)

Ever mindful of generational illness I asked Trina who survived uterine cancer several years ago if there was anything at the level of DNA that needed to be healed. She returned to eight maternal generations before where she simply received the gift, "My sexuality is wonderful!" We reinforced that with a couple of sacred tools, tapping and ringing the sacred bowls. Her soul messages revealed, "Never underestimate the importance of healthy sexuality," "Bless all relationships," "Remember oneness even in or especially in primary relationships."

Much of my work now revolves around ancestral healing. We are in an age where we cannot only impact the individual but the entire family soul lineage.

I am now seeing the grandchildren of some of my first clients, and their grandparents still return for tune-ups. I may not live to see the multigenerational research that needs to be done, and will occur in energy psychology and energy medicine. For now I will go on the faith that what my clients tell me is true that: **Long standing patterns in families are disappearing across the generations when only one or two people actually participate in this work.**

Points of interest for discussion from this chapter:

- Energy from your parents and ancestors is present in your energy field.
- This was evident in family therapy literature for several decades.
- I hypothesize and energy testing confirms that we can change our genetic/DNA make-up energetically.
- It is possible to communicate with deceased ancestral souls.

Chapter Sixteen
Karmic Energetic Origins

Initially, I approached past-life therapy curiously as another possible strategy for healing, with a mix of enthusiasm and skepticism. Although intuitive guidance tells me that the notion of time collapses on the other side, "past life" is a generic term that seems to work in communicating the concept with most of my clients and students.

In my personal work as a past-life client a couple of decades ago, I wondered if and how it might help me. I had much separation and loss from my now grown children and I could not seem to heal internally from that. I did past life regression and healing with a local healer, Ranae Johnson. I found myself in the dreamtime place of my being where soul knows what has occurred before. I was on a ship in pilgrims' attire gazing across the ocean at a shred of land on the horizon, hugging my toddler tightly, aware that a sick, dying child was left behind that I would never see again.

I wondered if I was making it up or if what I experienced was real. I was pleased with the results of that personal session many years ago that did not include energy psychology. I was very unsure at that time what past life material was or why it worked so well. I stayed in the closet as a past life therapist for a decade. I would only come out in the privacy of a session when a trusting client asked, usually sheepishly, if I knew anything about past lives.

Involvement with the energy psychology/healing field brought me out of the closet as a past life therapist. When we delve into the energy realm we eventually tap into the old information that is held in the karmic realm, in the soul. As a result of my years of experience I believe that nearly everyone will benefit from work at the karmic origins. I incorporate the notion of soul work and multi-dimensional existences as part of this work combined with energy interventions.

Past life work is an accepted and essential aspect of some of the energy psychology models but not part of other energy psychology models. I have now spent several years investigating, studying, practicing, and teaching past life work, not because I am convinced that past life work proves that reincarnation is real, but because the healing that happens for people in this work is profound. The notion of past lives or what I refer to as karmic energy is written about in the hypnosis literature, and of course, in many theologies.

When I had the more recent cancer episode, I realized that several times in my life a physician had looked at me, shaking their head and said, "Well, we don't know exactly what this is, you may have had it for a long time, and it is rarely treatable and you will most likely die from it." Or, "We have no clue about the course of this illness."

I thought, "There is an energetic pattern here to clear." So, as part of the work I did the year I was told once again I would die, I wrote an intention, "To heal and prevent all incurable, hidden, secretive disease through all time and all dimensions."

People come to me for resolution of their life issues, or because they are desperate for healing a chronic illness, unaware that past life work is an integral part of what I do. Only a few come to me intending to explore past lives. Some build a bridge from their trust in me as a therapist, to trust in participating in an initial past life session. Eventually they all seem to find a way to incorporate it with their existing frames of reference, archetypes, dream/metaphor, or for some actual reincarnation, because they feel so much better after a past life regression session.

Should you do Karmic work?

Marilyn, a devout Catholic, for awhile refused to do past life work. She asked me particularly not to do it with her 14-year-old daughter, who was eager to do it. I, of course respected these requests. A few months later she witnessed rapid and effective progress with some long-standing difficult issues in her friend, Joyce, whose story of healing was told earlier. She tentatively talked with me from time to time about the idea of past life work. I suggested that she read

Through Time Into Healing by Brian Weiss, MD. She found it was a very easy-to-read book describing past life sessions linked to common therapy issues such as depression, addictions, and loss. She came in shortly after reading Weiss' book and said, "I want to do this, after all St. Francis believed in reincarnation!"

Past Life work was a part of healing stress and illness and taking her from a middle management state job that she excelled at to creating a career out of her passion, art, clearly living her soul's purpose. She also founded a community service organization, Artists in Action www.artistsinaction.com. You can view a beautiful example of her work on our website, onedynamicenergetichealing.org./DEH Artists

Another client, Linda, had not thought of working with past lives before, but when I explained that past life work is a part of the DEH® model, she said, "Oh fine, I know I've lived before. I don't know how I know this, I just do."

John's Story

John found that past life work cleared the way for him to feel confident as an energy therapist with abused children and an energy coach with high school athletes. His example includes many of the pieces you will read about throughout the book.

During a DEH® class he discovers that he has a past life as a community spiritual leader and healer that needs clearing. We have learned over the years that clearing these are critical for becoming a successful energy worker in this lifetime.

Session One

His intention is,

"To heal my community spiritual leader and healer past life and be effective and confident with this work in my current life."

There are three past lives to heal...

We energy test that the first one is 23 lifetimes ago. I explain to him that numbers mean nothing in the other realm, but it is an effective inductive technique to get the conscious mind to line up with the sub-conscious mind.

We energy test that there is no disorganization or reversal.

He closes his eyes and develops his tunnel of light which he pictures as a metal culvert with light bulbs. He begins his journey...

"I am having trouble moving..." tapping

"I am worried I am not going to get there..." more tapping

"My family that I grew up with is walking with me..." tapping

"I see blue healing light." TAT *"I am a woman..."*

"Oh, I am in a time I have always hated...medieval times..." continue TAT

"There is a long staircase, I am at the bottom..."

"I am cowering against the wall. I am shouting, 'Why am I here?'"

"I am afraid..." taps

"There is fear in my body, I charge up the steps, and someone is standing in the doorway and they charge up the steps and they pull out a sword..." taps

"I cower back down...I escape."

"Next I see myself out in a crowd, talking to people..."

"This can't be true..." taps

"I feel sensations down my back, and my arms are weary."

He reported feeling neutral and there were no other DEH aspects to clear.

He received these Soul Messages

1. I am not a coward.
2. I am going to be free of this burden of feeling held back.
3. It won't be long now, I am ready to get on with things. I am excited and energized.
4. My heart is lighter, and I am opening more to the world.

Session Two

In our next session we returned to a lifetime that did not have a number because we used the somatic bridge induction. There were no reversals.

John focused on the tightness in his throat...I am a man...

"My heart is beating faster..." taps on heart center.

"There is a squeezing feeling." Taps on throat chakra.

"I see a guard coming down...my head is cut off..." holding throat chakra.

"This cannot be real..." taps meridian points.

Contract

We energy tested that there was the dark energy form that clients have labeled a satanic contract, discussed further in the chapter on contracts. I don't like these words, but they seem to work.

We energy tested that the contract was:

"If you let me live and give me safety and security, I won't ever use my healing gifts again."

In the sacred space we said a prayer, rang the Tibetan bell I received at a Buddhist temple in China when I adopted my last child, and did the TAT hold.

We energy tested that it was clear, neutral.

Dying Thoughts

"Oh no, why me..." taps

"I have so much to share..." taps

"I am leaving people behind who need me..." taps

"They will never know what I had to share..." taps

"I have thoughts of revenge...They will get punished eventually..." taps

"I am a coward for not fighting back..." taps

"Others will think I am a coward..." taps

We do heart center tapping for three minutes to establish energetic boundaries with the past.

Soul Messages

1. I'm free, freer.
2. I wonder what is next.
3. My heart is opening.
4. Now is the Time.

Session Three:

John reports using some of the energetic strategies with parents and children at his center, and he and they are appreciating the results.

We energy test that he is to go in the tunnel of light to a past life 25 lifetimes ago. He experiences it as blue and white healing light.

"I am curious what form I might be in...I see a flash of forest sunlight, flashes of people...I have a sense of clouds of gray light blowing by from the left to right...there is a high wind..." tapping

"I am in a big bizarre, like an outdoor market..."

"It is the time when Christ lived..." taps

"I feel heavy in my shoulders..." tapping

"I have a sense of milling around with people...I am a male prophet-like figure..."

"People come up to me, touch me, touch my clothes...." taps

"I shudder at talking about this..."

John is now noticeably shaking as he describes a wave of energy passing through his arms and chest...

"I am afraid..." tapping

"I feel Christ-like...I can't say that or people will think I am crazy..." taps

"I have love and connection to people, and I am a follower of Christ. I am in the Sinai Dessert and the hills are barren..." keeps tapping.

"I am teaching and preaching about love for one another..."

"A person in power objected..." tapping

"I am called before a sheik or a pharaoh..." tapping

"They are angry at me for my message..." taps

"He casts me out, and has me taken away..." tapping

John reports and we confirm with energy testing that this is neutral.

Shattered Energy Field of him as an individual, the community and the land...

John focused on the shattering of the fields, and did TAT until they were restored as light and bright.

Limiting Thoughts

"I am a coward..." taps

"I am lost..." taps

"I am weak..." taps

"I am not connected to anyone or anything..." taps

"I am a wanderer..." taps

"I feel white light and people's souls passing through me..." TAT

Curses

Cleared with prayer.

Forgiveness

"I cannot really offer forgiveness..." taps

"Well, I am nearly ready to offer it..." taps

"I'm mad..." taps

"I'm cursed..." taps and prays

"I am forgiving..." taps on heart center

"I have forgiven..."

"I'm lighter... jumping for joy..."

"Get on with it..."

Soul Messages

1. I am loving and connected to people.

2. I have a lighter heart.

3. I do not have to hide or defend myself.

4. *I am freer, I am breaking the chains from the past.*
5. *It's okay to go back now.*
6. *You get to know.*
7. *Enjoy the journey, it is your time now.*

Another client, Jo said eloquently after participating in and witnessing the Women of Power group which explores the past lives of women who were persecuted or betrayed for using their powerful divine feminine gifts,

"I don't know if I believe in this work or not, but I believe in the results!" In *the Women of Power process the trauma is healed and the gifts of the past are retrieved and restored for the present.*

In addition to the women of power themes, nearly any current life issue can have a karmic energetic thread that leads to a similar energetic theme. Loss, betrayal, anger/rage, fear and disappointment make up the emotional components of most illness, but cannot be fully dissipated until the karmic energy is dissolved. Most people with any chronic emotional-mental or physical illnesses will have one or several past lives to heal in order to collapse the energetic structure that holds the illness.

Bardo Healing

In the past life regression literature there are many references to work between lives. When we do past life work it is common that energy testing will guide us to the place right after the past life for souls that experienced trauma and betrayal to have an amends and forgiveness session. This place in Buddhism is called the bardo state. The prior soul being guides the session with suggestions from the practitioner like,

"Do you have any amends to make?"

"Are you ready to forgive at a soul level?"

"Do the other souls have amends to make to you?"

"Do they need to forgive you?"

Since the sub-conscious mind holds the energy in the trance state it knows exactly what needs to come through.

"Past lives" is the common way we refer to karmic energy. I am not really concerned whether my clients believe in past lives, theologically, I am only interested in the healing results. Karmic energy may be archetypal, metaphorical, or it may be the memory of a prior soul being. In fact none of the scholars that have studied spontaneous past life stories told by children, such as Ian Stevens, Ph.D., who was at the University of Virginia for 50 years studying this phenomenon, will say that reincarnation exists. We simply cannot know this other realm and how soul truly reveals itself.

Whatever the source of karmic work, I choose to focus on the remarkable results of exploring and healing "past lives." However one defines this energy, accessing it creates profound healing results and that is why we continue to include it in our work.

Points of interest for discussion from this chapter:

- Karmic/past life work may be objectionable to some.
- This soul realm may be archetypes, dream/metaphor, or for some actual reincarnation.
- I encourage karmic work because of its deep value for healing, not for theological reasons.
- Bardo level healing means the healing that occurs for souls between lives.

Chapter Seventeen
The Tunnels and Stories

The nature of light is to shine. The way of the river is to return home to its sea.

Chad Christopher Cobb

Induction in DEH

The Tunnel of Light is the imagined, guided realm that we most often use to return to the current, womb/birth, divine separation, ancestral and past life origins. It was given to me in a meditation when I asked for a safe, protected healing vehicle to assist people to return to these realms.

Intuitive guidance informs me that notions such as "past" and "future" lives are inaccurate and actually may occur simultaneously in other realms, and that the future impacts the present. So as we work in the tunnel of light and use careful language about "going" to our childhood experience, or to the experience of the ancestors, or to the karmic experience what really happens is that the energy and dreamtime memory of that time seems to flow to us.

One of the participants in DEH work got a message in meditation that the Celtic knot is a configuration about time, which supports the popular notion that the continual knot without a break represents infinity, eternity and our interconnectedness. The common image of a line to the past is replaced in our work with this spiral-like model. Further searching revealed,

"A standard answer to the meaning of knotwork question offered by many craftsmen and artists in recent times is that Celtic knots are endless paths and so represent eternity or continuum. The Scottish art teacher George Bain published the book *Celtic Art: The Methods of Construction* in 1951. This book became a standard reference and source book especially after its re-release in 1971. In it the author made a great deal of the single continuous path that is laid out in many ancient knotwork panels. This observation leads quite nicely to ideas about the "circle of life" or "never ending...love, faith, loyalty, what ever you want." Many ancient Celtic knots are not a single path, but several closed paths that are linked or woven together..." http://www.celtarts.com/in_search_of_meaning.htm

A nine-year-old child who graced my life with her old soul teachings and did her healing work through her tunnel of light worked on a creative project in one of our sessions. She wrapped a spiral piece of an old slinky around a decorated cardboard paper towel tube and proudly reported that this was the tunnel of light—a spiral.

Previous regression work I had done with breathing and counting or a silver thread had focused primarily on the destination rather than the journey of the person to the cause or event/s of the issue or symptom that was occurring for them. NLP and HBLU introduced me to Tad James' time line that emphasized the journey as well as the destination. However, the time line perpetuates the myth that time is linear. HBLU and hypnosis models offer other non-linear inductions; the somatic bridge, where one follows the body's sensation or physical pain to the origin, and the affective bridge where one follows feelings or the emotional pain to the origin.

As in traditional light hypnosis, the tunnel of light work takes people to what is known as the alpha state which is that realm we are in as we are "falling" asleep at night. We are relaxed but still aware of what is happening around us. From this place we easily connect with the dreamtime realms that the tunnel of light carries us to.

Also, in this trance-like place the energy strategies are very potent. I presented this work several times at the International Association for Regression Research and Therapies (IARRT), a prominent past life organization. The hypno-therapists in the audience pointed out that tapping the meridian points deepened the trance state and that the issues and feelings cleared more rapidly than with just hypnosis or just tapping.

The Story

As our therapies are sophisticated and artful and seemingly strategy driven we should not forget the age old healing that occurs when people sit across from their elders or peers and tell their story. Particularly if it is a story that has been forgotten, kept secret or not validated, it is very important to listen and hold the story as sacred before we do the energy interventions. Or sometimes the story is so traumatic that I do ask the person to tap gently on their heart center while s/he tells it. Sometimes when we energy test the number of origins before telling the story and after telling the story, many of the origins clear simply from the telling. One of the oldest form of reaching a trance state is story telling. Sometimes that is all that is necessary. The person will bring up all of the energy to clear the origin in the present with the energy strategies without the tunnel of light or another induction.

Many of my clients begin their session with the story of their week and tap or TAT while they talk.

Some clients energy test that no induction is necessary—in other words the energy can be accessed in the present. We then identify with ET what to work on and do energy interventions and find the aspects in the protocol while the story is told.

Time Travel

Should energy testing indicate that "time travel" rather than the story is a priority then follow the suggestions below.

ET for the priority induction to use to move to this realm: The tunnel of light, NLP time line, somatic bridge, telling the story or other inductions in your repertoire. If the priority induction is the somatic bridge say,

"Focus on where this origin/event/trauma is located in your body." When the person identifies the place/s MMT, "Is this in fact the somatic bridge?" If no, keep checking. If yes, say, "Expand this place in your body entering it to move to the event or events that requires healing today."

If the priority intervention is the time line...consult Tad James' book, *The Time Line*. He is an NLP practitioner.

If the priority is the affective bridge ask the client to identify the emotional feeling associated with this healing and follow the feeling back through time, eyes closed using language as in the Tunnel of Light or consult Bill Baldwin's *Spirit Releasement Therapy* for other language for inductions.

The tunnel of light for most is more comfortable and easier to access than many other regression strategies. The hypnotherapy world has borrowed my dream-like vision of light, (Rothman, Zimmerman, 1999) and it is widely used by other energy and hypnotherapists. Seasoned hypnotherapists and those new to energy work seem to find that it is an easy, elegant and protective experience for the client. The light seems to offer comfort and healing along the way. The color(s) of light are as individual as those journeying. On the journey people report floating in the light or being transported rather quickly by the light to the event/s that need/s healing.

We first determine with muscle testing a healing divine separation, conception or birth, current life, or ancestral, or past life origin that is the priority for healing. Then we return to the event/s using a tunnel of light, or another induction identified with energy testing or we sit with the story as healers have done throughout the ages. Then the practitioner guides the person in his/her usual practice to the event, i.e. past life, ancestral, inner child work, or womb/birth or divine separation work to dissipate the trauma and loss.

Remember only skilled professionals should determine if regression is appropriate with people with extreme trauma, dissociative disorder, or chronic PTSD. Often the origins can be accessed easily in the present traumatic reaction. Regression is contraindicated with schizophrenics. One could say they are in a full-time trance! They can, however in my experience, benefit from tapping regarding their delusions and other intrusive symptoms. Treatment of severe disorders can be very effective combined with the energy work but takes practice and supervision beyond the scope of this book. In advanced training and consultation I am glad to assist practitioners in applying energy work with these clients.

The Tunnel of Light

To return to the event/s using a tunnel of light, say to the person in this process or use the CD which is available on my website:

"Imagine a tunnel of light stretching…or winding…naturally & infinitely into your future…and into your past. Notice the color or colors and shape of the tunnel…" (Practitioner records the color or colors.)

As you observe the person, you will notice that the suggestion of the colors begins the trance state in which we work. If the tunnel is gray or black, test if there is dark energy to clear before proceeding in the tunnel. If yes, first go to the dark energy protocol(s) in Chapter Twenty, The Pathway to Light: Unveiling theMasks of Darkness. Then resume this process.

Take some deep breaths and relax into your chair. Relax, relax, relax letting go of the tension in your body. Now enter the tunnel in whatever way is natural for you and move at just the right speed for your optimum healing which of course is known to you…Move back, back, back, naturally and gradually in the tunnel of light moving, floating, winding, toward the event/s that call for healing…(repeat this as the client relaxes).

As you enter the events for healing today, instruct your subconscious mind to take you to exactly what needs healing (words from Larry Nims, Be Set Free Fast developer)…You may know something, hear something, feel something or see something regarding what needs healing…Moving to the time when/realm of (name the identified origin such as three life times ago, two maternal generations ago, or at three years old, etc.)

When events are extremely traumatic it may be a good idea to offer extra healing light before returning to the origin.

Choose a color or colors of healing light to radiate into the events. Then imagine that these colors of healing light are available in abundance from the Universe moving through your body, radiating the color or colors of healing light into these events…you will know exactly how long to offer this healing light…" One can ET for the number of minutes to shed the light or suggest that the person will know exactly how long to offer the healing light.

The practitioner then guides the person in his/her usual practice to the event, i.e. past life, ancestral, inner child work, or womb/birth work and through the rest of the protocol using the energy interventions to dissipate trauma and loss.

Once in awhile the events are healed completely with the healing light. Then ET, "Is it in the person's highest and best interest to collect the story?"

If yes, continue the protocol. If no, guide the person by saying "Move toward the present healing everything that is similar along the way."

Otherwise, the healing at the origin will continue supported by the light as outlined in the following chapters to continue healing the original intention.

Tunnels and stories, silver threads, timelines and bridges are all imaginary metaphors that connect us with the origins for healing and allow us to access that which needs healing.

Points of interest for discussion from this chapter:

- Induction means Mind-time travel.
- Time is non-linear, perhaps non-existent in other realms.
- The tunnel of light is a common induction in DEH.
- The energy is sometimes held fully in the story and released with energy work without induction.
- The affective (emotional) bridge and the somatic (body sensations) bridge and Tad James timeline are other inductions to choose from.

SECTION
FOUR

Healing at the Origins

Prelude:

Now we are at the heart of the work and the healing. There is a flowing intensity to this work which gently releases long imbedded problems.

Chapter Eighteen
Pathway to Freedom: Healing Trauma, Loss and Grief

In all chaos there is a cosmos, in all disorder a secret order.

Carl Jung

Aspects of Trauma, Loss and Grief

After the journey through the tunnel or by bridge, or into the story, we arrive at the event that holds the trauma.

Trauma holds illness with particular energy forms that bind the symptoms of the illness together. Most of the time when the energy forms are shifted to the light, the symptoms disappear and the illness is healed. The energy of depression and sadness, anger and grudges, shame and guilt, fear and betrayal hold the thoughts and feelings that are a part of keeping illness in place.

Trauma holds the classic stages of grief as outlined by Elizabeth Kubler-Ross in her work on death and dying: shock, denial, sadness/depression, anger/rage, and also fear, and betrayal seem to play their roles in keeping trauma intact. In each session we energy test which origins to heal and within the origins which of these aspects and the aspects in the subsequent chapters to heal.

In DEH, clients have taught us the other aspects of healing the energy field that are necessary for complete wellness and finding your passion. Energetic disturbances include the energy of death and darkness, collective trauma, shattered energy fields, energetic dissociation, soul loss, contracts and limiting thought fields.

The rest of this chapter deals with energetically clearing grief and loss associated with trauma and depression. The subsequent chapters deal with healing the other energetic disturbances.

Sometimes there are blocks to accessing trauma immediately as the person in the tunnel of light reaches the origin. During a DEH session while working on origins, it is not unusual for people to experience blocking as they proceed through the feelings or the story. Sometimes this happens immediately as they begin the induction, or muscle testing may indicate that they are in the right place to begin the healing, but they draw a blank. They may say something like, "I don't know what is happening," "I don't feel anything," etc. Blocks occur visually, in the body, or with thoughts. Proceed with the block as you would an aspect of the origin.

Thought Blocks

Thought blocks occur most frequently and clear by tapping or using the energy strategy indicated with muscle testing and focus on the thought, "I don't know what is happening," "I don't feel anything," "I don't want to go there," "I'm numb," "I cannot remember what happened." When these thoughts clear, then the story or feelings comes forward.

Visual Blocks

If there is a visual block, sometimes the clients will describe a wall appearing or fog, or darkness, or colors. Interestingly sometimes people know a visual block is there that they do not see. Simply follow their lead on what they intuit.

1. Check for dark energy and proceed with the dark energy protocols if it is present.
2. Return to check further for visual blocks after dark energy.
3. If there is a wall, but no dark energy, tap or use an energy strategy indicated focusing on the wall.
4. If there are colors, tap or use an energy strategy indicated and guide the client to move through the colors as they do the energy intervention.
5. If there is "fog," have them do the energy strategy while focusing on the fog.

The person will tell you when the visual changes to a positive.

Body Blocks

When a block is not obvious by the client's description, it may be stored in the body. (Swack, 1996) They may know where it is stored intuitively or you may know intuitively or by their descriptions of chronic pain, or body trauma. Once in awhile you will have to enegy test for the location in the body.

1. ET, "Is it in the head, neck, shoulders," continuing down through the body.
2. Tap or use the energy strategy indicated while focusing on the identified place(s) in the body.
3. While tapping, an emotion, thought, or story or picture will appear that holds the trauma. Continue tapping until it clears.

Shock

The moment of the gasp is when shock locks the toxins of fear or terror into the body which assists the locking down of the traumatic memories until healing them occurs.

I was 23, young, vibrant, mother of a two-year-old, beginning my career in early childhood education when my ob/gyn found a lump on my thyroid.

He suggested I have it checked out by a specialist. Now remember, I am from the family who at that point had ignored my father's major mental illness for almost 20 years. I was not the type to make a big deal out of a little lump. But my first moment of shock hit when I arrived at the door of the specialist and saw on the door that his specialty was not just endocrinology, but also oncology. No big deal, I thought. My next moment of shock was when Dr. M. turned white when he found out I had come to the appointment alone. The next moment of shock was when he told me that I would need surgery and that it very well could be malignant. In my work over the years I have done tapping and TAT on these moments of shock which have unlocked the trauma that helped hold illness and denial in place.

In discussing the developmental aspects of trauma, Pam's story about her auto accident and childhood abuse illustrated how to deal with the aspects of shock, and several stories have illustrated the aspects of loss and grief. Denial is a pervasive part of trauma that can keep us from getting well, seeing the truth, living our truth, and aligning with our soul's purpose. Denial also generalizes so that denial in addiction, for example, can assist denial of abuse or other trauma as Sarah tells in her story.

Denial

When something is too overwhelming, or happens when we are too young, we either forget it completely or minimize it. This defense protects us from being flooded with emotion or dealing with experiences that we are not prepared to deal with. Denial for awhile in our life is a protective friend, and then it turns on us and keeps us from purposeful pursuits, whole relationships, and realizing our dreams.

Sarah's Story

"Did I ever tell you that my first husband was most probably a rapist and a murderer?"

Nearly spewing my last swallow of water, I said, "No, you neglected to tell me that."

Trauma, I had long ago learned, lurks quietly in the shadows of our being, waiting patiently to steal more of our lives, or to heal.

Sarah and I had worked together since the day she sat before me with her bloated body and articulate tongue and explained to me the lists that she had to accomplish over the next month before she could leave for inpatient addiction treatment. "If she lives," I thought to myself. To her credit she had worked in and with institutions in her native Idaho for many years, and wanted to choose a place where she could truly engage and learn and where she would be treated respectfully. She returned weekly sometimes twice for energy treatments while drinking daily. I hoped the energy treatments would keep her alive until she finished her lists. She really was not interested in quitting drinking in the meantime.

She lived, she completed treatment at Betty Ford in Palm Springs, connected with others and found the Spirit of her understanding—connecting with mother earth through crystals and prayer. She stayed sober one day at a time after anethesizing herself for 20 years. She was no longer bloated, but beautiful and light—miraculous.

Denial, as a major part of the energy of addiction, had energetically spilled over and allowed her to deny some horrendous occurrences in her young adult life when she was married to Samuel. As we cleared the energy of her alcoholism, she could no longer deny the horror.

Sarah shared the details, and we tapped and did TAT to clear the denial.

There were many red flags, I know now that I simply ignored or minimized during my years of marriage to Samuel. I met him in an emotionally vulnerable state when I was 19 years old at the University of Idaho soon after I had broken up with my med school bound boyfriend of six years. We met at a freshman welcome, get acquainted dance where at first gaze I noticed his handsome face, bronze muscles, and piercing blue eyes which from that day forward put me in what I have come to call the "Samuel trance." We bonded immediately and were together from that day.

Nothing in my past except perhaps my family's tendency to ignore or minimize problems, prepared me for the events of the next decade. All through our relationship he treated me like a princess, courting me, taking me out to nice places, paying for everything, never being sexually aggressive, calling sweetly, "Sarry." By Christmas of our freshman year we decided to marry the next summer. No one suggested that this might be a bit soon, because we seemed like the perfect couple. Samuel appeared to be a blonde angel, a popular fraternity member and a church going gentleman.

We tapped on this set up for denial.

We went home by bus to the small southern Utah town he was from where his Dad had made his money in real estate, so he said, and was town Mayor. He had been adopted as an infant by his parents. He lived in a sterile house with few artifacts and little color with a blonde wood grand piano that had been stripped to bare wood which no one played, even though his mother was an artist. His house looked like a hospital and people would get confused and come to their house for emergencies.

We were given a wing of the house to stay in and those were my bulemic days and nothing was ever said about the fact that I got up every night to throw up.

We tapped on the meridian points regarding how they both participated in the energy of denial here.

I met his friends from high school at a party we threw at his parent's home with whom he had an odd and strange connection. His favorite English teacher visited and was boyish with the kids and later I found out that he had abused the boys as teens and then remained their "friend."

We tapped on the collective energy of denial at the party.

There were innuendos that his Dad may have sexually abused him and his siblings also. His brother was sexually deviant and his sister was a drug addict prostitute.

We did TAT on denial regarding abuse.

Back at school life went on and we announced to everyone we were getting married. There was so much that I ignored as did Samuel's family—his Mom was constantly rageful or suicidal, and his Dad had shady political and financial dealings.

We went back to Utah over the next Thanksgiving vacation and attended a big party in a small space with loud music and dancing. Samuel was a fabulous dancer and we always had a good time. I didn't know what Jamestown punch was and was clueless to its effects. But soon everyone was loaded and somewhere between happy and frantic. Soon we were trading partners, and Samuel disappeared with Fran.

We all passed out and spent that night together and woke up the next morning to find the plastic cups we had been drinking from had disintegrated. Samuel had returned and no one asked about Fran, everyone assuming he had taken her home.

Samuel continued to drink after we got home and became sexually inappropriate and aggressive. I grabbed a bookshelf and shoved it at him and he stopped. We went on with our day. I remember feeling terrible for hurting him! What was I thinking?!

We continued to tap on confusion and denial.

As I reflected later on that evening, I realized there were long stretches of time that I don't remember. It was a horribly fuzzy, confusing evening. We both left for work, but Samuel never made it. He was arrested on his way to work. He called and said he was in jail, "I have done something terrible and I should probably die. Do you want to come get me or leave me here?"

There was no question in my mind that there was obviously some big mistake and no question that I would get the bail money from his parents.

We continued to tap on confusion and denial.

When I picked him up, I heard the story that he had taken Fran out in her old station wagon at very high speeds to an isolated place in the bushes and had beaten her and raped her and beat her again and Fran knew he was trying to kill her so she pretended to be dead, and he left. The police found her covered with blood with a knife in her teeth.

We tapped on the energy of shock.

We drove home from the small town jail with the top down in our convertible in icy cold weather still both very hung over and exhausted.

After that it was all very hushed. We never spoke of it, and his Dad had one of his old fraternity brothers, who was a civil attorney and reportedly was afraid to take the case, refer him to a high powered attorney for such cases. This attorney cut a deal with the DA and Fran's family. They tried to question me about why Samuel would flee the scene and I was very uncooperative, still believing that it was all an exaggerated mess. Samuel never spent another night in jail for first degree rape and assault. He got five years probation and court ordered sessions with a psychiatrist named Elmer Fudge. Yes, that is his real name!

Energy generalizes; denial is denial whether it is abuse or addictions. Once the energy of denial is present then anything our system wants or needs to deny can attach to that field. We continued to tap on the meridian points to clear the fusion of trauma, fear and denial until energy testing indicated that this was 100 percent clear. Although the content of this story seemed to have little to do with her drinking, clearing this denial energy has been key to her staying sober.

Depression/Sadness

Depression according to the medical diagnosis has several symptoms—a depressed mood, inability to concentrate and complete things, negative thinking, confusion, disinterest in work or hobbies, and often over sleeping or sleep disturbance. When these symptoms are bound with neurological predisposition, clinical depression results.

When grieving, such as in death or divorce, these same symptoms persist for a period of time. DEH will heal clinical depression 95 percent of the time, and make the natural grief process much gentler.

Clinical depression often holds compounded grief—a build up of losses that go unresolved over a lifetime, or for many generations or for many lifetimes.

Patricia lost her father when he left, never to return, at age three, then her mother to depression and alcohol, her home at age 10 when they moved and her identity as a biracial Caucasian/Hispanic woman as she blended in and "forgot" her native language. She lost her first husband to death in Vietnam, and her next husband to addiction and divorce.

It took Patricia three hours to tell me these stories before we started the energy work. She didn't have adults who listened to her in her life and she had never told the stories before. I saw shifts in her energy and demeanor as she poured out the loss and trauma of her little girl and her young woman. Eventually we created an intention and energy tested the origins and checked her for reversal. But in the mean time she needed a mother-counselor to help her hold what she had been unable to hold until now.

She kept it in and became very depressed. We developed an intention,

"To 100 percent heal my depression, and to feel, light, energetic and focused."

We found several origins.

We traveled in the tunnel of light to her days of loneliness as a child when her mother worked long hours and siblings disappeared. We tapped on the meridian points, experiencing the loneliness and the sadness until the intensity of these emotions were at zero on a scale of zero to 10.

We revisited the energy of her mother the day her father left and cleared deep sadness and anger.

We returned to an ancestral origin four generations ago…Patricia speaks,

It is sometime in the late 1800s, and there is lots of work. They are tired all of the time. People are sick and dying, it is a rough life, and they are not near any hospitals. It is all about survival.

We tapped on the meridian points on hard work, tired all of the time, rough life, sick and dying, and it's all about survival.

This is some of the energy of depression. In another session we returned to a karmic origin. We returned 17 lifetimes ago to a past life.

"…I am wearing sandals and a white garb. I used to paint and now I am writing. I am employed as a servant. I am lazy and I don't do it right. If you do it right you get a proper burial in the end. I became paranoid and more lazy."

"Instead, in the end, I did not do it right and I was burned at the stake. As I am dying I think, "This is too hard, I am too tired, I cannot do it all, I can do this in the next lifetime.""

We did TAT to resolve this.

This level of despair gets brought forward with the soul for healing. It is important not to dismiss the power of karmic healing as too far out there for most clients. It is often the key to healing chronic mental and physical illness.

This is some of the deeper energy of depression.

Patricia is a stellar attorney on the west coast. Her profession, of course, involves much writing which she has to get right in order to win! She chooses to work, for the most part, on civil cases that improve situations for many and allows her to have an income to support her real love, horses. She communicates with animals and heals them energetically. She is healing her past life karma regarding writing, and using her gifts of healing. Sometimes in our sessions I have to ask twice if she is saying writing or riding...interesting. Her soul's purpose as a writer and a rider and an animal healer are being fulfilled.

The Anger Stage of Grief, and Energetic Grudges

Post Traumatic Stress Disorder

One of my Energy Psychology colleagues on the east coast had been telling me about her daughter in the northwest who had a recurring illness, and four small children and a husband with a very high stress job. She wished so much that her daughter would do energy psychology work but said she was just too left-brained and intellectual to ever do this work. Much of my work is done on the phone and I got a call one day from the very left-brained daughter who was desperately ill. When illness takes over, intellectual defenses drop. She did the work and liked the results and that is really all that mattered.

She told me she wished she could get her husband to participate, but he, she described, is very conservative and skeptical and I might be able to get him into talk, but he will never tap. I assured her that I could just talk and do a "normal" couples session. We made the appointment, and she called me twice before the appointment to remind me that he was NOT a tapper. They came in two or three times and we worked on parenting, communication, and touched on the stressors of his job and the stressors of being a full-time parent and ill at that.

He told me that he had a lifetime of grudges that he would probably never let go of. They each felt misunderstood. Kirk works for a police department in southern Washington. He alluded to some nightmares, witnessing horrific things, sleeplessness, and long held resentments and anger.

I was quite proud of myself. I had kept my finger tips off of my face and listened intently for three sessions. Things were getting better and I had their trust.

I said to him, "She really needs to understand how stressful your job is, and you really need to understand how stressful it is to stay home all day with little kids!" And so they talked, and are still talking. I then said to Kirk, "Sometimes stress at home is made worse by the job stress." I explained the fight-flight response that occurs within him when he is in tough situations at work. All the time he is shaking his head yes. Disguising the stories, I told him about the sheriff who brought his wife and children in for me to "fix," and he liked the results so well he did many sessions of treatment on his PTSD. I told him about the military guy who was determined to prove that this would not work for him, until his wife pointed out to him that he had stopped being angry, and so he continued the work with me until he was free of the PTSD symptoms.

I told him about the "weird" work that I do, but that I do it because people like the sheriff stop having nightmares and anger with their families. I asked him if he would be willing to try it with me. He said, yes!

His wife called before his session to tell me he was really nervous!

We developed an intention for him, "To 100 percent heal my PTSD, and be free of grudges, and be able to relax with his family and communicate well with his wife."

We found origins in all of the categories.

In the first session we cleared his haunting flashbacks of giving CPR to a teen who had committed suicide by gunshot and did not revive. He had a terrible grudge at a senior officer who he believed did not do the right things to save the teen earlier.

After the first session the flashbacks were gone and he did not think about the teen for the first time in five years.

In the second session we cleared another huge energetic grudge against women and authority due to the behavior of a female alcoholic colleague of his.

The next week he reported seeing the two people to whom he had held the grudge and reported having neutral feelings. He expressed amazement at how this works and how much better and lighter he feels.

In the third session we cleared a grudge at Dad, authority and God for horrendous childhood abuse. We tapped on the fear and terror of his helpless inner child and the betrayal.

A lifetime of nightly nightmares are fading.

He told me he and his wife and children had their best week in years! He told me also that he had made a commitment to his wife to come for at least four sessions. I energy tested that we had a few origins left. I said "If it takes longer than four sessions, is that okay with you?" He said, "Yes, if I keep getting to feel this good!"

Grudges in several healing models are defined as long-standing patterns of resentment. Cheryl Brinkman, a Neurolinguistic Programming practitioner identified these patterns in the addicts she worked with in her treatment center. Judith Swack in HBLU found that many disorders hold grudge patterns. We concur. Imagine, if you will, the energy of anger running through the generations or through a soul's lifetimes landing squarely in a childhood of abuse. This is the energetic grudge.

This is also the energetic view of the anger stage of grief and one of the explanations for why people get stuck in that grief. When released, long standing histories of anger dissipate.

Kirk says he knew by the time he was seven that breaking children's bones for discipline was wrong and vowed never to lay a hand on his children. He does not. This is a huge accomplishment for any adult child of abuse, but it is remarkable for someone whose PTSD is triggered daily at work. He is fulfilling a major piece of his family soul purpose by breaking the chain of abuse.

At this point in a DEH healing session we ask with energy testing if the trauma, loss and grief has cleared at the body, soul, conscious, unconscious, biofield, and chakra levels in this origin. If the answer is weak or no, we return to the events and ask for guidance as to what trauma or loss is still present. If the answer is strong or yes, we go on to the material in the next chapter.

Shock, denial, depression, loss, anger, betrayal and fear create the fertile energy which holds the death energy, the shattering, soul loss and erroneous beliefs. When the energetics of trauma begin to collapse, there begins to be space in the field for healing to begin.

Points of interest for discussion from this chapter:

- Trauma holds the classic stages of grief as outlined by Elizabeth Kubler-Ross in her work on death and dying: shock, denial, sadness/depression, anger/rage.
- Fear and betrayal play their roles in keeping trauma intact.
- Energetic blocks are common in this work; blocks occur visually, in the body, or with thoughts.
- Shock is the moment when trauma locks into the body.
- Denial is a part of all major illness and trauma as the body defends against the assault of pain or memories.
- Patterns of anger are referred to as "grudges."

Chapter Nineteen
Pathway to Life:
The Influence of the Energy of Death

"The purpose of reflecting on death is to make a real change in the depths of your heart..."

Sogyal Rinpoche, The Tibetan Book of Living and Dying

Clearing the Energy of Death

Embedded in trauma at a conscious or unconscious level is a wish to die or escape.

Birth, death, rebirth is a natural process according to our Buddhist teachers. On this plane, however, soul's deepest desire is to live fully and be fully alive and when our thinking is otherwise, something is terribly wrong. Sometimes the thoughts are conscious and a person will develop serious suicidal thoughts or a more serious a plan to carry it out. Sometimes the thoughts are unconscious, creating depression or physical illness. Sometimes the energy of these thoughts is left from a trauma or loss of which the person is fully aware. Sometimes the energy of death has its roots in womb/birth, ancestral or karmic origins, and is deeply unconscious. The energy of death acts as a drag on the energy field keeping our energy and spirit from activating our internal healing system.

"I really do not want to live any more," is expressed frequently by clients who come in to see me with mental/emotional, or debilitating physical illness. I used to get a sick feeling in the pit of my stomach when I would hear this. I would feel immediately extremely responsible for this person's life. Ethically, I am responsible to give them the support and muster the medical and community resources to insure that the person does not commit suicide. With energy work we can address this so simply and easily that although the life-saving responsibility is always present for health care practitioners, the fear in the pit of my stomach is no longer present.

For those new to working with suicidal people:

1. Get consultation and support for yourself.
2. Make sure a support system or in-patient care is available for 24-hour support.
3. Make a written contract with the client that there are no easy means for suicide, guns, knives, razor blades, or pills in their possession and that they will call you and others if they want to kill themselves. Put the names and phone numbers on the contract.
4. Follow the protocol for clearing suicidal thoughts. It usually takes a session or two, although, it will take 7-12 to resolve the clinical depression completely, and the suicidal ideation may recur until the depression is entirely resolved.

Judith Swack identified this energy as both the conscious and unconscious energy that, when energy tested indicates, "I want to die." We can measure the percentage of the death energy and energy test the percentage of the death energy. Over 50 percent is often the level where people have conscious suicidal thoughts. If people are 70 percent or above, quite often they need anti-depressants for a period of time for safety's sake while doing the energy work. As I teach in my Alive Again: Depression Free with Energy Psychology classes and in my writing, the DEH process results in all but 5 percent of my clients being depression and medication free. The other 5 percent are very accepting regarding continuing on their medication to remain depression free.

My experience with several hundred clients suffering from dysthymia (persistent low grade depression lasting more than two years), and chronic and major depression is that there are multiple death wishes that need to be collapsed. Death energy lurks in the energy field to create illness and block health, creating depression, pain, activating trauma, and endlessly contributing to illness symptoms such as cancer cells, congestive heart condition, or fibromyalgia.

Death energy also generalizes. A person may in fact have a plan to kill him/herself, however it may reflect the death of a part of the psyche that is emerging; the death one suffers from taking on an occupation that their parent wanted for them, the death of a relationship outgrown, the death of a value or idea about one's self. Sometimes death energy is disguised as escape wishes. The client verbalizes, I just want out of this job or this relationship.

Energy testing will confirm that the energy of death is present. Thoughts of the ancestors and prior soul beings regarding death also surface in the energy field for clearing.

These are the major energetic links to depression. When all of the death energy and trauma are cleared, clinical depression is no longer present. When depression is cleared, the immune system and cellular/DNA energy is strengthened and related physical and mental illnesses can be released.

Suicidal Death Energy

Jennifer said, "I have wanted to die everyday for years and I cannot stand it." I took a brief history and then taught her right away how to correct reversal and to tap. She was, not surprisingly, reversed on, "I want to live, I deserve to live, it is safe to live, it is possible to live, and it will benefit me and others."

We rubbed the neurovascular points stating, "Even though I do not want to live, I love and respect myself," and some color began to return to her face. She teared, "You know I do not believe this."

"I know, you will again soon," I said.

We continued... within five minutes she tested strong on, "I want to live," and each successive statement. I then showed her how to tap the meridian points and I asked her to tap regarding,

"I have wanted to die everyday," she said, "It will never go away."

I said, "I know it feels that way, but it will." I told her to tap while thinking, "It will never go away."

She continued...then she resumed tapping on

"I want to die..." Soon she stopped and took a deep breath.

"I feel better," she said.

"Will you kill yourself today?" I asked.

She teared, "I won't."

I said, "Will you kill yourself between now and your next session?"

She smiled and said, "No."

"Who will be with you to call me if you want to die between now and our next session?"

"My husband."

"May I call him and let him know to call me, or you could call me."

"Yes," she said.

As we worked together there were other pockets of death energy that revealed themselves in past origins that were feeding this current crisis. None were as life threatening as the initial suicidal episode. If you are or another is depressed, suicidal ideation should always be taken very seriously. It is my experience that suicidal ideation does not disappear completely in one session with major depression or PTSD. I want people to live and come back for healing sessions, because there is a time very soon when it never returns.

Unconscious Death Energy

Addiction

When energy testing tests strong on a wish to die and the person has no conscious knowledge of this thought, they feel rather disturbed and will ask, "What does that mean? I don't want to die."

Jay's Story

Jay was working on quitting a long nicotine habit. He had smoked for 25 years and it no longer fit his lifestyle or his image of himself. He is a leader in a state agency, active in his church and has a younger wife and two children whom he adores. But like so many, he became addicted to nicotine and has not been able to quit.

I taught him the standard EFT protocols to tap on the cravings and the stress. I have learned over the years that late stage nicotine addicts tend to do one thing to try and quit smoking and then come in and say they have been unable to quit. Unfortunately western medicine and our culture support these notions that you should "just quit" nicotine. However, our research shows that nicotine binds to the same receptors in the brain as heroin and therefore the craving is just as potent, and we have 60 to 90 day treatment programs for heroin addicts.

To suggest that a late stage addict can turn things around with a few rounds of tapping would be irresponsible. When nicotine addicts come to me, here is the plan they are given:

Nicotine Addiction Recovery Plan

PHYSICAL

Daily Exercise

Patches as prescribed

Gum

Healthy Foods

Herbal "smokers' tea"

Drinks with straws (satisfies oral craving)

Tap re: cravings and withdrawlal symptoms

EMOTIONAL

Notice feelings and stressors

Journal

Talk to trusted friend

Tap re: feelings that come up

MENTAL

Notice negative thoughts

Notice positive addiction thoughts

Journal and talk about

Read, *If only I Could Quit*

Tap on these thoughts

SOCIAL

Identify a non-smoking support group among friends and family

Attend a quit smoking class

Attend a 12 step group

Tap on resistance to developing support.

SPIRITUAL

Identify spiritual longings

Expand or begin or renew a spiritual practice

Tap on resistance to the spiritual component.

Christina Grof, Ph.D., co-developer of Holotropic Breathwork stated in a presentation I attended with her several years ago that, "addiction is misdirected spiritual longings." It has become my favorite definition of addiction. I understand that addiction is also a physical disease, but beyond abstinence there is no physical treatment for it. The "spiritual" that 12-step programs teach is the answer to redirect the longing.

Since energy strategies have their roots in indigenous spiritual traditions, they become a powerful adjunct to addiction treatment. We do not have research to date that would indicate energy work alone will cure addiction. However, addiction and withdrawal create energetic reversal, so simply teaching reversal correction eases the process. Tapping, combined with prayers for release such as 12 step prayers, is very powerful and will set the stage for less resistance for what it takes to be in full recovery, and greater success with abstinence.

Jay spent several weeks quitting and relapsing—I reminded him to tap and pray and do the other things on his list. We created an intention together,

"To be 100 percent nicotine free and to feel healthy, clean, and free."

There were several energetic origins. A pivotal one seemed to be an ancestral origin. We energy tested that Jay return in the tunnel of light to three generations ago on his father's side of the family.

I am moving from the tunnel of light observing my grandfather, a rough and tumble sort. He was a stump puller in the logging industry and the son of an Oregon Trail explorer. He was a circuit prize fighter as well. He was a very heavy drinker and abused his wife and was in regular bar fights here in Salem. Jay did tapping and TAT on this story, and then we found that great-great grandfather had deathwish energy which had been passed forward to Jay. Jay tapped on the meridian points while thinking, "I want to die," even though this was not conscious for him in the present. It was tied to limiting thoughts that, "What men do is drink and smoke."

In the end we energy tested that all was clear, and he was able to quit smoking.

Unconscious death energies are connected with almost every illness that walks through my door. Jay's story is just one example. Both physical and mental illness are bogged down with the energy of death.

Escape Wish

Sue's Story

"I am just not happy at work. My boss is crazy, and explodes at people and I am working at a job where I am underemployed." We had spent several months healing her PTSD from 10 years of illness followed by sexual abuse from a physician, as well as parental alcoholism and abuse. She grew up wealthy and Catholic and we had much to clear about the myths of wealth and religion. She is 48, but literally lost 10 years of her life with the physical problems. She was well-known in the arts field in Seattle and abandoned that in order to survive.

The job in which she is underemployed is the last thing left from her survival years. Through our work, she has no PTSD symptoms left, and is quite courageous, as the youngest child from her abusive and controlling family, about standing up to them. Her father now treats her respectfully. We are in the middle of her soul's purpose intention. She has returned to her art in her spare time. She is an extremely skilled fine artist.

Although we had cleared many wishes to die in many origins related to her 10-year vigil, we were both surprised that there was another one related to work, because her conscious thoughts were simply wanting out of her job! She energy tested to use TAT on this, and came up with thoughts about how toxic the work environment was for her. The people I work with often energy test for TAT when environmental or food toxins are present, so it is very interesting that the energy field codes the work situation as toxic also. In the end she tested that the wish to die related to work was clear.

She has decided to stay awhile for the benefits and to invest in the materials she needs for her future business. Her boss has been confronted and put on a work plan for her behavior by her superiors, and the workload is more reasonable.

Often times when we clear we find that things also clear in our surrounding environment.

Alcohol, Abuse and PTSD

Kay's Story

Dying would be the simplest way out, she thought. She had planned her death several times before I met her nearly 17 years ago. This was before I was introduced to EP. I have now known her as long as she was with "Mr. Jerk" as she now refers to him. She drank to numb the pain and her emotions. Of course alcohol just weakens the energy field, reinforcing the trance state that holds women hostage in domestic violence situations. I thought if she just got sober then she would see the "light." She got sober and then we began the grueling work with trauma in the only way I knew to do it then—painfully and slowly. We made plans for her safety, we did inner child work, she worked the 12 steps, we did reality therapy to assist her out of denial about abuse.

And she stayed, and we continued the work, and she stayed. She finally revealed that of late he was threatening to kill her if she left. He had a gun in the house. She had nightmares and to my surprise I began having nightmares. It was a long five years before the fateful night he slammed her up against a wall and broke her nose. Somehow she escaped and never returned. She said she knew the next time he would kill her. Her nightmares did not stop and neither did mine for awhile.

She lived in constant terror for the 17 years that she was with Mr. Jerk. She said she never knew what would make him explode. She tried to figure it out. She would keep the house perfect, but if she missed a dish, he might knock her across the kitchen. She did not miss that dish again. If she was late from work due to errands or other necessities, she might get a beating. He yelled at her constantly and controlled everything from the food in the house to her weight, to what they bought, and when and how the bills were paid. If they did things which were fun, he planned it and he was in charge of when they went and how they got there. It followed the script of the film, Sleeping with the Enemy.

I did what I knew how to do then. I assisted her in managing her PTSD symptoms. I encouraged her to rely on trusted friends to teach her how to live normally. She had married Mr. Jerk at 19 and had never kept the checkbook, or made a budget.

Fortunately she had a good job. By the time she was away from him for 18 months she bought her own home. She had much anxiety and sleepless nights, because she had been brainwashed to believe she never did anything right.

Whenever she traveled, she had panic attacks. Stress at work would plummet her into nightmares or flashbacks. My nightmares stopped, hers did not.

In the following chapter on Healer Preparation you will read about my work with vicarious trauma related to my work with her.

About three years after her escape I discovered energy psychology and began to put together the tools in this book. I had prayed for teachers and she was one of the reasons.

When I returned from my first training, I said, "I believe I have found something that can help you even more." Well neither of us would have ever imagined 11 years ago just how much help energy work would offer her.

Abuse survivors have a different quality to their PTSD than the survivors of combat we originally studied. After all that was war, and trauma is to be expected. Home, however, is supposed to be safe, and the betrayal runs deeper.

She grew up not surprisingly with addiction and and parental abuse, but with an unusual outcome. Everyone got sober and clean when she was in her teens and her father got treatment for abuse, unusual in those days, and they developed a close relationship over the years. Ironically, part of her denial system was the expectation that like her father, her husband would recover from his abusive nature, still unusual today.

We did an intention, "To heal all abuse and PTSD through all time and all dimensions, and to feel confident, competent and safe in my life."

Dying Thoughts

We worked through many origins, but a pivotal one that she had been aware of consciously for many years was that in her last life she had been a woman in the Air Force who longed to fly in World War II. She told me this story when she was still married. As a woman in that era, she was forced into a desk job. She died of alcoholism with the thoughts, "I would rather die than live," and "I will never get to have my true love." We tapped on the meridian points regarding these dying thoughts. Energy testing confirmed that they were clear.

A high point in her current life was a love who was a prior soul being in the WWII lifetime with whom she shared the joy of piloting small aircraft. She did become a licensed pilot this time around!

Clearing the dying thoughts is often required in several karmic and ancestral origins where untimely or traumatic death occurs or is witnessed, for example the death of a great grandmother during childbirth. This is very important because the energy of the dying thoughts carries forward, and holds karma and/or death energy for the future. Working with dying thoughts applies primarily to past lives. Past life writers, Woolger, Bowman, and Stevens all trace current life issues and problems to the material and energy contained in the dying thoughts.

Dying Thoughts Healed

Kay went to an earlier lifetime to heal more trauma and dying thoughts.

"My hands feel light and tingly...I see other women, all holding hands in a circle around a flickering fire in a dense forest with lots of rich green foliage. We are runners. We run to gather our food, we run to escape the warrior men. I am sad because I cannot be a mother...I run long distances for the clan and it is difficult to run with milk filled breasts...others in the clan are the mothers and their breasts are full, mine are not..."

I guide her to clear the sadness with tapping.

"It's night time...there is drumming; they are dancing, skipping...in the circle in the dark..."

I ask her to look at her feet and to see what she is wearing...

She says, "I'm barefoot and I'm wearing a tannish brown animal hide skin..."
I ask her to ask where she is and when it is. She says, "It's New Zealand and it's 1863...and clear, although sometimes the climate here is rainy." ET indicates that this is true.

I say, "Ask what your role is in this community."

"I am a leader, but no one can know or I'll be killed...I have a special leader's necklace so the women know...I'm not the only leader...there are warrior men with dark energy who will kill me."

I ask her to focus on what she is feeling.

"I have tightness in my chest, I am tense all over...I'm very afraid..." I guide her to tap on the eye, under nose and collar bone points. The fear releases. She says, "The tapping is like the drumming in the circle. It is a joyous time. The dancing and singing is a group trance...a dreamscape in dreamtime."

Kay approaches her dying thoughts.

"The dark energy of the warriors wants me...it got two other women before me. I knew what was happening, but I couldn't stop it."

I guide her to tap throughout…

"Two women rise up to protect me. I cannot allow this. I gave myself away and they got me…I'm dying…It got me."

Dying Thoughts:

"I had to die to protect the other women…I died for the love of my tribe."

Soul energy is core energy that is extremely strong and powerful. In Women of Power lifetimes the dying experience and thoughts are the energetic origins of co-dependency and violence against women. They hold the energy that is passed on with the soul that accumulates victim/perpetrator and co-dependent energy. Tapping the meridian therapies also clears the dying thoughts.

Will to live

We end a segment of clearing the energy of death by energy testing whether or not the person is at 100 percent will to live. We have found over time that the absence of death energy does not necessarily mean the full embrace of life. Thus, one origin at a time, one death energy piece at a time, the person will return and maintain the will to live. One can also do an energy strategy such as holding chakras one and seven, sending the energy down from seven to one to strengthen the will to live.

Since death is natural, the energy of death is inherent in the energetic process. However, it becomes stuck in the body-energy field impeding wellness. Clearing the influence of death energy is imperative for complete health, and retuning to our natural will to live.

Points of interest for discussion from this chapter:
- The energy of death holds specific energy forms which impede healing.
- Suicidal people need precautionary intervention as well as energy work.
- Addiction requires some traditional strategies and treatment as well as energy work.
- Dying thoughts affect the soul and come forward.
- The absence of death energy does not necessarily assure 100 percent will to live.

Chapter Twenty
The Pathway to Light:
Unveiling the Masks of Darkness

Knowing your own darkness is the best method for dealing with the darkness of other people.

Carl G. Jung

The dark side has been part of our archetypal world from Shakespeare to science fiction. Accepting the notion of "dark" energy is really just a matter of thinking about archetypes as energy.

Clients who have lived in the depth of depression, addictions or post-trauma do not blink an eye when I say energy testing is telling us that there is something dark here. Their responses are:

"Of course, I have lived in the doom of depression for years."

"Oh sure, the black hole is where I go when I am really depressed."

"Oh yeah, that black pit I am in when I wake up from being loaded."

"Since childhood I have felt like my family lived in a dark cloud."

Recognizing Dark Energy

People with the dark energy influence say things like,

"I am not myself."

"Something comes over me."

"It's like something takes over."

"It's like I'm possessed."

Also language like "hate," and "terrified," or

Tibetan bell

suicidal or homicidal thoughts tend to hold dark energy. Chronic physical symptoms and issues tend to hold dark energy also. I sense a heaviness in the room, or the client may begin choking slightly when dark energy is attempting to release.

We notice that as practitioners strengthen and raise the vibrations of their healing field, much of the dark energy clears with the trauma, and we do not have to deal with it separately.

Historically, work with dark energy was left to the realm of theologians in the form of exorcism. This has been portrayed as dramatic and dangerous. Our work with dark energy is **not** dramatic and is extremely safe. In the therapeutic realm we have worked with dark energy for sometime now. It is disguised as rage, shame, fear, or addictions. When we simply name the "dark energy" more specifically, the result is that it clears more thoroughly.

Scott Peck, MD, well known for his landmark book, *The Road Less Traveled*, also wrote a much lesser known book, *The People of the Lie*, in which he bravely discussed addressing evil in the therapy setting. He challenges the field of psychology to address evil in our work with clients. Twenty years ago when he wrote this he made no suggestions on how to do this.

He tells the story of a family who gave the gun that one of their sons committed suicide with to their other son the following Christmas, and saw nothing wrong with this. I remember thinking as I read this how right Peck was that therapists consider themselves too intellectual and sophisticated to acknowledge evil. I was left, however, wondering how one might work with the dark side effectively in therapy.

From studying the writings of William Baldwin in *Spirit Releasement Therapy,* and S. Modi's, *Remarkable Healings,* Fiore's *The Unquiet Dead* and training in Supernatural Interference with Judith Swack, my colleagues and I have developed simple clearings for dark energy. Most of the time we use the term "dark energy" to make it the opposite of "light energy," rather than to use words loaded with fundamentalist religious consciousness. However, sometimes, particularly when there has been major individual or collective trauma, words such as "demonic" or "satanic" need to be brought into the field in order for the clearing to be thorough. **Remember, this a therapy of the energy of language.**

Baldwin found that in western cultures where he practices hypnotherapy that these are the terms that clients identified.

We need in other words to tap into the larger established collective unconscious regarding dark energy. As long as there are traumatic and toxic experiences in the world, dark energy is present. With few exceptions we find that it is not a dramatic or frightening encounter. We have, however, developed a healthy respect for its existence and its agenda to divert us from our soul's purpose.

I will not cover this subject in-depth here, but encourage you to come to our trainings to learn how to work with this energy effectively.

Most of the time energy testing will identify that there is dark energy in the field and we clear it with:

1. TAT or EFT
2. Prayer
3. Sound: Tibetan bell or crystal bowls and/or
4. Smudging

Sometimes energy testing will indicate that you need to name the dark energy in order to clear it.

Curses

We work with the energy of anger, which can land squarely in another's energy field when damned or cursed. It is imperative to clear anger and grudges and not project it on another.

Sally, who had suffered abuse from her brother growing up stated during a trauma clearing that it seemed like the women in her family were cursed. We energy tested and found that five generations previously one of her female ancestors had been murdered by her husband. This was the ultimate curse that had lessened in intensity over the generations but still brought unwanted energy to the family.

We used prayer and the Tibetan bell to clear the curse.

Soul Stealing

During a major transition in my life I found myself giving up some further strands of co-dependency. While working with a DEH colleague we discovered that I had allowed all of my former partners to "steal" or use a piece of my soul. Gradually, we visited the times in my life when this had occurred and used the energetic strategies, prayer and sound to reclaim these stolen pieces.

Energetic Attachments

Baldwin, Swack and Modi all write and teach about earthbound spirits.

I was so very curious about this phenomenon in my early trainings. Sometimes dark energy accompanies them, sometimes not. If energy testing reveals dark energy, release that first and then work with the attachment as described here.

Apparently when death is sudden or premature, spirits will attach to the souls of another rather than move to the other side. Sometimes the soul choice is random, as if after death they simply land in someone's field. Sometimes a loving relative will "stick" around to care for a loved one. Other earthbounds wish to experience the qualities of the soul to which they attach. In any event, they need assistance to complete their experience here.

I had known so many who went to Vietnam in the late 1960s and early 1970s who met an early death, or met the death of their soul, returning as a hollow form of their former self. It impacted me to the point that I would leave the room during conversations about the war, and I could not read a book or watch a movie about Vietnam. I got stomachaches if I was exposed to anything about this war.

In Swack's training my partner and I determined with energy testing that I had an earthbound spirit that came into my field in 1968. I was connected with several returning vets during that time. I closed my eyes and returned to this time and found that a spirit that had died in Vietnam and had jumped from one of my friend's energy field to mine. It was almost 30 years later…could this be? I spoke with the spirit and he told us of his torment and pain and the uselessness he felt about losing his life in this way. I could feel his pain and grief like it was my own. I had felt it as my own many times.

I explained to him that he was stopping his soul development by staying with me and that he could find more peace on the other side with God, and that many of his buddies were waiting for him. My partner said a lovely prayer, and sounded the bell, while I did TAT and asked the spirit to return to its rightful place.

Since his departure 12 years ago, my torment about the war and my friends who lost their lives or themselves has calmed. I can stay in the room for a conversation, and watch a documentary if necessary.

Earthbound spirits cannot continue the important tasks of their soul development until they release and move on.

Bob and I were in a college class together. I had known him in recovery groups where he shone as a charismatic leader. Even though he was a leader, he had difficulty staying sober for more than a year at time. We dated during one of these periods of sobriety. We talked about God and life and kids, and work. We drove to the snow on a moonlit night and wondered about our futures. Before I knew it he was off again on a cocaine run, seduced away from me by the high of the white powdery stuff.

I went on with my life, and I heard through the grapevine that he was still struggling. Three years later I got a call from my friend Jess, who had also loved him—few did not—that he had died of a cocaine overdose. We had coffee and reminisced about the roller coaster of knowing Bob and the lessons he taught us about life and death. Jess and I shared gratitude for our gift of sobriety and life.

A few years later I was doing another personal healing on illness and we discovered Bob as an earthbound attached to me. When I asked him why he had stayed with me he said that he had never had the opportunity to experience long-term sobriety and now he had with me, and his soul voice expressed his admiration for my perseverance in staying sober.

Again we released him with a prayer and a bell. Now I experience him every once in awhile as a guide, especially when I am dealing with men. He knows I need all the help I can get in that area!

These two experiences made it easier to accept and be compassionate with the spirits when my clients and I discover earthbounds in their fields.

We send light to black holes and cosmic voids and release contracts made with the dark. We release entities and demons and earthbound spirits all in the name of health and well-being.

Shatki Gawain sums up my experience of working with the dark,

"Evil (ignorance) is like a shadow. It has no real substance of its own, it is simply a lack of light. You cannot cause a shadow to disappear by trying to fight it, stamp on it, by railing against it, or any other form of emotional or physical resistance. In order to cause a shadow to disappear, you must shine light on it." (1979)

Points of interest for discussion from this chapter:

- Work with dark energy is archetypal.
- Clients easily recognize the dark energy connected with their disease.
- The names for dark energy were labeled by clients

Chapter Twenty One
Reclaiming Wholeness

Internal and external are ultimately one. When you no longer
perceive the world as hostile, there is no more fear, and when there
is no more fear, you think, speak and act differently. Love and
compassion arise, and they affect the world.

Eckart Tolle

This chapter will cover other ways that, in my experience, the energy field loses life force. The energy field may shatter, the soul may split, or an energetic part may leave the body.

Shattered Energy Field

When I was a young woman, a long-time partner left one day without explanation, never to return. In the months that followed I told a friend that I felt like a piece of glass that had shattered and that if someone would drop me I would break into pieces.

Years later, I remembered that feeling when I discovered the shattered energy field with C. L. She came in with psychotic symptoms and also debilitating shooting pains down her spine diagnosed by a neurologist as an organic neurological disorder. In other words she said, "He doesn't have a clue!"

Over the course of a year we reduced all of her symptoms dramatically. For the first few months, however, her energetic boundaries weakened frequently. I asked with energy testing if there was an energetic origin to her frequent loss of strong boundaries and we were guided to return to her Women of Power lifetime, a lifetime I had discovered with many that contained a significant loss of personal power.

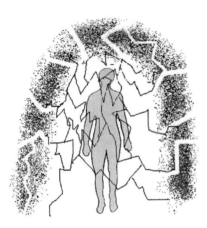 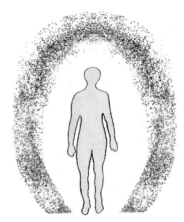

Shattered Energy Field   *Restored Energy Field*

We intuited and then confirmed with energy testing, that her whole field had shattered and needed repairing in this origin. We then were guided to ask about a shattered energy field in all DEH healings. Her need to repair boundaries went from daily to monthly. Currently, she only needs to do energetic boundary work when she makes a major life change. Healing the shattered field also greatly improved her paranoia and completely relieved her psychotic symptoms.

This shattered energy is carried forward by the soul projecting through illnesses such as depression, bipolar disease, or post traumatic stress disorder (PTSD), dissociative disorder, schizophrenia, psychoses, and chronic physical illnesses. It is the origin of energetic boundary disturbance, when the boundary work discussed earlier does not stick.

Harv's Story

I was to learn more about this from Harv, 42, a health care professional in a very high stress job who had been diagnosed with bi-polar disorder five years earlier and had been treated with lithium. He also had been sober and clean for 15 years and uses a 12 step recovery program. He was unable though to control the explosive anger that often accompanies bi-polar disorder.

We created an intention, "To be anger free and to 100 percent heal bi-polar disorder."

I have not yet seen anyone 100 percent heal this disorder but I always have people go for that possibility with any illness.

We worked through many origins, did couples counseling and energy work with his wife who had been the brunt of his anger. He tapped daily on his stresses and anger. He said that tapping had became so second nature to him that he found himself downtown on a street corner waiting to cross the street tapping away until he noticed people staring!

One evening we were guided by energy testing to a paternal ancestral origin, four generations ago—apparently the origin of the illness in his lineage. There had been the trauma of poverty, abuse and alcoholism, and we cleared this trauma with tapping on the meridian points. Energy testing helped us identify dark energy and a shattered energy field in the brain. First we cleared the dark energy which he described as "in his brain." Then we used TAT to heal the shattered energy field until Harv felt/saw his brain filled with light. From this session on he was able to reduce his lithium to half the previous dose and manage his anger effectively.

June's Story

Another client with bi-polar disorder also benefited from this work.

We worked on clearing the fight response for June because her neurological responses were easily triggered when fear was present.

June suffered from bi-polar disorder and had the accompanying bursts of rage at unpredictable moments that often accompany this disorder. It seems that the body/brain produces fear easily with the ups and downs of a bi-polar person, and reactive anger results.

Although most people with chronic mental illness have earlier trauma in their lives and need to address that energetically in the course of treatment, it is impossible to heal the illness without recognizing the neurological trauma that occurs day to day for the chronically mentally ill person and do energy work directly related to that. In other words the illness itself causes on-going trauma.

June describes her husband forgetting to turn the heat on for her when he gets up in the morning and flying into a rage at him as soon as she was out of bed.

I had her return in her mind to the moment she woke up and felt her jaws tighten and her body tense, and we tapped on the meridian points until her body relaxed. Then I had her re-do the rage state in her mind at her husband and tap regarding that until the rage neutralized. She said, "I can't believe I acted like that."

Then I asked her to imagine what occurred in her brain during this time and to tap about the misfired neurotransmitters and the brain's inabilities to calm itself. As she tapped, she uncovered dark energy and a shattering of the energy field in her brain, and soon she saw her brain filled with light and peace.

June went on to be more contented in her marriage, was able to reduce her bi-polar medication, and establish a business based on her creative endeavors. She says in spite of her illness she is living her soul's purpose!

Thus after the trauma is cleared, we then focus on clearing damage to the energy field. Major traumas and losses can cause a disturbance, a shattering of the energy field, which has to be focused on specifically to be restored. Each individual describes what is seen or experienced in the field differently. S/he may describe it as heavy, damp, collapsed as well as shattered, fractured or disturbed. Shattering is the most common descriptor.

The shattering can be to the individual, family, group, or community and land. The shattered field must be cleared with focus and intention.

If the shattering is in a past life, such as the Woman of Power lifetime, where the woman was a community spiritual leader, the field of the whole community and of the ritual artifacts may be disturbed or shattered. Dark energy forces move into this vulnerable space, blanket the community and the land. Or in the case of a smaller energetic individual or family field, the dark energy may enter the individual fields and the surrounding earth.

This healing may occur but does not always occur through telling the story, clearing the trauma, or the death energy.

Soul Loss

Soul loss is significant in healing trauma and illness. Usually the lost part is a positive quality left behind in trauma's clutches. Once in awhile it holds pieces that still need healing. It is a simple, sacred, and powerful soul retrieval.

My shamanic teachers drum and journey and retrieve the soul part for another.

I continuously ask for guidance to empower individuals to do their own work, and several years ago the voice whispered tap, do TAT or chakra balancing and say "soul loss" as away of releasing the loss and retrieving the lost part. This idea seemed too simple and disrespectful to my shaman friends, so I asked again and got the same answer, so I decided to try it. That was several years ago and the results from this simple process have been amazing.

Lyn, 64, came to me questioning her purpose and her journey. She was depressed and stressed and had a continual yet changing list of physical symptoms. She lives alone and is retired from teaching due to stress. Due to her discomfort many energetic parts separated from her body.

She returned to a paternal ancestral origin several generations ago when the "land could not provide." We identified soul loss with energy testing and as she did TAT to release the loss, she retrieved the lost soul part of "happiness." She immediately felt less depressed and more hopeful about healing and her future.

Abused or otherwise traumatized children will retrieve lost innocence, hope, and self-worth. Depressed people often retrieve joy, and anxious people may retrieve relaxation. The release and retrieval is usually gentle and unemotional leaving people with their natural positive birthrights.

Out of Body

There are several levels and extremes that occur when people leave their bodies. At the level of personality an inner child part that suffered trauma may have split off. Swack calls this an autonomous part. Sometimes an entire energetic part will dissociate, and sometimes a whole other personality will form.

There is a continuum of dissociation from natural to disordered that I came up with several years ago. There are the times when we "space out" staring into the trees in the woods or watching the waves in the water lap in and out, or on those long drives where we do not quite remember everything we passed along the way. There are the times of "natural trauma" as children—a broken arm in sports, thunder and lightning that scare us and cause us to leave our bodies for awhile. Then there are the more frightening traumas—automobile accidents, abandonment, assault. Some of these may cause more permanent dissociation. Repetition and duration of the trauma make a difference in severity of the dissociative disturbance.

Hans' Story

When Hans was 10 and his mother was 32, a male intruder broke into their home, waving a gun and a knife and held them hostage for a week. Hans ran the gamut of feeling terrified to feeling sorry for his captor, as is common in hostage situations. He has vague memories of the man dragging his mother away and assaulting her and raping her, and threatening to kill them if they told anyone. The week seemed like a year. In a moment on the last day Mom somehow got them out the door and to safety. The man was arrested that same day. Hans is sure they would be dead otherwise.

Hans is 32 now and is very depressed, ever protective of his mother, and cannot sustain adult relationships. He has memory problems and is very anxious and fearful. He meets all of the criteria for PTSD—anger, a sense of foreshortened future, nightmares, flashbacks and avoidance, hyper-vigilance, sleep difficulty, and exaggerated startle response. We revisited the trauma to clear the PTSD symptoms. To heal dissociation we check with energy testing when the moment was that Hans left his body in the captive situation. It turned out to be when his captor threatened to kill him. We stay at that moment and energy testing guides us to do frontal occipital holding while he focuses on "I left my body." This calls the parts back into the body, and restores the energy field to wholeness.

As is common with extreme current life trauma there were also karmic issues and ancestral origins as well related to the hostage trauma.

There are volumes of mental health and hypnosis literature that attempt to explain and research the process of splitting and dissociating as a problem of the sub-conscious and the personality. When addressed energetically it becomes much simpler. In my advanced trainings we cover the material to heal the personality splits in dissociative disorder and energetically integrate the person to wholeness.

The shattered energy field is often a key to healing major neurological and physical illness. There is a two-fold explanation for this. One, there is an origin where there was such severe trauma that the body or brain was damaged and the energy field did not repair itself. Then, the illness itself—panic disorder, bi-polar disorder, anxiety, addictions, or a heart condition continues to re-traumatize and weaken the energy field and continue the shattering.

Again, I want to emphasize that severe illness is re-traumatizing and if this is not addressed, no matter how many origins or events are revisited, the illness will not heal.

Restoring the field to wholeness is key.

Points of interest for discussion from this chapter:
- Energy fields may shatter split, or fragment.
- Souls may experience lost parts.
- Shattering of the field is key to healing serious illness.

Chapter Twenty Two
Creating Gratitude and Joy

Gratitude unlocks the fullness of life. It turns what we have into enough, and more. It turns denial into acceptance, chaos into order, confusion into clarity.... It turns problems into gifts, failures into success, the unexpected into perfect timing, and mistakes into important events. Gratitude makes sense of our past, brings peace for today and creates a vision for tomorrow.

Melody Beattie

Limiting Thought Fields

I was to learn a thousand times over that clearing trauma and negative thoughts leads to the body-mind-spirit's expanded ability to hold the positive energy of joy, gratitude, peace and love. Beliefs have biological and energetic connections as described earlier in this book. My colleague, Mary Sise, LCSW, has articulated the Energy of Belief in her recently published book by that same name.

We entered the rooms for our 100 hours of Neurolinguistic Programming (NLP) training, wondering how in the world we could manage this commitment with our busy practices and our young families.

NLP is the study of the use of language and imagery to create change in people. Its developers, Bandler and Grinder, studied the top therapists of the last generation to discern how clients responded to their language and nonverbal behavior. They then created formulas and exercises based on the expert's language and behavior to create an elegant system for change. NLP became controversial in the last few decades as the developers took it to the corporate world and taught people to make sales with these strategies!

Our instructor, Washington state counselor Ragini Michaels, brought NLP to a much higher level. We immersed ourselves in travels to the language of the body and the subconscious mind. There we discovered the limitations and the expansion possibilities for thoughts and feelings. Presented in great detail were the thought fields for change.

Cognitive Therapy, based on thought change, has been a major model in counseling for several decades. The idea that you can change your thoughts and feel better has also emerged from New Thought churches such as Unity and Religious Science. The film and book, *The Secret,* have brought these ideas to the mainstream.

Callahan, you recall, titled the first model of energy psychology *Thought Field Therapy.* He proposed that thoughts are energy and therefore changeable with energy strategies. This is the crux of most of energy psychology and many of the aspects of Dynamic Energetic Healing. Intention, trauma, grief, grudges, and soul loss, along with the descriptors of death energy and dissociation, for example, are simply thoughts. We tap, TAT, or hold and they balance or change to the positive.

They change to the positive because positive is our natural state. All forms of therapy and support groups have the intention of talking through the negative to let it go. Our methods simply allow you to let it go more quickly and gently.

Generally, energy testing guides us to use Emotional Freedom Techniques-tapping on the meridian points.

Sometimes the limiting thoughts are part of the origins work; sometimes we use a fairly traditional EFT or TAT model.

Limiting Thoughts about Change

Signing up for an energy psychology or DEH session, class or workshop ultimately involves an admission that you need to change something. A common response to change in the psyche is resistance. At the beginning of a session or a process we will often tap on resistance by way of shifting reversal...

"Even though I do not want to change, I absolutely love and respect myself."
Within a couple of minutes, *"I want to change,"* energy tests strong.
Or we tap on the inner objection about getting healthier...

"If I get over my depression, I will have to take more responsibility and work too hard."

After a few rounds of tapping, "It will be better when I am not depressed and I can monitor how much I work."

"If I recover from my back pain, I will no longer be eligible for disability and I won't be able to support myself."

Eventually we find ourselves tapping on the positive, "I can change my attitude—if I no longer have back pain, I can get a good job and support myself."

We then tackle the limiting beliefs...

"It is hard to change old habits." To..."I can easily change."

"My mother's depression never went away and neither will mine." To...

"I have tools my mother did not have and my depression will go away."

Limiting Thoughts in Illness

There are thoughts that are part of the structure of illness that when in place perpetuate illness and when energetically cleared help heal the illness.

"It seems that no matter what I do I never get better."

"Every one in my family has this condition."

"Heart disease or cancer runs in my family."

"Every holiday season I get a cold."

"Every spring I get allergies."

These are some of the energetic thought fields of illness. When the energy of the thoughts shift along with the energy of the previous trauma, the energetic structure of the illness collapses and the illness ceases to exist. (Swack, 1996)

My clients will say, "But this is true—everyone on my mom's side of the family has heart disease!"

Working at the energetic level challenges what has always been true. The first generation that contracts an illness plants the seeds for the future thought fields to grow, and once it reaches the third generation the belief system is rooted and true. We tap or TAT to clear what has always been true.

Sharon had two failed surgeries on her irregular heart rhythm, which was causing blocking and pain. By the time I saw her she could not work and only had four to six functional hours per day. She had PTSD from childhood issues and the heart arrhythmia caused her to startle, and trigger her PTSD. She was anxious and losing sleep.

We did many sessions on the origins of her PTSD and then tapped on the beliefs that were keeping her debilitated.

"I am afraid the surgery will not work again."

"I am going to be like this forever, and I will never work again."

"The pain never completely goes away."

"The stress in my life keeps me from getting over this heart condition."

The third surgery was a complete success and Sharon is back at work full-time and is about to get a promotion. She is pain free, has reduced her personal stress, cares for five dogs, and helps out her elderly grandmother!

Limiting Thoughts in Relationships

"My husband will never change." I have heard this many times over the course of my career as a professional counselor. There are many ways to address this. I could ask the person to tap on, *"My husband will never change"* and notice what comes up. Often it is something like, *"well I guess he did quit smoking."* And then she will rattle off several other ways that he has changed.

I could also ask her what is bugging her about her husband, and have her tap regarding her feelings about him.

"I am so angry," soon changes to …

"I am so disappointed when he treats me like that."

"I am afraid that things will never change."

There are several possibilities here. One is that the person would end up in a positive place.

"Oh, he's not so bad."

"I can choose other reactions."

"Things could change if we both work at it."

If it is an abusive situation generally the thought field tapping will assist the person in her emergence from denial.

"He really is scary,"

"I am not safe with him."

"He is one sick guy."

Later, when she is out of the abusive situation and safe we will work some more on safety and fear in general.

The other possibility is that as she taps she realizes in both the non-abusive and abusive situations that she can change how she feels and reacts.

208

So with the husband that bugs her we might end up with…

"I can look for the good in him."

"I can let him know how I feel."

"I can ask him to work on things with me."

In the abusive situation…

"I can take care of myself and my children."

"I am a good person."

"I am a smart person."

"I can create a safe and happy life."

Of course, sometimes the outcome is that a person becomes clear that the relationship has succumbed to a slow death and they are to move on.

Another possibility for change in our relationships is to think of the law of attraction which is described in the film, *"The Secret"* as a universal law that like attracts like and energetically that similar vibrational fields seek their sisters.

We can use the mirror approach that I spoke of earlier.

In the law of attraction as my mirror model, I would tap on the way that I hurt others. This fits well with the *"keep the focus on yourself model"* that I teach couples who come to me to work on their relationship issues.

Recently, Sally was feeling hurt and judged by her partner. After she tapped on *"I feel hurt and judged,"* I asked her to tap on when she is judgmental and hurtful to her partner or others. She joked, *"How dare you suggest that I attract this!"* She is aware of the law.

She tapped on,

"I hurt my husband when_____."

"I judge my mother because_____."

The principle in the energy of relationships is that what one field holds so does the other—there is an overlap, an emeshment, or a reflection in the mutual fields. When we clear our own feelings and limiting thoughts, and the mirror of those feelings and thoughts, the field is truly cleared and possibilities exist for deeper understanding…and even for her husband to change!

Limiting Emotions

Emotions are also thought fields. Often an uncomfortable emotional state—rage, grief, panic are what drives people to seek help. They are amazed that simply tapping or doing TAT on these feeling states can bring such relief and comfort.

Rage

Dave's Story

Dave, 25, was arrested for beating up his girlfriend. Fortunately she is okay physically and is receiving emotional help from one of my colleagues. Dave's father, who left when he was nine months old, was abusive to his mother. Mom has been tapping and doing TAT on her abuse history for several months, and she and Dave came in together to tap on the family rage. Dave continued in treatment with me to tap on a rage filled mind since childhood.

He had difficulty keeping the focus on himself and so we tapped on blame, "she makes me react that way," "she makes me feel jealous and then I feel angry." His neurology seemed hard-wired for blame and deflection. We spent many sessions tapping on the rage at various stages in his young life and in many generations.

He reports several years after treatment that he still gets angry now and then, but has not been driven to the edge of violence since our work together. I am hopeful we have broken the chain of abuse in this family.

Grief

Pat's 11 year old daughter had been abused by a trusted neighbor, and as she spoke of her guilt Pat's grief filled the room. "My baby daughter," she sobbed. I had her tap on her heart center as she cried and talked. She then tapped about her guilt and her sadness. "I couldn't protect her; I should have protected her." Heart center tapping again…

Over several sessions as both Pat and her daughter tapped regarding these incidents, the sadness and the grief began to release.

It became a life changing incident that brought them closer as mother and daughter and closer to the energy of forgiveness.

Panic

Fear freezes our process and our actions, and panic stops us dead in our tracks. Your heart rate increases and you become restless and uncomfortable. Melanie grew up with parents who were devoid in abilities to give emotional support. When as a now young adult she would lack support for work, finances or from her boyfriend she would re-experience the childhood fear that no one would be there for her and she would panic. As well as doing origins work we tapped repeatedly on,

"*No one is there for me...*"

"*I feel abandoned...*"

"*I am all alone...*"

"*I cannot make it...*"

"*My heart is pounding...*"

"*I'm panicking...*"

"*This will go on forever...*"

Finally she could tap on, "*Calm, I'll be okay, I am loved...*"

Success: The New Comfort Zone

During times of change or times of setting and reaching new goals our energy field needs to expand with us to this new place. I call it the new comfort zone.

Once during a time of great change for me my friend Sharon Rommel reminded me that I had been talking about my discomfort for well over a year. Instead of saying, "*Shut up and get on with it!*" she said, "*Why don't you tap on feeling uncomfortable in this new field and strengthen it.*" We tapped together.

We tapped on:

"*Uncomfortable in this new place...*"

"*Don't deserve to be in this place...*"

"*Afraid of messing it up, of not doing it perfectly...*"

The telling sighs emerged, and we continued tapping while smiling and I said,

"*This is the new comfort zone.*"

We tapped on, "*New comfort zone...*"

In the following 24 hours I wrote three articles, a chapter I had been stuck on for this book, and received two opportunities to do research and a new business venue.

The new energetic comfort zone is serving me well!

Contracts as Energy Fields

Some believe that we have contracted before we enter this life with those whom we love and those that we are challenged by to grow spiritually. I work with this notion with others as their prior soul beings meet the prior souls of their loved ones and their enemies.

And the ancestors also reveal the patterns that apparently were agreed upon before birth. We clear the trauma and the karma, and the DNA, and their soul messages tell them that they all agreed before on the love and the challenges.

I also struggle with this notion, because I am not sure that the holocaust was agreed upon before, or that children agree to be abused. And what about free will used for good or for evil?

I have come to terms with this by following the guidance of energy testing. If there are contracts to clear then we clear them, and what the overriding theology is really doesn't matter to me if people get well and find their passion.

There are several forms of contracts we have discovered. There is a co-dependent contract where literally your soul promises to take care of someone forever. That may or may not serve you or them.

Then there is the sacred contract that Carolyn Myss talks about in her book of the same name. This, according to Myss, is the contract that leads you to your soul's purpose.

And there is sometimes a satanic contract made in desperation to avoid pain.

Codependent Contracts

Codependent contracts seem to emerge when people find themselves growing beyond certain intimate relationships, but are unable to release them. Codependency implies that one is giving to another to the detriment of their own mental, emotional and physical well being.

Dianne's Story

Dianne, a recovering alcoholic, had been married to Sam for 19 years. He had never gotten sober or pursued a spiritual life, which was growing more and more meaningful to her. She came to therapy to sort through her conflicts about letting go of the relationship. A part of her still loved him, needed him, and another part of her was finding a new and brighter life that he would not join with her.

In a session we worked on her co-dependent contract. We returned to a past life, she saw the mountains in the background, and the river that sustained them. She was a healer for her family as women were in ancient times. She also offered her healing to other community members.

Her past life husband contracted a mysterious disease, one that we could name now but she could not then. She followed the usual guidance for herbal and crystal remedies. She used her God filled hands to move the illness from his body. For the first time she failed in her healing, and it cost her the love of her life.

She tapped on her heart center, remembering the grief. We did TAT on a grudge against God because she perceived that God had failed her also.

As her husband died, she promised to love him forever. They have returned many times together to work this through. Now it is time.

She did the TAT hold while she focused on:

"I have to love him forever."

Finally she opened her eyes filled with tears and said, "I can love him without being married to him."

We energy tested that her co-dependent contract with him was complete. When a karmic contract is complete, one is totally free to be in a relationship with the person or not.

Satanic Contracts

The hypnotherapy literature (Baldwin and Modi) use this term to describe an agreement made unknowingly with the dark side at a point of desperate fear and pain in one's life, ancestry or past life. I find the word a bit dramatic and I'm not sure at all about satanic entities, but I can wrap my head around the idea of a significantly sinister dark energy that is created by this desperate fear and blocks health.

Caren had been sick with fibromyalgia for a number of years when I met her. We did many origins including a past life where she had an ill child who was in constant pain. In a moment of desperation before her child in that life died she cried out, "I will carry your pain."

That energy remained in her soul and is coming forth to heal through her illness.

A common satanic contract that blocks many from their soul's purpose is connected with karmic energy where a healer or community leader felt responsible for the death of one or more community members. In their grief they cried out that, "I will never serve as a healer or leader again in order to avoid this pain."

We work with satanic contracts as dark energy with prayer, TAT, and sacred sound or smudging.

"Sacred Contracts"

Carolyn Myss opens her book, *Sacred Contracts,* with,

"We all want to know why we are here. What is our mission in life? Those people who know it are easy to spot, their lives shine with meaning...Many people, however, are confused—or completely in the dark—about their reason for living."

Living Your Soul's Purpose™ is for those who are mystified about their reason for being, and to assist them in finding their callings. This book is also for those who have the vision, know their calling, and cannot seem to realize it. And too, this book is for those who know their calling and who keep clearing for the next steps in their soul's development.

We find in this work that there are turning points or "choice points" as Gregg Braden (2001) calls them, where we stay on track with our purpose or we do not. This work takes us back through our history in this life, in our ancestry, and in our karmic history to the exact energetic moments where we got off track and allows us to correct them. With the medicine of our body's wisdom we clear the blocks and limitations at these choice points.

Bri was 23, anxious, and clueless when we first met about her destiny. She had daily panic attacks, and had been depressed for years. Her sleep was disturbed and she reported she could "barely function" in her work and in her marriage. She was raised in a home with a verbally abusive father, and her parents divorced when she was eight years old. Her mom became very depressed and Bri felt like she was left on her own. She hid out in her art and in her books. A very bright student, but socially inept, at 15 she moved away from her small coastal home town and came to the city to go to college. This was a choice point that created conflict that we later cleared with TAT. Although she was happier and felt as if she fit better in a college environment, she missed her family.

Here she met Bill, four years her senior, who is kind and gentle. They became close and married when she was 19. This was the next choice point, to marry young for safety and security. They had a child. Within six years she decided that she had married for the wrong reasons and left.

As often happens in safe relationships, what was unhealed came up to heal. She revisited the anxiety and depression of her childhood and became less and less functional. This was a choice point to get help.

We developed an intention, "To 100 percent heal panic attacks, anxiety, and depression, and to feel calm, relaxed, energetic, focused and fully alive again!"

Energy testing indicated there were seven current life origins, 13 ancestral origins and 11 karmic/past life origins that held the blocked energy to Bri's illnesses. I explained to her that energy origins clustered and that we generally do DEH with about 50 percent of the origins.

Her first origin, indicated by energy testing, was to clear a verbal attack by peers at 11 years old. We cleared trauma, shock, hurt, panic, a shattered energy field, and a wish to die. In addition she had a limiting identity that she was "changed forever by that event." She was given insights that she was okay and would not feel that way forever.

In our next session she cleared the trauma of being taken from her home, abruptly and forever, when her parents separated. She tapped and did TAT to clear the trauma that fed her anxiety and tendency to freeze emotionally.

In addition in that session she did EFT at a maternal ancestral origin three generations ago where her great grandfather abandoned her great grandmother— he went out for cigarettes and never came back. She was carrying the ancestral energy of abandonment, hurt, and not being worthy of love.

By the third session her daily panic attacks were no longer present. She interviewed for art classes without fear!

We continued the origins work on anxiety and depression for six more sessions, which included additional current life, ancestral and past life origins with the energy of death in all of the origins. If all origins are clear with the death energy, our experience is that clinical depression and anxiety does not return.

I saw her again nearly three years after our initial session. She is still depression and anxiety free. She is in school to become a Licensed Massage Therapist and has plans to become a Nurse practitioner. She and her baby's *father remain good friends in parenting. Her mother, no longer depressed, is supporting this phase of her life financially and emotionally. She is back with me to do some deeper soul's purpose work and to strengthen her commitment to be a better parent! These are choice points to more fully carry out her sacred contracts and live her soul's purpose in family and career.*

Clearing unwanted, negative contracts and the blocks to our sacred contracts that align us with our divine nature that paves the way for the freedom of forgiveness, divine connection, and reclaiming gifts.

Points of interest for discussion from this chapter:
- Limiting thought forms are a part of all energy psychology models.
- Limiting thoughts can block healing and success.
- Emotions can be energetically limiting also.
- Some limiting thought fields are contracts at the soul level.

Chapter Twenty Three
Resurrection and Hope

We are saved by the final form of love, which is forgiveness.

Reinhold Niebuhr

When I first began energy work, I described it as getting sober all over again at the energetic level. Walking through the energy of my traumas to the light was as profound as walking from the powerlessness to the awakening in addiction recovery.

The thought transformation that occurs through this work is sacred. In the end of this process forgiveness work, messages from within we call soul messages, talking with the ancestors and prior soul beings, and collecting gifts from other realms are the revelations of a healed energy field. It is the material of a personal energetic resurrection.

Christians might say being born again at the energetic level. Buddhists might say finding a deeper place within and Jews and Muslims might say finding a clearer view from the mountain. Those who are more spiritual than religious describe it as being more connected with nature and love. There is a place of awe that arises when one connects with their inner healing system.

Those feelings, qualities and relationships that seemed to forever haunt us find a place in the quantum light that holds them for us so that we no longer need to carry them.

Incredibly, we do not have to go the route of revisiting one laborious trauma after another in order to heal. Since energy clusters, we can visit one energetic origin and find that we have cleared/healed one of many traumas all at once because with this one origin we have gotten to the energetic underpinnings of them all.

Forgiveness

When I was a younger therapist and working with sexual abuse survivors, I was relieved to hear from some of the leaders in that field that forgiveness was not a requirement for healing. (Bass, Davis, 1994) I could not imagine forgiving the horrors I was hearing in my office that were perpetrated on my clients.

Over time, however, I began to notice that those who truly moved beyond being a victim of abuse and began to thrive, talked about finding a place within themselves to forgive their perpetrators.

Listening to my clients nudged me to embark on my own journey of forgiveness of people who had hurt me much less.

I then began to speak with a different voice about forgiveness to new clients. I now say, "Forgiveness is not a requirement for healing, but with this work you may eventually find that place within you that is open to forgiveness."

Through journeying to the origins and doing TAT, or tapping or frontal occipital holding, many would find that place of clearing where they would naturally say, *"I can forgive and be at peace now."*

Many clients feel demands from their personal theology to say they have forgiven when energy testing reveals that there is some deeper energy of unforgiveness. To relieve their conflict I simply say, "A part of you has forgiven but other energetic parts still need to heal to reach complete forgiveness."

Or, for others whose spiritual life or process does seem to require forgiveness, we simply do an energy intervention on, "I cannot forgive…" until there is the recognition, "Oh, I can forgive."

Most of the time I wait for the client's lead. They say things like,

"I feel like I should forgive…" or even, "I will never forgive."

I say, "What would it be like if you forgave him/her?"

Usually they respond with, "I would be free…"

I say, "Do you want to be free?" I have never gotten a "no" in return.

Then we TAT or tap,

"I cannot forgive her/him…" until the body's wisdom takes us to,

"Okay, I forgive…"

You are thinking, "It cannot be that simple." But it is this simple because forgiveness is our true nature. Energy psychology and energy medicine simply takes us to our true nature—to love, to gratitude, to joy and forgiveness. Why make it more difficult than that?

Forgiving God

It is common when injustices and deep losses occur that we express anger at God. Sometimes that anger is so great that we turn away from our faith. In light of this, I tell clients, "Any deity worth his/her salt can handle your anger or mine!"

It seems that this anger at God can build up energetically over the generations or soul lifetimes and end up as an energetic grudge.

Julie lost her 17 year old daughter to suicide. She was usually a happy, go lucky kid, extremely ADHD, and unmedicated. Julie thinks she just wanted to see how many pills she could take before she got sick rather than actually wanting to kill herself. She took one too many. I listened to her grief and her guilt and she used her strong support system effectively. She did energy work on related origins and finally came to her anger at God for taking her daughter.
She tapped,

"*I am really angry at God.*"

"*I don't trust God.*"

"*Why would God do this?*"

Soon she was saying,

"*God didn't do this.*"

"*I can be at peace.*"

"*I can rebuild my relationship with God.*"

"*My daughter is at peace now.*"

Working with the Ancestors

Over the years I have accompanied hundreds of clients to thousands of ancestral origins. That realm became as familiar to me as my living room. At the same time, my field strengthened through my own healing, through becoming a Reiki master, a shaman and ordained. As my relationship with Divine Mother strengthened, so did my abilities to commune with souls on the other side. It was revealed to me that the person's energy is also still connected to the souls of their ancestors, and as grace would have it, the ancestors' souls heal also.

Remember that some of the information I get comes from intuitive experiences that I have grown to trust over the years, and have expanded intentionally with energy work.

One evening during one of the Living Your Soul's Purpose™ groups at my office in Salem, (no it is not lost on me that I live and work in Salem…) after a very moving ancestral origin healing, suddenly the faces of the client's ancestors appeared, and said "Thank you, you are healing our souls too." I have not figured out how to do a scientific study on the healing of the souls of the deceased ancestors. For now I am just trusting it, for this message has come many times since.

It follows the logic of our work; we think we can heal, we think that the source of that healing is divine. We believe deceased souls are connected in the home of the divine. So why wouldn't they be healing?

Soul talk has become a natural part of the work that we do. The soul of Karen is mentioned in the first chapter. She is not Marlene's biological sister. However, her soul comes to therapy with Marlene frequently as her soul sister. Unfortunately Marlene's life has followed Karen's death with many other losses and changes which keep her coming to tap and TAT.

Karen accompanied Marlene through another friend's death, and yet another friend's chronic illness. Karen would show up in my office just to say, "You will be okay." Marlene's job was eliminated in her school, and as the best reading teacher in our district with seniority, it was never an issue that she would be employed. However, in this district with over 100 elementary schools, Marlene and I were thrilled when Karen, from the angel realm, "arranged" a job at her old school. Marlene will now work with all of Karen's former colleagues, be present to the shrines to Karen throughout the school, and move through the halls that still hold her energy.

As the therapist, in Marlene's life I was often comforted by Karen's presence also. It is difficult at times to hold another's hand through so many losses.

As I am writing this, Karen pops in to say, "Remind Marlene often that she is loved."

Gifts

Another offer of hope is the gifts we collect from our prior soul beings and ancestors.

In many energetic origins, not only are there issues to heal, but there are also gifts to collect. We find them most of the time in the karmic origins as our prior soul beings reveal to our present soul and consciousness the gifts from prior realms.

Some resolution is achieved through retrieving the gifts possessed in past lives because of twists of fate or twists in history that cause the soul to discard the gifts. Witnessing people rediscover their remarkable gifts is an inspiring part of this work. Some use words they had not known before, or make sweeping gestures with their hands as they move the ancient energy for healing. They relearn ancient, delicate hand-made art; and they relearn the deep knowings they held as wise men or women. They come into fullness with their intuitive abilities. When they retrieve the gifts, they are able to use some of them immediately.

Other gifts require more study or development in this life. However, when the traumatic events, loss, grief, and dark energy are cleared, the participants have clear internal access to where the gifts reside within. Previously unaware of the past life trauma, the participants all report that they had vague fears about cultivating their gifts. They were hesitant regarding their intuitive knowing, feared psychic abilities, denied their propensity to heal with touch and their attraction to the earth religions, or the gift of leadership. Through this work, they replaced this fear with a deep desire and longing to pursue the development of these gifts.

As the following story reveals we go slowly and meticulously through the tunnel of light and into the karmic realm to pick up the gifts. We often use TAT to absorb the gifts and then we enhance the gifts with imaging color and light and imagining or creating sound, and strengthen the gifts in the field with heart center tapping.

Kay returned as I guided her, to the time in her past life New Zealand in the 1800's when her gifts were at their peak.

I began, "Kay, now return to the time in this life with the women in New Zealand when you were thriving and practicing your gifts." With eyes closed again she relaxes, and tilts her head. She began by speaking of the gifts of all of the women, because her gifts were no more important than their gifts. "We are in the same beautiful land...It is winter, but mild. We don't have much of a winter here, just a bit of snow...There is an ocean, but it is several days away...We are very cooperative, peace-loving...We are skilled. Each woman has a craft such as making jewelry out of beautiful rocks...The jewelry is used in the rituals. They are bathing rituals...there is something to drink like in what we would call a baptism...it's an initiation...an entry...flowers in hair...special oils and leaves in the bath...someone in tribe does the oils, another does the herbs...much ritual here...

"There are horses...Not everyone has horses, but many of the women do have horses...We share our horses...we ride bareback...the horses are psychic and we have a psychic connection with the horses..."

I asked Kay what her specific gifts were..."I am the decision maker about critical things in our community...I take care of the food supply...Runners go out and scan the land to let me know where abundance lies, and to determine safety...I decide where and when to hunt and gather...we can't carry too much with us...in the winter we save up for the short snow season...in the summer we don't need as much...I use my psychic abilities to make these decisions and the guidance of the sun...we go in a circular fashion from season to season...we move often. I am a Shaman, I guide my tribe...

I also am close to and teach the children...the children were strong...I did not nurture them individually as we might today, but rather nurtured and valued the gifts in children so that they could come to fruit in adulthood...

On our travels we help people...we offer protection to those who need it, and comfort to those in trouble...We sometimes enter other communities to help and share our gifts, but we are not always welcome...to our surprise we find that some people don't want to be free...

Most of us also had the gift of healing touch...we would lay our hands on one another's injuries, wounds, or pain..."

I asked Kay to identify where the gifts were held in her body. She said, "They are held in my heart." I guided her to add a color, a sound, a smell to each gift. She sat in meditation with this.

I then asked her to associate, move into her body and absorb the gifts at the body, soul, conscious, unconscious, and in the aura and the chakras. I asked her with MMT whether the gifts have in fact been absorbed at all five levels. I then guided her to integrate the gifts combining the colors, and sounds, with the gifts. Then I guided her to, "See yourself using these gifts in a week, in a month, in a year, easily creating jewelry, making decisions, knowing the right time to move, the healing with touch, teaching, leading, valuing the gifts in children...Notice the body feelings and emotions that go with this experience."

I then asked her with energy testing if the collection of the gifts was complete. She indicated positively.

To conclude you might journal regarding your gifts and plan a ritual regarding reclaiming your gifts.

Wendy Jensen, LCSW, Diplomate, Comprehensive Energy Psychology is a superb EP/DEH practitioner in Portland Oregon. She is also a skilled hypnotherapist and has been guiding clients to past lives not only to heal trauma but also to find gifts to enhance their current life.

She generously offers this story of her work:

"I have been doing trauma-release work for many years using energy psychology techniques. One particular client, a new mother, had come to me for help with overcoming years and years of anger and fear about her own mother that had been exacerbated by recently becoming a mother herself.

"My client's mother had suffered from mental illness for all of her adult life and had been emotionally and physically abusive throughout my client's childhood. My client had desperately wanted to believe that she could be a good mother to her own child despite the role modeling that had existed for her from her own mother. However, when doing energy testing, my client tested strong for many negative beliefs about her ability to be an adequate mother.

"After many sessions of doing trauma release and working on dismantling those negative limiting belief systems, we were moving towards collecting the gifts from that work that we had completed. Although we had done this in earlier work, the gifts collected did not seem to sustain my client for long. She was very stuck on the belief that since she had not experienced a loving, nurturing, adequate mothering, she could not find it in herself to be all of those things.

"I am a hypnotherapist, and I use regression and induction techniques throughout my sessions. I intuitively decided to regress my client to a previous time in her existence where she had experienced a loving and nurturing mother. I had a strong hope that she could find at least one lifetime where she had experienced positive and adequate mothering where we might be able to gather gifts and resources from that lifetime to bring forward into her current life.

"She did, in fact, regress to a lifetime where she was raised by a strong, loving, powerful grandmother, who was very fond of her and took excellent care of her, teaching her many wonderful things and showing her unconditional love and acceptance. My client immediately knew that some of the mothering skills she was showing her own child had come from this lifetime with a loving grandmother. We collected many more gifts and resources to bring with her to current time and space. She collected gifts such as patience and intuitive knowing of what her child needs. These are qualities she had never witnessed in her own mother. She commented in the following weeks that she had felt, for the first time, the confidence that she could be a good mother and would not repeat the mistakes of her own mother.

"Gathering gifts from other lifetimes has become a frequent process in my work with clients since this positive parenting lifetime experience. It is particularly useful when the client struggles with finding anything positive about a particular piece of their history, albeit current life or past life."

The universal energy is so generous.

Karmic Soul Talk

In the end the prior soul beings may have messages for us we energy test if that is the case. I assume that our psyches tap into the ancient energy held within to hear this deep, still voice. Hear these messages:

"I read people's fields and I know what is the matter physically and how they are feeling emotionally, and then I know where to lay my hands and what herbs to give."

Marilyn, Salem Mass. 1688

"Use your powers to heal womankind no matter how long it takes. Women will heal the planet. Use the power with care."

Mary's past life, Germany, 1283

Soul Messages

We end each session with energy testing if there are soul messages as a result of the healing just experienced. I was curious about where these messages come from. In my second year of EP practice I energy tested 50 clients and ET revealed that some of the messages came from our higher selves, some from spirit guides and some from Creator.

Here are some examples in addition to the ones you have read in the cases throughout the book:

Soul messages are a gentle, meditative means to end a process.

Go to our website, onedynamicenergetichealing.org to receive daily soul messages.

Resources to Maintain the Healing

Energy psychology and energy medicine offer many of the answers for immediate and long term healing. However, sometimes other resources are helpful associated with the person's spiritual path or needs for health maintenance. So we may energy test that continued meditation or prayer is necessary, or perhaps one of the mind-body spiritual paths such as Yoga, Tai Chi, or Qigong would enhance the person's well-being. We may energy test that chiropractic care, acupuncture, or a naturopath is advised. Western medicine care may be indicated. Sometimes energy testing advises homeopathy, certain supplements, aroma therapy, essences, or a particular crystal for healing.

Of course a healthy diet, and exercise are always a requirement. Energy testing may guide you to certain foods and kinds of exercise.

The body loves the energy of forgiveness and hope. In that positive energy field it is easier to maintain over all well-being.

Points of interest for discussion from this chapter:
• Forgiveness must be approached gently as one is ready.
• People who think they have forgiven are often surprised to find that there is still energetic forgiveness work to do.
• Resentment at "God" may be cleared for greater emotional freedom.
• Ancestors and karmic soul beings often hold "gifts" for us to retrieve.

SECTION FIVE

Imagine the Possibilities

Prelude:

Over the years I have developed energy psychology and DEH protocols for working with children, couples and families, groups, organizations, and communities. This section invites you to "imagine the possibilities" for healing beyond the individual.

Chapter Twenty Four
Children, Play and Energy

Children are the living messages we send to a time we will not see.

While I was growing up, my mother encouraged my creative play, and by the time I was eight I did not play with doll houses, but turned my entire room into a doll's home that I built with my friend Susie. I didn't have your average lemonade stand; instead I turned our lengthy driveway into a restaurant with decorated tables serving juice and treats. At nine I instigated the first of several annual neighborhood carnivals, turning Carolyn's backyard into booths and entertainment. It was 1956, when Moms stayed home, and there were 100 kids per block in our southern California middle class suburb—plenty for a neighborhood carnival!

This part of my childhood was a natural entré to my career that started out in early childhood education leading to play as healing children and children within.

Play therapy was my initial therapy model with children. It is still miraculous to me to watch a child, young or old, naturally choose play materials, without suggestion from me, that will cause the necessary regression to create healing from trauma. Working through the trauma simply with play could be slow and painful, however, and I have been excited with the results now that I combine play therapy with energy psychology which speeds up the results for the children and their families by about 60 percent. Children I used to have in therapy for a year now need about four months, and children with more severe trauma that I used to have in therapy for three years are now in therapy for about one year.

I am a great proponent of play as child therapy (Schaefer, Hammond-Newman, 1992) because it is more natural for them than talking, and acts as an induction to the origins of their trauma.

Energy psychology, especially EFT, TAT and DEH, has assisted both children and families. Energy psychology has helped in simple matters such as tantrums, simple phobias and compulsions, to more complex matters such as saving the sanity of several families that adopted traumatized children, and saved a family's life that was caught in domestic violence.

Children also improve social skills, raise their grades and reading abilities, and increase their performance abilities in the arts and sports.

During the play and art sessions in a special room in my office, as the children draw and play through their fears and grief stricken moments, we will pause and tap on the heart center or meridian points. Instead of all of the resolution of the trauma having to be accomplished through the expressive therapies, a substantial portion is resolved through the energy system.

Phobias

Roger Callahan, Ph.D., (Callahantechniques™), Gary Craig's original teacher, put meridian points on the therapy map with his book, *The Five Minute Phobia Cure* a couple of decades ago with criticism from the psychology establishment for such a claim. Some issues are this easy with EP, some are not. Kids have many fears or phobias, some warranted some not, but all should be taken seriously. Yes, in five sometimes stretched to 10 minutes, I have watched children from five to 15 dissolve their fears of ants in the bathtub, walking across bridges, riding on elevators and escalators, being in their dark rooms at night, and loud noises, by tapping on the meridian points.

You might be thinking that children for generations have grown up with those fears and that they usually work through them naturally by the time they are grown. However on-going simple phobias may lead to anxiety disorder later in life, and it is sensible to free up the energy system for more fruitful endeavors than dealing with phobias. And there are some phobia healings that can be life saving—for instance neutralizing the fear of water.

My daughter, Amber, was very afraid to learn to swim. By energy testing we determined that she had a soul experience where she had drown. Amber and I in a dreamtime state "remembered" being mother and daughter and as a toddler she drowned right in front of me. I noticed that she played often about rescuing the babies, and now we tapped on the meridian point. I cried, and soon the experience was neutral for both of us. Amber has not been afraid of the water since this session five years ago, and has gone on to be a strong swimmer.

Tantrums and Attachment

Johnnie had been abused physically, perhaps sexually and neglected in the first couple of years of his life, and was then moved to two different foster families by the time he was six. He was adopted by a lovely caring family with older children who desired to give Johnnie a second chance. They were vaguely aware of reactive attachment when I met them and after a year or so in their care, Johnnie, by then eight years old, began having tantrums and nightmares. He raged during the day and screamed at night. Reactive attachment means when hurt children attempt to attach to a new, safe parent they react from their place of pain, and without intervention, block the love. We worked in my play therapy room with the toys of healing—sand, animals, cars, dollhouses and art materials. He would play the things he missed as a toddler and pre-schooler, and then we would tap on the meridian points regarding his sadness and rage. It was exhausting for all.

Closeness brings up memories of abandonment and pain for little ones who have been abused, so it is just safer not to feel close. I asked him and his mother to stay close if he felt afraid or mad rather than being pushed away. He played and tapped and played and tapped. He reduced his tantrums from once a day lasting 30 minutes or more to one or two a month lasting about 10 minutes.

After several weeks of playing with the "scariest toys" in the room in sand tray and tapping regarding his fears, his nightmares subsided.

I also worked with the Mother. Her story is next.

Before I found energy work, this kind of therapy used to take three years or more and was not always as successful as I experience with the addition of energy psychology methods. With energy psychology interventions and the participation of brave parents in their children's healing, attachment work is only taking about nine months.

Parents as Partners in Healing

Attachment

Whether it is a simple issue that takes only a few sessions or more complicated work like abuse, parents are essential in the healing process. Birth and adoptive parents share an energy field with their children. So, when parents work on their blocks and issues there is automatic healing for their children. One must think about this energetically. We believe the premise from energy psychology that thoughts and feelings are energy.

Since Johnnie and his mother are so close, their energy fields overlap and impact one another—in the problem and in the solution.

Johnnie's Mom worked on an intention, "To heal everything in my energy field that blocks the attachment process for Johnnie."

We worked on origins where Johnnie's mother had an estranged relationship with her mother. In addition Johnnie's reactions caused her to feel hesitant and lack confidence in her parenting. So while Johnnie was feeling and carrying the energy of hurt and fear and yet acting angry, Mom was carrying the energy of estrangement, hesitancy and lack of confidence. We worked together on her patterns in relationships and her style in parenting with counseling and tapping, and soon she reported feeling strong and confident and loving with Johnnie.

Expressing love became easier.

Domestic Violence

Sally was 14 when she married her 28-year-old husband. Imagine his motives and imagine the parents who allowed this marriage. By the time I met Sally she was 26 with two children. She had a new step-mom who could easily see how awful and abusive this situation was. Step-mom paid for treatment and Sally spent three to four months tapping about the past, her terror, and the impact on her children, and her hope for a better life. She got stronger and stronger.

Children in Domestic Violence

Research in the last decade revealed that children who witness violence grow up with post trauma as severe as children who are abused.

Her two girls 11 and 5 came in with her and drew pictures and talked and tapped of their fear of their father, his drinking, drugs and abuse of their mother. Mom could not deny their terrified faces and the blood in the drawings. They cried and tapped together. The children came in together and individually to play and draw and tap about their fears and their grief at not having a normal father, and their hope for escape.

Sally's step-mom called me four months after our initial session to say they had escaped, and they were in another state. Sally had a job and no one knew where they were! Domestic violence cases prior to energy psychology had often taken years for escape to occur or there was no escape and they simply stopped coming to sessions. I cried when I hung up the phone after talking with step-mom. The power of these tools for change, I knew, were unlike anything I had ever experienced.

Four years later I ran into step-mom at a local restaurant. She said Sally and the kids were well and safe. Sally had moved up in her company, and had also met a wonderful and kind man. I smiled with the warmth that EP practitioners get to experience daily.

The Lighter Side

Most children come to me from rather functional families with normal family "stuff." They are upset about divorce or a parent's rules. Some have social or learning problems.

Ted came in when he was 12, a high functioning autistic child, who had trouble making friends and difficulty with reading. We tapped about his insecurities, feeling different, fear at talking with people. We uncovered some depression and tapped on some unconscious energy of death. Soon he reported no depression, greater ease at talking with friends at school, and increased reading scores.

Jill was eight and dyslexic. We added an energetic intervention for neurological disorganization to the DEH and EFT repertoires and in just a few months of daily energetic practice, the words on the page were turning around. By the end of the school year her reading scores were up two grade levels!

Ted was 16 and came for a variety of teen issues. I taught him to use the under nose point for his golf game as a member of his high school golf team. He reported significantly better scores.

Whether for healing or success, energy work greatly enhances the work of children and teens.

Points of interest for discussion from this chapter:

- Combining energy psychology with play therapy reduces the time needed for therapy.
- Children are naturally in tune with their energy systems.
- Children may heal attachment, depression, phobias, anxiety.
- Children can improve reading skills, dyslexia, ADHD, and behavior problems.
- Sports and arts performance can be enhanced for young people with energy psychology

Chapter Twenty Five
The Energy of Love: Couples in DEH

Love is patient, love is kind.

I Corinthians 13:4-8

Over the decades, the world of therapy has dissected the world of couples to try to figure out the mystery that really is not a mystery. Couples can maintain fairly healthy relationships when there is the absence of addiction, abuse and mental illness. They can enhance their experience greatly when there are the following qualities, which I want us to think about as energy, for our healing purposes:

- A deep desire to be together
- A purpose that is more compelling than the relationship
- Mutual values
- Working communication
- Respect and courtesy
- Agreement on physical closeness and sexuality
- Some shared activities
- A willingness to grow and change over the course of their lives.
- A support system of family and friends

I have always loved the challenge of working with couples who seemed to have impossible, complex issues. I enjoy assessing which issues are individual and which issues are truly couple's issues, and I am clear with couples that it takes two healthy people to create a healthy relationship and that some of our work will be done individually because of that.

I am also clear that if there is addiction or abuse I will expect that person to work on those issues, while we do the energy work together.

This protocol that I use with couples developed over time.

In the first session I ask them each to write down or tell me their main concerns so that I can understand why we are here together. Then I explain that we cannot deal with a decade of problems all at once, but we will address these things one at a time in discussion and energy work. "For now," I say, "let's put those aside and go back to the beginning of your relationship and tell me what it is that you liked and loved about one another that got you together to begin with."

I ask them to face one another while they share those thoughts and feelings.

Most couples soften as they return to the feelings, the energy, of the beginning of their relationship.

If there is a mental health or addiction problem with either one of them then we deal with that first. If either of them feel unsafe, we talk about temporary alternate living.

In the next session I begin to teach them energy work. Using the lists that they developed the week before we write an intention together. They usually look something like this:

"M. heals her depression and lack of trust. J. is addiction and anger free. We work cooperatively on projects, have open, honest, kind, loving communication, we spend time alone, together and with friends and family. We come together on parenting issues. We are affectionate and have a great, mutually satisfying sex life."

We then energy test for the number of current life, ancestral and karmic origins for their couple's field. Couples have a unique energy field that can be energy tested for both of them by one individual.

Each session we spend some time working on communication with standard energy strategies that have proved to be valuable over the years. I ask couples to plan Couple's Meetings at home using this model:

1. Create sacred space in your own way.
2. Pick one topic and stick to it.
3. Partner A speaks.
4. Partner B really listens and then reflects the content and the feelings that s/he hears. When complete then...
5. Partner B speaks.

236

6. Partner A really listens and then reflects the content and the feelings that s/he hears. When complete then…
7. If there is a problem to solve, then brainstorm win-win scenarios and choose one.

Couples are encouraged to take breaks and tap or use the TAT pose if tension or anger escalates during communication sessions or at any time strong feelings need clearing in order to communicate effectively.

In sessions with a practitioner we practice this model and do the energetic protocols in this book.

We check in each session for reversal using words from the intention and statements like:

We want our marriage to heal.

We deserve to be happy.

We can resolve our differences

We deserve love.

It is safe to love.

It is possible for us to heal our relationship.

There may be unconscious objections such as:

If we heal, I will have to be married forever.

If I love, I will be hurt.

If I heal, I will have to grow up and I do not want to.

It is scary to commit.

If we heal, I will have to have sex more than I want to.

Couples typically will visit traumas in their childhoods that hold mutual issues such as not being listened to, being hurt, feeling less than, feeling unloved etc.

They visit their ancestors who lost loves prematurely, hurt one another unnecessarily, had progressed addictions and unmonitored violence. It wasn't so long ago that abusing women and children in western cultures was a man's right as it still is in some third world cultures. We are still healing this.

It is common that couples have had soul connections before, frightening or filled with loss, as well as positive and loving. We heal the karma of premature deaths, and unallowed love due to class, age or race. We heal untold abuse and murder of our former soul mates. We recapture lost love and unachieved mutual dreams.

In these origins we heal the trauma, loss and grief and the energy of death and darkness, soul loss, and other dissociation, and limiting thought fields. We retrieve our shared gifts and resources for the present.

We speak with the ancestors and the prior soul beings, gleaning their wisdom to carry our relationships into the future.

Points of interest for discussion from this chapter:

- Couples have a shared energy field.
- Long term problems can be shifted with origins energy work.
- Think about the complexities of coupleship as energy, therefore changeable.
- In my experience the following creates healthy relationships:
- A deep desire to be together
- A purpose or God that is more compelling than the relationship
- Mutual values
- Working respectful communication
- Respect and courtesy
- Agreement on physical closeness and sexuality
- Some shared activities
- A willingness to grow and change over the course of their lives.
- A support system of family and friends

Chapter Twenty Six
The Energy of Families in DEH

The family is one of nature's masterpieces.

George Santayana

When a family comes to my office all at one time, I know it is both urgent and sacred. For a family to come in together there has usually been a crisis that threatens the health or life of one of their clan, and the pain is so great that they cannot contain it on their own.

The sacred space in my office, my attention to grounding myself and holding healing energy, allows them the safety for their story to unfold.

Cheryl was 13 when I first met her. After talking with her a bit I determined that she was very depressed. Some of that was circumstantial and some of that was familial. Mom was anxious and stressed, and depression ran on mom's side of the family. When I met with Dad he was stressed also. Both worked at high stress jobs. Cheryl's eight year old brother had severe learning challenges and took much of the parent's time in the evening. Cheryl was doing poorly in school after having done well for most of her school life. She had been active in sports but in the last year lost interest. She had told her mom that she wanted to die but did not know why. There was no apparent history of severe trauma.

Recognizing that all of the family members had stress and some degree of depression and that they were distanced from one another, I invited them in to meet together. They each described feelings of love for one another, and feelings of loneliness.

I taught them to tap and we tapped together on the family loneliness.

They began talking about things they could do together.

Mom and Dad tapped on their stress and too busy lives.

Mom asked for more help from everyone.

We created a family intention,

"To heal the stress, depression, loneliness and anger in all of us, and to have more fun and relaxation, to get the family work done easily and for the kids to be more successful at school."

We found several current life, ancestral and past life origins for all of them. The following were the key ones.

We went to the origins of the kid's feelings of low self esteem when they were younger in school and did TAT on that. I taught them to do the three thumps and the marching exercises every morning before school.

Several times we went to the mother's lineage to heal the origins of depression. Mother's father had died a few years back and she said that her mother was really stuck in her grief. They cried and tapped.

Dad revisited the stories of his ancestors losses and the build up of stress through the generations.

Brother tapped about his feelings of worthlessness for his learning problems and kids making fun of him.

After several sessions Mom wondered if it would be okay for Grandma to come in to learn to tap about her grief. She came twice and felt tremendously better.

After several origins and several months the kids' grades were going up, and Cheryl was back in sports. Mom and Dad were tapping everyday to deal with their stress. They were laughing again and having fun.

Progress Not Perfection

I met Alice twenty years ago when her kids were young teens and she had identified herself as an adult child of an alcoholic. They had lived all of their lives in a small farming community in Oregon. Her parents were first generation immigrants from the Netherlands and dairy farming went back for generations.

Dairy farming, I was to find out, was not the only generational pattern. As her story unfolded over the months, I was to hear about a home as much like a war zone as I have heard before or since. The brothers beat up one another, and Dad beat up them. There were indelible pictures of blood and bruised bodies in Alice's mind. We told the stories, drew pictures and did imagery and breath work. Her memories and the fear calmed.

She told more stories of drinking with the violence, and realized that all of her siblings as well as her father, now deceased, had problems with alcohol and violence. She and her husband broke the chain. After scaring herself by spanking her children too hard a couple of times, she never hit her children again and no one got beat up. Every year or two they come for help with their drinking or their kid's depression and drinking. She sent in her sister for several sessions who embraced tapping. Her brother came to work on his anger, violence and drinking. I have seen all of the children as teens and adults—most have addiction issues. None of them hit their children. I have helped with interventions, relapses and the spouses' co-dependency.

I have felt elated, discouraged, hopeless and resigned. I am not impacting this family to the degree I had hoped with the generational addiction except that everyone talks about it now. I know from my work with addictive families over the years that this is a huge step.

I have rarely seen a family filled with such love and perseverance.

If I am getting the truth from most of them, they have broken the chain of abuse and tremendous violence which is generations old. Many of them have worked on their karmic and ancestral origins and many use tapping to relieve their on-going stress.

We do energetic boundaries between all of them and I do energetic boundaries with the clan.

I have seen a few of the grandchildren as their parents' addiction has impacted them, and expect to see more. I have seen second and third spouses and girlfriends!

If nothing else, I have built trust and they do not need to repeat the family story.

I continue to encourage Alice and her husband to stay sober. I see progress in that no one has been beaten for two generations and addiction is out of the closet. Everyone has lived a normal life span thus far.

I share this story not because we got dramatic "ride into the sunset" results with this family, but because it is the real story of a real family who has overcome that which is most hurtful, but still has a long way to go.

We do not always achieve perfection with this work or in our families, but we progress and wiping out generations of abuse is progress!

Points of interest for discussion from this chapter:

- Families have a shared energy field.
- When one person in the family changes the energy field of the entire family shifts.
- Family healing is relative.

Chapter Twenty Seven
The Path to Becoming an Energetic Healer

"Our deepest fear is not that we are inadequate. Our deepest fear is that we are powerful beyond measure. It is our Light, not our darkness that most frightens us."

Rev. Marianne Williamson

When I was working with Kay, the woman who was brutally and continuously abused by her former husband, I mentioned that I began to have nightmares about him also. I had no idea what was happening until literature came out regarding vicarious trauma (Pearlman, 1995) where they described therapists and others in the helping professions having symptoms like those they were helping. The nightmares caused me to question my sanity, my effectiveness and my ability to maintain control.

As my client found safety and the energy tools her nightmares subsided, as did mine.

The single most career saving experience for me was to have a means to no longer carry vicarious trauma. As my abuse survivor clients would tell their stories, draw their pictures and change their images the trauma would remain in my heart and in my body. I would startle for them, get anxious for them, reject men for them, and have their nightmares. Since I began tapping with my clients, that no longer occurs.

The next year I began my energy psychology training and found Pearlman's book, *Trauma and the Therapist*. Now I tap or do TAT with my clients, and at the end of the day do TAT to clear whatever is left. I immediately clear any vicarious trauma symptoms. I stay healthy and focused on the positives in my work, and find the path of the healer to be gentler now.

Ultimately DEH and many energy psychologies and energy medicines take you on a path to become a healer. Some of you will end up using it for your own and your family members' healing. Some of you will find yourselves incorporating the notion of healer into your more traditional health care or leadership role, while others are motivated to study a health care or leadership profession, or a healing tradition and meet the requirements in their state, province or country to practice a career as a healer. And some of you are already healthcare professionals who would like to enhance your skills.

My intention when I found energy psychology was to add these strategies to my counseling practice. I knew right away that there would be personal and professional benefits. I was delighted to find that this path paved the way to healing serious illness beyond what I had imagined before, and to assist people to break through completely to their soul's purpose.

There are many paths to becoming a healer. One can train in Reiki, Shamanism, Yoga, or Qigong, and many paths to ordination have a healer pre-requisite. It occurred to Nancy Gordon, LCSW, and Howard Brockman, LCSW, and I that we could use intention and clearings to grow our businesses and to be more comfortable in our growing roles as healers and teachers.

What has developed in my teaching is the energetic path to becoming a healer. I have come to believe it is an essential path to be protected, and have energetic strength as you work with others.

Traditionally, healer has meant that something mysterious is done to the person who is ill that causes a miraculous recovery. Again, I hold a more client-centered modern lineage where the person who is ill also aligns their divine nature and is as active participant as possible in her/his healing. Being an energetic healer then means preparing your energy field for the healing experience.

It seems that karma and ancestry conspire to make it difficult to fully embrace oneself as a healer. If I have heard the following statements once I have heard them 200 times…

"I am afraid to let people know I do this work."

"My family thinks I am crazy, because I am into this."

"I don't trust my energy testing."

"I can't see energy."

"I know I get intuitive information, but I don't trust myself."

My approach to the blocks with my clients, students and other would-be healers, is to use the model you have been reading about and use EFT or TAT on the limiting thought fields and then create intentions to enhance your healer potential.

Healer Intentions

Here are examples of intentions that we used and others have used on the journey. Shape your intentions in words that suit you.

"To let go of my fear about my healing abilities and to trust my energy testing, and to let go of my fear of being judged."

"I see and sense energy when I work with people and when it is in my and the person's best interest."

"I trust my intuitive and psychic abilities 100 percent."

"I align my work with the divine that guides me."

"I am aware of and know my spirit guides."

" I am comfortable and accepted in my community as a healer."

"Expand the ability to hold love, and joy."

"Expand the ability to hold gratitude and abundance."

"I assist clients in healing all illnesses and trauma."

"To work effectively and safely with dark energy."

"To be effective in assisting with healing physical illness."

These intentions propel us with energy testing to assess the origins and complete the protocol and use the energy interventions to clear what is in the way of becoming a viable healer.

It is not a matter of doing one intention and having the job of being a healer completed. It is a matter of using intention and this or any effective energy psychology protocol as an energetic practice along with your spiritual practice to deepen yourself as a healer. It is not a neat package…heal all of your traumas and illnesses, and then do intentions to become a healer. It is much more in the celtic knot or spiral form—heal an illness, deepen as a healer, heal some trauma, deepen some more as a healer, heal limiting thought fields, deepen even more as a healer.

YOU HAVE THE PICTURE NOW

By now you realize that your soul's purpose most likely involves healing—healing yourself, your family, your clients/students or customers, your community, your corporation or organization and the planet.

When you create these intentions, you are joining an energetic field that goes back to ancient traditions and is a powerful field that demands your attention one way or another.

Developmental Process on the Healer Path

Let us return to my ever-faithful developmental model to discuss what happens as you are on this healer path. This is what I experience and what many have reported to me. As you do your work the vibrations in your energy field rise, resulting in a strengthening and expansion of your energy field. So, during the shifts there are physical, emotional, mental, relationship, environmental and spiritual changes.

Your body holds your individual energy field, and responds to that expansion in an interesting fashion. Your back or ribs may go out. You may unconsciously gain weight to expand with your field. You may feel ill if you are running too much toxic energy through your body instead of calling in the divine and running it through your energy field. The more you practice a mind-body tradition such as Yoga or Qigong, there is a minimization of these physical reactions. I practice yoga, and I go to the chiropractor!

Since the vibrations rise in your field emotionally and mentally, another layer of issues will come up to heal. Sometimes this is confusing because it seems that as a healer we should be "done" with our issues. Rather, it turns out that healers are on an accelerated personal path of healing, and actually more comes up for them to heal along the way. This is not because you are sicker than most; it is because you seek more than most.

In my trainings I always say, "Stay at least one week ahead of your clients!" This makes my students laugh but also helps the newer practitioners relax and realize that they are on a journey. There is not a destination as a healer—once on the path the journey carries you where you need to go and the journey nudges and, yes, demands deeper work and further self-healing.

Balancing time for personal growth and time to expand as a healer with personal relationships is a challenge. We must have partners who come along

246

on this path at some level or distance develops. Some find they can use the energetic tools to sustain their relationships effectively, while others find they cannot and let go of relationships.

The environmental changes are interesting. Most of us find that our tolerance for the canned, fast food, fast paced plastic world greatly decreases and we have to do clearings on environmental and food intolerances frequently. I highly recommend Sandra Radomski's Allergy Antidote work for this clearing solution (allergyantidote.com).

Spiritual development is inherent in this work as you learn to use the energy work in all situations that clears the way to the still voice within.

Sacred Preparation

A spiritual path brings some to this work, or a spiritual path evolves or deepens with DEH and other EP work. The voice within that guides us becomes clearer and we grow to trust it. We increase our abilities to see or sense energy by working with it and by writing and working through intentions.

At a spiritual level we create sacred space in our offices and our homes daily. Although we all have an office or a room where we do our work, energy does not know boundaries. Our own need for healing, insight, or our lifestyle as healers can be held in the sacred space of our homes.

We are drawn to spiritual practice and community.

We all meditate and/or pray from our different traditions. This wasn't so for everyone as they began—it evolved over time.

Working with Guides

If working consciously with guides interests you, then create an intention something like this: "I work effectively, clearly, and safely with guides that serve my and my client's best interest aligned with my spiritual path."

Again, follow the protocol—checking for reversal, boundaries and origins as well as limiting thought fields to clear.

I was amazed by the results as I did my intentions to enhance my abilities as a healer over the years.

I have an enhanced and lovely relationship with Divine Mother who guides me in my work and my life.

In a Woman of Power group our friend Janine introduced us to Kryon whom is a being that is here to work with us to save our dear mother earth. Kryon has taught me that guide relationships are reciprocal, and collaborative in this era. It is no longer necessary to leave your body to get messages. Kryon says to be in conversation with your guides and to not follow blindly. True guides will only ask you to do loving things.

Friends also introduced me to the brotherhood of light in Maechelle Small Wright's work. These beings act much like inner physicians performing healing on physical issues. They have adjusted my back, stopped a cold in its track, healed stomach aches pain, and digestive problems, and have participated in DEH healing. They have worked on organ systems and prevented serious consequences. They assist me and my clients with healing physical symptoms.

Many times during this work ancestors and guides of my clients present themselves to assist us.

Protection

Emerging as a healer you will come to understand that it is not your energy that does the healing. In fact it is not safe to use your own energy and you will quickly deplete, if not become ill, if you are using your energy in the healing work. All of the personal clearing you do of past traumas and illnesses strengthen your field to be a clearer conduit for the universal energy.

For daily protection, call in divine healing energy through your crown chakra or your heart center, and allow this energy to expand into your energy field as you work with yourself or others. Continue to silently ask for guidance throughout the sessions from your Universal source and guides.

The Path of a Healthy Healer

First of all, clear all major traumas and let go of addictions. Work with other energy practitioners of like philosophy for on-going clearings. Most of us need to do that at least weekly. When working with clients, make notes for yourself regarding similar issues you may have to clear or for which you may need to do energetic boundary work. Create a personal energetic practice in addition to your spiritual practice.

Daily creation of sacred space, completing intentions, an energetic and spiritual practice, a conscious diet, exercise, time with other healers such as acupuncturists, chiropractors, massage therapists, nutritionists, other energy workers, working with guides and your divine connection are the necessary ingredients for life as a healthy healer.

The other level of working as a healer that I ask of advanced DEH practitioners is working with collective energies. There are many levels of working with the collective field through energy psychology and DEH. We can work with the individual's connection with the collective, we can work with groups, and as Gary Craig says, "borrow the benefits" of the group field while working on individual healing.

We can also use the energy of a group to work on one collective intention such as, "creating peace in the world," "balancing the collective masculine and feminine," or "healing addictions at the collective level."

On this path we can "tap" into faith, hope, confidence, joy and love.

Points of interest for discussion from this chapter:

- Energy psychology can assist the practitioner in avoiding vicarious trauma.
- It is common for practitioners to question what others will think as they pursue this unusual work.
- A practitioner can use this model to enhance healing skills.
- Developing a spiritual path is essential for the healer.
- Working with guides may develop over time.
- Ask for divine protection while working with others illness and toxic energy.
- Healthy healers are addiction free, work on clearing their traumas, have a healthy diet and exercise program.
- Healers generally have a connection with a collective community and develop abilities to heal collectives.

Chapter Twenty Eight
Soul's Purpose:
The Journey and the Work

"It is about putting on a lens through which we can see our lives as a process of calls and responses."

Gregg Levoy, *Callings*

In 1993 as I prepared to have my third child through the birth canal of the Chinese government, and the divine feminine began to speak through me whether I wanted Her to or not or whether I understood it or not, a friend asked me what I thought I would be doing next work-wise. And out of my mouth came…"Oh, I will be doing soul work." She said something polite trying not to roll her eyes while another part of me inside was screaming, "What did you just say?! What does that mean, and what the heck is soul work?!"

The still voice within knew that I had just spoken my truth. Still, I did not set out to learn or do "soul" work. As I said before, I prayed for teachers. I was led to my energy psychology and energy medicine teachers. Soul work evolved.

Since these prayers I have been guided to adopt another child from China, separate from and five years later divorce my second husband. Guidance also brings me to share this work and my love for it with you.

I have developed many aspects of work in energy psychology, assisted many with their healing through counseling and teaching. I was ordained, share Divine Mother messages, and joined the national leadership of energy psychology. I continue to heal with my grown children and to create relationships with my young children and grandchildren that will not require so much healing. I have been guided to strengthen my program of sobriety that I have been successful with for over a quarter of a century. And I tap and TAT and write and teach.

I am living my unfolding soul's purpose.

As trauma subsides, soul unfolds and reveals itself more fully. As I healed and participated in the work of over a thousand people, this work emerged. It is a simple formula. Heal the emotional, mental and spiritual aspects of illness and issues, and heal the physical to the point you are able, and then use the same protocol to find your passions and your purpose.

It is wonderful, it is simple, and anyone can do it.

Gregg Levoy, in his book, *Callings*, invites us to notice the nudges, the inner whispers that may eventually become callings. I have learned to listen, and to teach others to listen.

People come in to do this work with me at various stages in their calling from clueless, to skeptic to star!

Intention and Process

I live my soul's purpose as an individual, in relationships, family, career, community and the world.

We then energy test which of these aspects of soul's purpose need to be healed for clarity to emerge, and then we proceed with the protocol.

Success Leader Finds More Success

Sonia Miller always knew her work was to inspire people to be their best. For 10 years in Sonoma County, California, she was a leader and mentor in a women's leadership organization. She taught, counseled and led women to their inner and outer stardom.

Despite this success, she had the normal pulls of family let-down and family love, early wounds and relationship work. I met her a couple of years after she moved north to work on her family's soul purpose; to own a vineyard and live in the country.

Her mother, who has cancer, is living in a cottage on their property. She wanted to strengthen and expand her work as counselor, teacher and energy healer. Sonia came to do more healing on herself.

Her initial intention was,

"To 100 percent heal her relationship with her mother and be loving towards her. And to feel safe, unafraid and supported with her siblings."

252

Origins energy tested: six current life, six ancestral and two past life.

There was no reversal.

Inner Objection

If I heal these relationships, then I will not have a purpose.

She did TAT on this objection and in the end said,

"Healing this is my purpose!"

First Origin: Healing Divine Separation

She had no reversals, and usually objections are related to the intention not the origin.

She returned through the tunnel of light to a time of oneness with her Creator…She said, "I have an undramatic knowingness, a state of beingness."

With my direction she basked in this place of oneness…remembering that this sense of oneness is only a tunnel of light away.

After a few minutes I asked her to remember her soul moving toward this realm…toward her mother's womb.

She tapped and cleared the following:

"Mom's energy is pulling me, she is very needy."

"I am pulling back, I do not want to go."

"Okay, here we go, say good-bye and bless all about her."

"I am resigned, no choice, loss of freedom."

"It's inevitable."

"Mom has child energy, innocent, there is no maliciousness to her neediness."

"Mom can be joyful and humorous."

"I am ready to feel free."

Soul Loss

There was one soul loss.

She did TAT while repeating soul loss and retrieved, "Lost Joy."

She received two soul messages.

Soul Messages

1. *It's okay to be child-like with your mother.*
2. *As you heal in your relationship with your mother, you create the space for her to heal also.*

Next Session

In our next session she returned through the tunnel of light to a past life six lifetimes ago…

"I am seeing horses. I am outdoors in wide-open spaces...I see more and more horses...It seems like Wyoming...I am a woman...my relationship with my husband is discontented."

"We are aloof, distant with one another..." taps the meridian points...

"We have not been able to get over the grief regarding the death of our child..." Taps on her heart center

"I see my husband holding our dead child." Continue heart center tapping.

"We are western cowboys, something awful happened..." heart center tapping

Death Energy

"We are in despair..." tapping meridians

"We are like walking ghosts...dead inside..." TAT

"Life will never be the same." tapping...

Soul Loss and Dying Thought

"We cannot connect with joy." TAT

Soul Messages

1. That was then, this is now.
2. Joy restored!

Energy testing determined that the soul of the lost child was the soul of her mother.

Bardo Healing

We returned to the time between lives for soul healing.

The soul we now know as Sonia asked the child-Mom's soul for forgiveness for not being able to save her then.

The child-Mom soul replied, "That was our journey...no forgiveness needed."

We energy tested that the intention was complete.

Apparently, there was not only healing for Sonia but also for her mother. Their communication and closeness improved, and Mom has lived triple the time that was predicted.

Sonia has continued personal work, DEH, EFT and Yuen training, and is greatly expanding her business, Success for the Soul, successforthesoul.com!

Her book is available at her website. Recently she began some online classes based on the Law of Attraction principles, and is working on her intention to hold the collective field more fully for this endeavor.

Skeptic to Star

I met Greg Warburton in 2000 as a student in a DEH® class that Howard Brockman and I taught together. Greg is smart, asks good questions, and is sensitive in his work with others. Despite former injuries, he is still an avid athlete. When the class ends, although he has gained many skills, he still cannot really imagine himself doing this at work. He is employed at a counseling center for high risk children with mental-emotional problems and their families. He lives in Corvallis the home of Oregon State University.

I began getting e-mail and phone calls during the 2007 College Baseball World Series with messages, "Did you see the Oregon State University pitcher, Jorge Reyes, tapping in the dugout before he went out to pitch?" The announcer said, "He is using acupressure points to focus his energy." For a couple of days I asked around and finally got word that Greg Warburton, MA, LPC, whom I had not seen for several years, was teaching the OSU players these techniques.

There were e-mails coming in from all over the country, and there was an article in the Oregonian, Portland's newspaper, about this strange phenomenon, called Emotional Freedom Techniques or "tapping."

Greg and I went to lunch to celebrate his new fame, and the OSU Beavers victory in the College World Series. He showed up at my favorite local deli in his orange Beavers t-shirt.

He caught me up on his life. He had resigned from working at the adolescent day treatment program a few years ago and works now for a child abuse clinic part-time and has a private practice. He had done some personal work with Howard off and on, and continued to hone his energy psychology skills.

Dan Spencer, the OSU baseball coach, worked out at the same gym in Corvallis that Greg does and over the years they became friends and he showed Dan EFT. Greg is soft-spoken and yet enthusiastic. He said, "Because Coach Spencer trusted me, when I approached him about working with some of the team members, he agreed.

"I began working with them mid-season 2006. I introduced the energy work to the pitchers and the catchers. I met with them one time and I taught them EFT, heart center tapping, Cook's Balance, and three thumps and cross crawl. I checked in with a couple of players during the season. They have given me permission to tell their experiences."

Center fielder Kevin Gubderson told Greg that he used EFT and heart center tapping for mental-emotional issues related to a hamstring injury. As a result he lost no innings where he was needed. Kevin also used tapping before each game. He tapped only on positive statements, and pitched the final game and the final out!

Coach Spencer thanked Greg and said, "Let's make this a regular part of their routine starting with fall ball." In the fall, Greg then re-introduced the techniques to most of the pitchers and catchers, meeting with them twice for 30 minutes each.

In 2007, Greg worked on eliminating self-defeating behaviors with pitchers Jorge, Joe, Eddie, Anton and also Mitch, the catcher, who reported a significant decrease in his ERA.

Another pitcher, Blake, had always had learning difficulties and taking finals on the road during the series made studying even more stressful. He reported using the cross crawl and tapping to get through the stress and found that his struggles with learning were lessened!

Greg beamed as he pondered the future with his work, and gave me a copy of the Oregonian article. The story was also picked up and published in the New York Times.

Unfortunately for Oregon, Coach Spencer accepted a coaching position in Texas. Greg is going to videotape an interview with him before he leaves. He will meet soon with the OSU basketball team. He also met with several OSU coaches to introduce the energy strategies to them, and he has the support of the current Athletic Director.

I invited him to speak at my next Practitioner's Intensive, and we hugged good-bye and promised to keep in touch!

Greg is available to work with athletes individually and with teams, and he promises that you do not have to go anywhere in a tunnel with him unless you really want to! He will simply teach you to tap your way to greater success.

Courageous to Community Leader

Kim called me in the late 1990s for counseling for her and her husband. They had a young son, busy jobs and were having trouble communicating without anger. They did intentions regarding what they would like to achieve in their relationship and reducing their anger.

Kim cleared several origins that were significant. Her first husband died suddenly when they were in their twenties and it had always been difficult for her to trust that love could last. Then she was in a relationship with a controlling, somewhat older abusive woman for about 10 years. There was much trauma to clear from this.

From the time she was very young she had thought that she preferred women, but the abusive experience coupled with anti-gay childhood religious beliefs, caused her to want to "get over that!" She thought if she married a man and had children that she could just go on and live a "normal life." Gently, I worked with her in a client centered, energy centered style teaching her to follow her body's wisdom to find her truth. One day soon after her second son was born and 18 months into their therapy she came in and said, "I cannot live a lie anymore, I have to have the courage to tell him that I am really lesbian and let things unfold as they will."

Needless to say, her husband was shocked and hurt. We met individually and worked with his pain. He joined an online support group for spouses of gay partners.

Admirably, Kim continued to work with her conflict about her truth, the God of her childhood, and societal norms. She and her husband lived as roommates for two years while they cared for their young sons.

Finally, they separated and she began to live the lifestyle that expressed her wholeness. She was serene and content. She wondered how to meet people in our small, conservative city, especially lesbian women with children. She decided to put out the word and throw a potluck. Over a dozen families showed up. Kathy and her two teenagers came from southern Washington. It was love at first sight for Kim and Kathy. They have been together ever since.

For many years I had worked with this population of women who were stymied about how to meet people in our city and surrounding farming communities. It was not an unusual story for lesbians to move to this area for a job and to have it take a year or more to meet another woman in their lifestyle.

Kim came into see me after the first potluck and expressed her amazement. She said, "We decided to do this monthly." I said, "So you didn't know that lesbian women have never organized here." She said, "No." I said, laughing "I think you just have."

Kim then attended one of my first Living Your Soul's Purpose™ classes. We did a community spiritual leader past life clearing…

She said soon after, "I feel that providing community for lesbians is my calling."

The potlucks continued, as did parties, field trips and service work. Love and emotional support filled their lives and greatly enhanced the lives of the others in their community. Kim is a computer buff, so she built a website, and their core group chose their name, lavenderwomyn.com Within a couple of years there were about 200 women, some with kids, some not, signed up on the site and coming to the events. Kim and Kathy bought a large house with a huge yard for them, their four children and the ever growing potlucks. People started coming from hours away as Lavender Womyn's reputation for clean fun and good people grew. Kim spent many hours running the website and responding to inquiries.

A chapter developed in Eugene and then in Portland. As of this writing there are about 650 people on the website and attending events.

Recently, Kim brought Kathy to a Living Your Soul's Purpose™ class so that they could work together on some individual and relationship soul's purpose intentions. They wrote about their experience afterwards.

Kathy and I have decided to pursue our creative sides and market our photography and writing skills—it's slow progress trying to balance this with family, full-time jobs, taking care of a home, and running the Lavender Womyn's group. I know, I know…tap on "there's never enough time." :-)

Anyway, we came up with a business name, "Windfeather Expressions" and have a few photos to work with, but that's about it so far. We'd like to do greeting cards, pictures, etc. The lesbian community doesn't have much to choose from when it comes to greeting cards, so we'd like to be able to give them some wonderful choices. My ultimate goal would be for this business to replace my income at my corporate job. I'd love to quit working graveyard, and working for a corporation. And then, for it to replace Kathy's income so we could travel the world, see some incredible sights, and capture some awesome photos!

Drugs to Minister

I have told some of Roy's story earlier.

Roy was divorced from his children's mother and then his girls were abused by a man outside of the family. Their mother had moved so many times that Roy could not find them. He had been on a path of drug use that took him away from Bible College where he was an aspiring minister, away from his children to menial jobs and loneliness.

Along the way he met June, the love of his life, and realized that to keep her he would need to change his ways. He gave up drugs and reconnected with his comforting God. One day after not seeing his girls for several years, he came home and found a note on the door informing him that his children were in state custody with a number to call. Within 24 hours, two shocked, frightened young girls were reunited with their Daddy.

June is the consummate protective mother. I have asked her if she would give step-mother classes! Their addicted mother lives out of state and calls periodically. She was saying things that caused upset for the girls, so because Roy would get too reactive, June began monitoring the phone calls. She made an agreement with the girls and their birth mother that they could write to one another. Both June and Roy feared potential kidnapping and they did not reveal their street address, so June got them their private mailbox with their own key—metaphorically the safe key to their mother.

After the girls had been with them for a couple of years, June and Roy had a baby boy together. June readied the girls by including them in doctor appointments, having them attend the birth and allowing them to help care for their new brother. All were thrilled.

Roy had been working two jobs that paid the bills but didn't satisfy him. Remember, he was the skeptic who set out to prove that tapping wouldn't work and was so surprised when it did. He ended up doing his own work with me and did DEH on his former drug use, and his pain and guilt regarding his girls, and his anger at his ex-wife and the abuser. When this was complete, we did a soul's purpose intention and energy tested that he had origins to clear on career and community.

Two years later he called me and said, "You had to be one of the first to know. The minister of our church just asked me to train to be his assistant minister and work with the youth. This is my dream and my soul's purpose, you know."

I know.

From Counselor to Healer

George had been dissatisfied with his role in a mental health agency and longed to do deeper work with people. He came in with the following intention:

"I find my right place in my career."

There were two current life and three ancestral origins to clear. We energy tested to return to three generations ago on George's father's side of the family.

He entered the tunnel of light. He experienced lavender healing light encircling him, and blue and white healing light being offered by the divine. He arrives...

"I see trees, I stand up, look around...my body is tense..."

I energy test if this is also a past life since he is saying "I" instead of "they." It is. He taps...

"I am a boy, I cannot do a man's job, glad they are leaving me alone, I want out of this..." taps

"I want out of being a burden, people do not believe me."

"People shouting, you don't believe in yourself..."

Earthbound Spirit

"A human-like form walks out of my body through my mouth..." TAT and prayer.

"I am free..." Heart center tapping...to anchor the positive energy of freedom in his body.

His intention was complete! He soon went from case manager to healer with traumatized families.

Health and History Converge

Anahid came in to generally improve her health and ability to handle stress. She was referred by her chiropractor. She is a graduate level pesticide specialist for the Department of Agriculture. She works daily with farmers to achieve the balance of maintaining their livelihood and protecting the land and consumers. She is passionate about the earth and its relevant damage and health. She is an activist at many levels for the oppression of people and the planet. She is happy in a relationship with a loving partner.

Over several months Anahid learned to manage the stress of her job and many activist activities both with energy work and by cutting back on some of her organizational work. She felt harassed by a new co-worker and was able to clear her feelings and set strong energetic boundaries.

She talked about her Armenian history with grief and pride. She had grown up in an Armenian-American community with four siblings.

Intention

"To have a healthy physical body and to do my life's purpose, and to connect my mind and body."

Session One

Anahid returned in the tunnel of light to a past life, 17 lifetimes ago. She says, "I failed my people, did not show enough leadership during a war..." She tapped the meridian points. She cleared the trauma. She then cleared the collective energy of death with TAT.

An inner objection arises before we enter the ancestral origin...

"If I overcome my overeating I do not know who I will be." Clears with TAT.

She then visited Armenia through her father's lineage two generations ago, returning in the tunnel of light...

"There is starvation and terror..."

"She is sad... she is attacked, her earrings are ripped out...she is raped..." continues to tap

"She is oppressed as a Christian Armenian..." tapping.

Death Energy

There is individual and collective death energy connected with "starvation." TAT

"If I speed up my metabolism, I will die..." taps

Out of Body

"Grandma left her body to avoid the pain..."

Anahid taps on this family dissociative tendency.

"Her metabolism saved her life..." taps

Session Two

Anahid again traveled in the tunnel of light to a maternal ancestral origin three generations ago on her mother's side of the family.

"This a bad place, not good for women..." begins tapping

"My great grandmother had 12 children..." tapping

"They have immigrated from Serbia to Pennsylvania..." tapping

"She is married to a violent alcoholic..." tapping

"My grandmother, her daughter, is happy when she dies..." tapping

Dark Energy

Anahid says, "I want to push this energy away, I feel contaminated." TAT

Merging further into the tunnel of family history she resumes tapping as she says,

"My great-great grandmother was sold as a slave in her teens because her family could not afford all of their children and needed the money."

Soul Loss

Tapping… "My great-great grandmother then had to be with a man she didn't love."

"Oh, I am retrieving the lost soul part of true love."

A few sessions later

Anahid returned to four generations ago on her father's side of the family through the tunnel of light to a brutal time in Armenian history where they were under Turkish rule.

"It is warm and familiar. I see a young woman in a small Armenian village… It is warm and dry, filled with the scents of their crops—olives and apricots. She feels trapped in a cult-like religion, ruled by males only."

Begins tapping until clear.

Death Energy

"She feels like there is no place she can go." TAT until clear.

Soul Loss

Continues with TAT…focusing on soul loss and then retrieves,

"Be whole in order to be free, then and now."

Next Session

"Dad's father escaped genocide in 1915…He was a Christian in Armenia under Turkish rule by extremist Muslims who wanted to cleanse Armenia of Christians," Anahid said, after traveling through the tunnel once more. Tapping…

"He lost family and friends…" continues to tap…

"It was all over corrupt politics and greed."

Death Energy

"He wanted to die, but instead escaped…" TAT

Soul Messages

1. Stay whole.

2. Have a strong leadership role.

Anahid and her partner attended a Living Your Soul's Purpose™ weekend.

Soon after Anahid came in and said, "I am applying for a volunteer position where I would work in Armenia for several months teaching farmers about pesticide management. There is an organization that sponsors some of the costs, and assists in making the connections."

After a couple of months she was accepted and tapping on her mix of anxiety and excitement. She has communicated with the department where she will be working, and they wondered if it will be a problem that she is a woman... TAT, TAT, tap, tap.

Healing illness and relationships, and enhancing inner qualities is made possible with energy psychology and energy medicine, and then the process of aligning with the divine moves into place with greater ease. The joy and the challenge of consciously co-creating soul's purpose with the divine is a remarkable journey. The still voice, the nudge, the calling creates the conscious intention. The sacred tools of energy work forge the path of light so that we may actually see our soul's purpose as an individual, in relationships, family, career, community and the world.

Points of interest for discussion from this chapter:
• Living Your Soul's Purpose™ is an unfolding, developmental process.
• Energy work takes the mystery out of clarifying one's soul's purpose.
• Wellness and purpose alignment go hand in hand.

Epilogue
My Vision for the Future

My grandaughters' grandchild will live in a world where the information in this book will be simple energetic hygiene, and living her purpose will be her natural expectation.

When she walks into the emergency room with a family member, after the paper work is complete, they are sent to the waiting room where there is a fountain, and soft music and a staff person who teaches tapping and does frontal occipital holding.

On other floors energy practitioners offer pre-op sessions to prepare the body for the upcoming assault of drugs and trauma, and the family for their worry and fear.

Post-op the energy practitioner then returns to assist the "customer" (no longer called a patient) with her pain and her family's stress.

On any given morning at her daughter's school, right after the bell, all rise to do the three thumps and the cross crawl, and tap on their heart center for anything that is bothering them that would interfere with their learning that day.

The reading teachers then repeat this exercise along with reversal corrections for struggling readers.

Put downs by self or others at small community schools are handled in the halls or on the playground by the assistant teachers all trained in meridian tapping and TAT.

Energy psychology and energy medicine are the standard in university schools of counseling and social work required by the National Health Insurance which will require it because of its cost effectiveness.

The business world is inundated with a new generations of young adults with indigo auras and androgynous minds that can only think about the effects on the whole—caring for their individual energy fields is second nature taught to them by their mothers and grandmothers.

In the long run I envision energy psychology and energy medicine leaders teaching the world the relationship between individual energy and health, and the relationship between individual health and organizational and community health, and the relationship of collective healthy energy to the health of the planet.

The Association for Comprehensive Energy Psychology (energypsych.org) research and certification and the International Society for the Study of Subtle Energies and Energy Medicine (issseem.org) along with many training programs are creating a professional arena for energy practitioners and their work. They also provide humanitarian work for communities and countries in need.

Donations for research and humanitarian work are always appreciated.

I think this is the part of the book where I am supposed to say that I enjoyed writing this while gazing at the Pacific surf or on a mountaintop in a rural Oregon cabin...

The truth is I am an older single Mom of two beautiful Chinese girls who at publishing are eight and 13. This book was written at my dining room table, in my office, living room, and on my bed often to the background sounds of High School Musical, or Sponge Bob Square Pants. It was written between soccer practice and music lessons, shopping trips and carpools. It was written before and after road trips to Redding where my grown children and four grandchildren live. It was written when I had time and when I didn't, when I was in the mood to write and when I wasn't.

It was that important to share with you.

August 2007 Salem, Oregon.

Appendix One
Daily Energetic Routine

I like to encourage people to come up with their own daily energy routine. It makes a difference if it is a routine to continue healing or a routine for maintenance. Your body's wisdom knows. You will energy test differently for different needs, so re-check about once a week.

1. Energy test if you are at 100 percent energetic boundaries with whatever your major concern is.
2. Energy test if you are at 100 percent energetic boundaries with whatever you want to achieve.
3. Energy test if you need to do general boundary work daily? Weekly? Number of times a day or week? Time of day?
4. Energy test how many times per day or week for reversal points.
5. Energy test daily, weekly marching and tapping for ND correction.
6. Energy test how many times a day you should clear stress or other emotions.
   • TAT, number of times a day. Time of day?
   • EFT, number of times a day. Time of day?
7. Energy test a routine for physical pain if that is an issue.

An example of a personalized energy routine:
1. Three thumps and cross crawl routine every other morning.
2. Energetic boundary work in the morning for three minutes.
3. TAT if tired or have unwanted dream.
4. EFT mid-morning.
5. TAT while resting after work for five minutes.
6. Boundary work before dinner.
7. Chakra balancing in evening.

Appendix Two
Soul's Purpose Circles

I encourage you to begin Soul's Purpose Circles and to discuss the points at the end of the chapters, and to do clearings together. Check our website, **onedynamicenergetichealing.org** for practitioners that you may consult with along the way.

Guidelines for Circles
- Have a different person lead each time following these guidelines.
- Read one chapter per week.
- Create sacred space together.
- Use a sacred talking stone. Pass to each person to hold as they speak.
- Begin with a check-in time to report on soul's purpose progress, three minutes each.
- Take turns leading discussions on a point or two from the chapter of the week.
- Plan a closing ritual that you use each week that respects all of the group members' spiritual orientation.

Appendix Three
The Steps in Dynamic Energetic Healing®

Dynamic Energetic Healing®:
Energetic Origins Process At a Glance
copyright 1999 Mary Hammond-Newman, MA, LPC,
Howard Brockman, LCSW, Nancy Gordon, LCSW

1. Create Sacred Space/Seal the Room
2. Energy Testing Calibration. Ask: Yes, No, blocked MMT? Pull hair while testing, checks for hydration, lateral and over-under
3. General psychological reversal, ET I want, deserve, safe, possible, will benefit me and others?
4. Check for Homolateral/ Neurological Disorganization
5. Intention/ Check specific psychological reversal
6. Inner objection/conflict
7. Energetic Origins ET which and number, divine separation, current life, conception/womb/birth, ancestral, past life.
8. Energetic Boundaries before returning to the origins?
9. Induction/Regression tunnel of light or?
10. Healing light imagery, sacred sound or other resources?
11. Energetic Boundaries before entering the origin?
12. Healing Trauma/Loss? Intervention? Position? Blocked Access? Shock? Denial? Anger? Depression? Sadness? Despair? Fear? Shame? Grudge?
13. Death energy? Dying thoughts?
14. Out of Body
15. Shattered energy field?
16. Dark energy
17. Bardo (Between Lives) Level Healing
18. Gifts to collect? soul messages, messages from the ancestors or prior soul being
19. Returning to present
20. Fully (100 percent) back in body in present time? Other limiting beliefs or identities? Energetic origin is clear at conscious, unconscious, body, soul, and chakra, levels
21. Check periodically: will to live

Appendix Four
Resources

For all websites mentioned in this book go to
onedynamicenergetichealing.org/links

Bibliography

"Scientific thought, then, is not momentary; it is not a static instance; it is a process."

Jean Piaget

Adler, Alfred, Ph.D. *Understanding Human Nature: A New Translation,* St. Paul, Minnesota: 1998.

Andrade, Joaquin, M.D. and David Feinstein. *Energy Psychology: Theory, Indications, Evidence* published in *The Promise of Energy Psychology,* Tarcher/Penguin, New York, New York: 2005.

Andrews, Ted. *Animal Speak; The Spiritual & Magical Powers of Creatures Great and Small,* Llewellyn Publications, St. Paul, Minnesota: 1993.

Arrien, Angeles. *The Four-Fold Way: Walking the Paths of the Warrior, Teacher, Healer and Visionary,* Harper and Collins, San Francisco, California: 1983.

Bain, George. *Celtic Art: The Methods of Construction,* Dover Publications, New York, New York: 1973.

Bandler, Richard and John Grinder. *Trance-Formations,* Real People Press, Boulder, Colorado: 1979.

Baldwin, William. *Spirit Releasement Therapy,* Headline Books Inc.,Terra Alta, West Virginia: 1992.

Beinfield, Harriet. *Between Heaven and Earth,* Random House, New York, New York: 1992.

Callahan, Roger. *Five Minute Phobia Cure,* Enterprise Publishing, Wilmington, Delaware: 1985.

Benor, Daniel, M.D. *Consciousness, Bioenergy, and Healing,* Wholistic Healing Publications, Medford, New Jersey: 2004.

Black, Claudia, Ph.D. *It Will Never Happen to Me,* Ballantine Books, New York, New York: 1991.

Bohm, David and B. J. Hiley. *The Undivided Universe,* Routledge, London: 1993.

Bowen, Murray, M.D. *Family Therapy in Family Practice,* Jason Aronson, New Jersey: 1990.

Bowman, Carol. *Children's Past Lives,* Bantam Books, New York, New York: 1998.

Brennan, Barbara. *Hands of Light*, Bantam Books, New York, New York: 1998.

Bradshaw, John, Ph.D. *Healing the Shame that Binds You*, Health
Communications, Florida: 1988.

Briere, John, Ph.D. *Principles of Trauma Therapy*, Sage Publications,
Thousand Oaks, California: 2006.

Brockman, Howard, LCSW. *Dynamic Energetic Healing*, Columbia Press,
Salem, Oregon: 2005.

Capra, Fritjof. *The Tao of Physics*, Shambala, Berkeley, California: 1975.

Childre, D. and H. Martin. *The Heart Math Solution*, Harper,
San Francisco: 1999.

Church, Dawson. *The Genie in Your Genes*, Elite Books, Energy Psychology
Press, Santa Rosa, California: 2007.

Deepak, Chopra, M.D. *The Seven Spiritual Laws of Success*,
Amber-Allen Publishing, New World Library, San Rafael, California: 1994.

Courtois, Christine. *Healing the Incest Wound*, W. W. Norton & Co.,
New York, New York: 1988.

Craig, Gary. *Emotional Freedom Technique: Steps Toward Becoming The Ultimate
Therapist*, Training Manual and DVD, San Francisco, California: 1998.

Dass, Ram, Ph.D. and Paul Gorman. *How Can I Help?* Knopf, Michigan: 1985.

Davies, Brenda. *The 7 Healing Chakras*, Ulysses Press, Berkeley, California: 2000.

Dossey, Larry, M.D. *Beyond Illness; Discovering the Experience of Health*, New
Science Library, New York, New York: 1984.

Durlacher, James V. *Freedom From Fear Forever*, Van Ness, Tempe, Arizona: 1995.

Diamond, John. *Life Energy*, Dodd, Mead & Co., New York, New York: 1985.

Dyer, Wayne. *Power of Intention*, Hay House, Carlsbad, California: 2003.

Eden, Donna. *Energy Medicine*, Tarcher/Putnam, New York, New York: 1998.

Eisler, Riane. *The Chalice and the Blade*, Harper and Row, San Francisco,
California: 1988.

Erickson, Milton H., M.D. and Ernest Rossi, Ph.D. *The February Man*, Routledge,
London: 1989.

Falter-Barns, Suzanne. *Living Your Joy*, Ballantine Books, New York,
New York: 2003.

Feinstein, David, Gary Craig, Donna Eden. *The Promise of Energy Psychology*,
Jeremy Tarcher, New York, New York: 2005.

Fleming, Tapas. *Reduce Traumatic Stress in Minutes,* TATLife, Torrance, California: 1996.

Gallo, Fred, Ph.D. *Energy Psychology,* CRC Press, New York, New York:1998.

Gallo, Fred, Ph.D. *Energy Diagnostic and Treatment Methods,* W. W. Norton & Co., New York, New York: 2002.

Gallo, Fred, Ph.D. *Energy Tapping,* New Harbinger, Oakland, California: 2000.

Gallo, Fred, Ph.D. *Energy Pschology in Psychotherapy,* W. W. Norton & Co., New York, New York: 2002.

Gawain, Shakti. *Creative Visualization,* Whatever Publishing, Mill Valley:1979.

Glasser, William, Ed. D. *The Quality School,* Harper Collins, New York, New York: 1990-98.

Goodheart, George and Frost, Robert. *Applied Kinesiology: A Training Manual and Reference book of Basic Principles and Practices,* 2002.

Harner, Michael. *The Way of the Shaman,* Bantam, New York, New York: 1982.

Hawkins, David R. *Power vs. Force,* Hay House, Carlsbad, California: 2002.

Hellinger, Bert. *Love's Own Truth,* Zeig, Tucker and Theisen, Germany: 2001.

Hillman, James. *The Soul's Code,* Random House, New York, New York: 1996.

Hover-Kramer, Dorothea. *Creative Energies: Integrative Energy Psychotherapy,* W.W. Norton, New York, New York: 2002.

Huston, Jean. *A Passion for the Possible,* Harper Collins, New York, New York: 1998.

Ingerman, Sandra. *Soul Retrieval: Mending the Fragmented Self,* Harper, San Francisco, California: 1991.

James, Tad and Wyatt Lee Woodsmall. *Time Line Therapy and the Basis of Personality,* Meta Publications, Capitola, California: 1988.

Judith, Anodea. *Eastern Body Western Mind,* Celestial Arts, Berkeley, California: 1996.
Wheels of Life, Llewellyn, Woodbury, Minnesota: 1987, 1999.
The Sevenfold Journey, Crossing Press, 1993.
The Boxed Kit Chakra Balancing, www.sacredcenters.com: 2003.

Jung, C. G. *The Archetypes and the Collective Unconscious,* Princeton University Press, Princeton, New Jersey: 1981.

Kaptchuk, Ted J. *The Web that Has No Weaver: Understanding Chinese Medicine,* McGraw Hill, New York, New York: 1999.

King, Karen L. *Women and Goddess Traditions: In Antiquity and Today,* Augsburg Fortress, Minneapolis, Minnesota: 1997.

Hover-Kramer, Dorothea and Midge Murphy. *Creating Right Relationships: A Practical Guide to Ethics in Energy Therapies,* 2006—available through http://www.midgemurphy.com/Book/Book.html

Krieger, D. *Accepting your power to Heal: The Personal Practice of Therapeutic Touch,* Bear & Co, Santa Fe, New, Mexico: 1993.

Levoy, Gregg. *Callings,* Three Rivers Press/Random House, New York, New York: 1998.

Lipton, Bruce, Ph.D. *The Biology of Belief,* Mountain of Love/Elite, Santa Rosa, California: 2005.

Mandala, Nelson. *No Easy Walk to Freedom,* Penguin Classics, New York, New York: 2002.

Matt, Daniel C. *The Essential Kabbalah,* Harper One, San Francisco, California: 1995.

Ragani, Michaels, MA. *Neurolinguistic Programming Training,* Portland, Oregon: 1998.

Millman, Dan. *Living on Purpose,* New World Library, Navato, California: 2000.

Mindell, Arnold. *Working with the Dreaming Body,* Routledge & Paul, Boston, Massachusetts: 1985.

Mishlove, Jeffrey. *The Roots of Consciousness: Psychic Liberation through History, Science and Experience,* Random House, New York, New York: 1975.

Modi, Shakuntala. *Remarkable Healings,* Hampton Roads Publishing, Charlottesville, Virginia: 1997.

Mountrose, Phillip. *Getting Thru To Your Soul,* Arroyo Grande, California: 2000.

Nims, Larry. *Be Set Free Fast Training Manual,* 1998.

Myss, Carolyn. *Sacred Contracts,* Harmony, New York, New York: 2001,

Oschman, J. *Energy Medicine in Therapeutic and Human Performance,* Butterworth-Heinemann, Newton, Pennsylvania: 2003. *Energy Medicine: The Scientific Basis,* Churchill Livingstone, London: 2000.

Palmer, Helen. *The Enneagram,* Harper and Row, New York, New York: 1975.

Pearlman, L and K. Saakvitne. *Trauma and the Therapist,* W. W. Norton & Co., New York, New York: 1995.

Pratt, George and Peter Lambrou. *Instant Emotional Healing,* Broadway Books/ Random House, New York, New York: 2000.

Pert, Candace, Ph.D. *Molecules of Emotion,* Simon and Schuster, New York, New York: 1999.

Bruce Perry, M.D., Ph.D. *Attachment: The First Core Strength,* Early Childhhood Today, Scholastic 10/2001.

Radomski, Sandra, ND, LCSW. *Allergy Antidotes Basic Manual,* allergyantidotes.com: 1999.

Ray, Sondra and Leonard Orr. *Rebirthing in the New Age,* Celestial Arts, San Francisco, California: 1983.

Rogers, Carl. *Client Centered Therapy,* Houghton Mifflin, New York, New York: 1951.

Roth, Gabrielle and John Loudon. *Maps to Ecstasy: Teachings of an Urban Shaman,* New World Library, San Rafael, California: 1989.

Satir, Virginia. *Peoplemaking,* Souvenir Press, New York, New York: 1990.

Shapiro, Francine. *Eye Movement Desensitization Reprocessing,* Guilford Press, New York, New York: 1995.

Scaer, Robert C., M.D. *The Body Bears the Burden,* Haworth Medical Press, New York, New York: 2001.

Shealy, Norman, M.D. and Dawson Church, Ph.D. *Soul Medicine,* Elite Books, Santa Rosa, California: 2005.

Simpson, Liz. *The Book of Chakra Healing,* Sterling, Sterling Publishing, New York, New York: 1999.

Sheldrake, Rupert. *The Presence of the Past,* Park Street Press, Glen Falls, New York: 1995.

Shumsky, Susan G. *Exploring Chakras: Awaken Your Untapped Energy,* Career Press, Franklin Lakes, New Jersey: 2003.

Siegel, Bernie, M.D. *Peace, Love & Healing,* Quill, New York, New York: 1998.

Sise, Mary, LCSW. *The Energy of Belief Energy,* Psychology Press, Elite Books, Fulton, California: 2007.

Stanislav, Grof, M.D. *Beyond the Brain: Birth, Death, and Transcendence in Psychotherapy,* State University of New York Press, Albany, New York: 1985.

Talbot, Michael. *The Holographic Universe,* HarperCollins, New York, New York: 1992.

Thurston, Mark. *Soul Purpose: Discovering and Fulfilling Your Destiny,*
St. Martins Press, New York, New York: 1997.

Tolle, Eckhart. *The Power of Now,* New World Library, Novato, California: 1999.

Van der Kolk, Bessell. *Traumatic Stress,* Guilford Press, New York,
New York: 1996.

Villodo, Alberto. *Shaman, Healer, Sage,* Harmony, Chatsworth, California: 2000.

Warren, Rick. The Purpose Driven Life, Zondervan, Grand Rapids MI: 2002.

Wilbur, Ken, Ph.D. *No Boundary: Eastern and Western Approaches to Personal
Growth,* Shambala, Boston, Massechusetts: 2000.

Zukav, Gary. *Seat of the Soul,* Simon and Schuster, New York, New York: 1999.

Index

C

Callahan, Roger, 56, 70, 79-80, 81, 206, 230

Callahan Techniques, 79-80

Callings (Levoy), 252

Capra, Fritjof, 13

Celtic Art (Bain), 162

Celtic knot, 161-162

central meridian, 83

Chakra Balancing (Judith), 100

chakra interventions, 113

chakras
    additional resources about, 100-101
    balancing, 16-17
    as an energy system, 100-101
    fifth of the (throat), 108-110
    first of the (root), 101-103
    fourth of the (heart), 106-108, 113-114
    in Reiki, 20
    second of the (sacral), 103-104
    seventh of the (crown), 111-113
    sixth of the (brow), 110-111
    third of the (solar plexus), 104-106
    the way of the, 97-100

change
    limiting thoughts about, 206-207
    the new comfort zone, 211

chi, 11, 16, 19-20

children
    in domestic violence, 233
    phobias in, 230-231
    play therapy for, 229-230
    social and learning problems, 76, 233-234
    tantrums and attachment in, 231-232

Children's Past Lives (Bowman), 149

Chinese medicine, 11, 19-20

choice points, 214-216

Chopra, Deepak, 21

Christianity, 6-8, 17

Church, Dawson, 9-10, 15, 148

circulation meridian, 85

clients, resistant and in denial, 69-71

codependency, 212-213

Cognitive Therapy, 206

collarbone, tapping under the, 75

collective energies, working with, 249

collective soul, 9-10

collective unconscious, 5, 195

color(s)
    of the chakras, 99
    energy as, 12
    Tunnel of Light, 164
    in the Tunnel of Light, 164-165

Combs, Allan, 51

comfort zone, 211

conception, energetic origin at, 143

conception meridian, 83

connectedness. *See also* oneness
    collective energies, working with, 249
    the collective soul, 9-10
    the collective unconscious, 5
    with the universal, 20

Consciousness, Bioenergy and Healing (Benor), 21

contracts, 212-216

controlling vessel meridian, 83

Hurricane Katrina, 42

Hurricane Rita, 42

hypnotherapy, 164

hypnotism, 20

I

illness, limiting thoughts in, 207-208

indicator muscle in energy testing, 63

Ingerman, Sondra, 6

intent, defined, 124-125

intention

    energetic, 123-124, 129-130

    examples of, 130-131

    inner objections, 132

    and the law of attraction, 131-134

    as a process, 124-131

intuition and energy testing, 59, 61-62

J

Jackson, Wayne, 6

James, Tad, 162, 163

Jensen, Wendy, 223

Jesus, son of Mary, 17

Johnson, Ranae, 153

Johnson, Scott, 95

Jones, Deborah, 95

joy

    body language for, xxii

    creating, 205-216

Judaism, 7-8, 17

Judith, Anodea, 100, 105

Jung, Carl, 5

Jungian theory, 10

K

Kabbalah, 17

karmic energetic origins, 153-160, 189-191

karmic soul talk, 224

Kendall, Florence, 57

Kendall, Henry, 57

kidney meridian, 84

kinesiology, 57

Krieger, Dolores, 21

Kubler-Ross, Elizabeth, 169

kundalini, 101

Kwan Yin, 82

L

large intestine meridian, 84

Lavender Womyn, 258

law of attraction, 131-134, 209

learning problems in children, 76, 233-234

Leary, Timothy, 28, 144

Levoy, Gregg, 252

Liebeault, Ambrose-Suguste, 20

life, pathway to, 181-191

Life Energy (Diamond), 58

light, pathway to, 193-198. *See also* Tunnel of Light

limiting emotions, 210-211

limiting thought fields, 205-206

limiting thoughts, 206-209

Link, Nancy, 95

Lipton, Bruce, 14-15, 150

liver meridian, 84

love, the energy of, 235-238

lung meridian, 84

M

N

O

The Authors

Mary Hammond, MA, LPC, Diplomate in Comprehensive Energy Psychology

Mary began her career in Early Childhood Education after she was educated at California State University, Dominguez Hills. During this time Mary read and studied the complete works of Jean Piaget. She owned and taught in the first private mainstreamed open classroom school in Orange County, California for infants through third graders.

Play Therapy was the bridge for Mary from early childhood educator to therapist. Children induced trances and exhibited energetic shifts through play long before Mary knew the language of energy.

She taught Early Childhhood Education, Psychology, Play Therapy and Chemical Dependency at several colleges.

She is a therapist, trainer, consultant, writer, and healer in Salem, Oregon. For over twenty years she has practiced the art of assisting people in finding their truths and healing their illnesses. Since 1990 she has immersed herself in the new frontiers of healing by studying and exploring Holotropic Breathwork, Transpersonal Psychology, Eye Movement Desensitization Reprocessing (EMDR) and finally Energy Psychology, in which she is trained in many modalities. She is guided in work and in life by the presence of Divine Mother and Christ Consciousness. She develops work which combines her background in Human and Child Development, Addictions, Play Therapy and the inclusive Divine Feminine Spiritual path with the energy psychotherapies. She teaches in colleges and privately. Mary and Howard Brockman, LCSW, published "Dynamic Energetic Healing: Soul Work at the Origins" in *Energy Psychology in Psychotherapy* by Fred Gallo, Ph.D. She is published in play therapy and the hypnotherapy fields. She is a current board member for the Association for Comprehensive Energy Psychology and is committed to professionally leading Energy Psychology with Energy Medicine into the mainstream.

She parents grown children and two daughters from China and is Grammary to four grandchildren. She enjoys walking, music, dancing, time with friends, traveling, and serving.

She can be contacted at mhnheart@comcast.net

Ruth Crowley, Ph.D., lives in the Sacramento, CA area. She holds a Ph.D. from Stanford University and taught for 10 years at the college level. She is trained in Dynamic Energetic Healing and is a Reiki master. Over the last decade she has studied dreams, poetry, myths, and archetypes and is currently involved in a project on dreamwork, colors, and the chakras. She teaches workshops on The Goddess in History, Myth, and Archetype and has led several dream groups. She is available for DEH® sessions, Reiki or dreamwork in person or by email or telephone: r.a.crowley@att.net; 916-599-4641.

Mary Hammond lives her soul's purpose in the Northwest US loving her two young children and grown children and grandchildren as well as her work as a therapist, consultant, and teacher. As well, she loves walking and being among the beauty of her surroundings.

Mary Hammond may be contacted at
503-585-8992 or mhnheart@comcast .net
for private sessions or trainings in your area.

CPSIA information can be obtained
at www.ICGtesting.com
Printed in the USA
FFOW04n1527190214
3664FF

9 781427 631480